Nashville: Music City USA

Nashville: Music City USA

by John Lomax III

HARRY N. ABRAMS, INC., PUBLISHERS, NEW YORK

PROJECT DIRECTOR: Margaret L. Kaplan
EDITOR: Lory Frankel
DESIGNERS: Raymond P. Hooper and Andrea DaRif
PHOTO RESEARCH: John K. Crowley

Library of Congress Cataloging-in-Publication Data

Lomax, John, III.
Nashville: music city USA.

Bibliography: p. 211
Includes index.
1. Country music—Tennessee—Nashville—History and criticism. I. Title.
ML3524.L65 1985 784.5'2'00976855 84-2860
ISBN 0-8109-1345-3

Published in 1985 by Harry N. Abrams, Incorporated, New York

Printed and bound in Japan

Acknowledgements

This is the part of the book where the author thanks the many people whose contributions were of vital importance in the creation of the book.

My grandfather, John Avery Lomax, is due thanks for beginning the Lomax family tradition in American music. He began collecting the songs of working people one hundred years ago and published his first book, *American Ballads and Folk Songs*, in 1910.

My uncle, Alan Lomax, and my aunts, Bess Lomax Hawes and Shirley Mansell Lomax, are also due thanks for carrying that tradition forward into the next generation and for always providing a warm place to stay along with sage advice.

My parents, the late John Avery Lomax, Jr., and the late Margaret Marable Lomax, are owed my everlasting gratitude for exposing me to music and the people who make it, inviting me into the family tradition rather than forcing it upon me. To them I also owe my curiosity, tenacity of effort, and a warm love for those who create any type of music.

My brother, Joseph Lomax, has been a continual source of advice, an understanding business partner, and a warm friend throughout.

I'd also like to thank Helen Greenwood, my English teacher at Lamar High School in Houston. That regal woman nurtured my desire to write with wise criticism of poor work and hearty approval of better efforts.

Jack "Cowboy" Clement and Paul Soelberg were the two men who first hired me when I arrived in Nashville in 1973, providing me with the means of survival in a strange city.

Bill Ivey of the Country Music Foundation has been my only other "boss" in Nashville. It was during my stay at the Country Music Foundation that I learned of the incredible resources of that organization's Library and Media Center, the most complete repository of knowledge about American popular music in the world.

Songwriter, author, and all-around good person Carol Hall introduced me to her agent's partner and thus set in motion meetings that led to my contract.

That agent, Phyllis Winder, is due thanks for taking on a writer who had no previous books and convincing one of the world's finest publishers, Harry N. Abrams, Inc., to take on the project.

I am grateful to Paul Gottlieb and Margaret Kaplan at Abrams for giving the green light to the project for "another country music book."

My editor, Lory Frankel, deserves praise for going above and beyond the call of duty. She took a disorganized mass and shaped it into the book you hold in your hands. Her patience and diplomacy with an inexperienced writer were a source of continual amazement to me. Ray Hooper and Andrea DaRif created the design and overall look of *Music City USA*, and they are due my gratitude for an obviously outstanding job.

Ronnie Pugh, K. C. Cauthon, and Bob Pinson of the Country Music Foundation Library were especially helpful during my many visits to the C.M.F. Library and Media Center.

My colleague Robert K. Oermann has dispensed advice, facts, and encouragement during the darkest hours. In addition, his friendship has helped me to weather stormy seas in my personal life.

My wife, Jeannie, and our children, John Nova and Amanda Margaret, have suffered the most during the two years it took to produce this volume. They cheerfully put up with a person preoccupied with this book at the cost of their time and attention. They were remarkably understanding throughout.

Contents

Introduction

It's exciting, it's star-studded, and it's one of America's most popular tourist attractions. It's composed of songwriters, guitarists, singers, publishers, engineers, managers, producers, agents, "go-fers," groupies, executives, session players, and more. It has its own radio programs, it's a site for major Hollywood films, and it produces so many television shows that a TV network was created just to air them all. It's Nashville: Music City USA, a city whose heart pulses to the stories, melodies, and rhythms of the songs heard around the world.

This book will take you into that world, behind the closed doors of recording studios and executive suites, into the minds of the songwriters, singers, producers, and musicians who create the music that has earned Nashville, Tennessee, a unique place in the cultural history of the world.

Nashville is alone among the cities of the world because it is the only large population center that has become primarily known for music rather than some form of commerce. New York City has Wall Street, Los Angeles is the film capital of the world, Dallas and Chicago are national marketing centers, and Houston has its oil, but none of these cities has quite the hold upon the attention of the heartland of America as does Nashville.

In 1950 disc jockey David Cobb of station WSM in Nashville coined the phrase "Music City USA" to describe the activities here. The term stuck like glue because it rang true and because the members of the then-fledgling industry tirelessly worked to lodge the slogan in the public consciousness.

It's interesting that this phrase preceded the city's designation as "The Country Music Capital of the USA," as well as a truly significant amount of national music success upon which to base such a lofty claim. In this sense Cobb was more of a prophet than the creator of a slogan, for the city had tasted little of the incredible success that has followed in the thirty-five years since Cobb launched his sobriquet.

At the time Cobb coined the phrase there had been only three No. 1 hits recorded here, and pop singers were about as likely to record in Music City as they would be to make albums of Eskimo chants. Nashville was then known as the home of the "Grand Ole Opry," WSM radio, and a few publishing companies.

Through the years the two phrases "Music City USA" and "The Country Music Capital of the U.S.A." have done battle with one another for slogan supremacy. Today both are true characterizations of the city. Nashville is clearly the center of country music for the U.S.A., the world, the solar system, and, for all we know, the galaxy. And the city is also the location of the creation and recording of enough music to justifiably claim the broader title. Nashville is proud of these titles and it works hard to retain them, buzzing along creating words and melodies for the world's music lovers.

Several themes are presented in this volume. The first focuses upon country music's rise from a popularity slump in the late 1960s to a position today as a vibrantly healthy form that is enthusiastically embraced full-time by over 2,200 of America's radio stations—almost 25 percent of all U.S. radio outlets. The story of how country music climbed to the top from a period of declining popularity occupies a good portion of this book.

But Nashville is more than just "The Country Music Capital of the U.S.A." Over the years, this city has produced much of the popular music in the nation. Nashville's songwriters have penned numerous pop smashes, the city's studios have hosted hits in the fields of rock 'n' roll, blues, adult-contemporary, gospel, pop, and even disco music. In addition, a great many of Nashville's artists have "crossed over" from the country charts to the highest levels of national success in pop and adult-contemporary music. Surprisingly, Nashville has also played host to many top artists in the black music field. Today, Nashville is much more than just the home of country music; so, too, the scope of this volume embraces more than merely Nashville's country success.

Historically, *Music City USA* will present a detailed study of the events in country music since 1968 as seen from the perspective of Nashville. In addition, it will tell the story of Nashville's rise to prominence as a source of many other kinds of music, a tale that began in 1947 when Francis Craig and his Orchestra logged the city's first major recorded success: "Near You," a No. 1 *pop* hit for three months that year.

Although there is a brief rundown of the important events and trends in country music prior to 1968, this book primarily focuses upon subsequent events for several reasons. The success of country music in the last seventeen years has been nothing short of phenomenal, in view of the form's standing prior to 1968. At the time, country was fighting for its very existence following a radical change in the way popular music was presented. The story of how country music met this new challenge is an exciting one. The fact that country music went on to post its most amazing gains in the years from 1978 to 1982, when the recorded music industry as a whole suffered sluggish sales, only underlines the magnitude of country music's victory.

In addition, Bill Malone's book *Country Music USA* published in 1968, gives a detailed account of the important events in the field up to that time. It doesn't make a lot of sense to plow the same furrow. Parts of *Music City USA* are intended to supplement Malone's fine work.

It's also my hope that *Music City USA* will become a valuable reference tool for scholars who wish to trace Nashville's influence in noncountry music areas. Much of the information in these sections of the book has never been published before; perhaps those of a scholarly bent will explore these areas of Nashville's music contributions at greater length.

Music City USA is more than just a book of words; it also features over three hundred photographs provided by more than forty photographers and sources, most of them based in Nashville. The images they have supplied present unusual glimpses of the men and women who have made this city the musical capital that it is today. In selecting the pictures, I have tried to show these people engaged in activities besides merely standing on a stage singing into a microphone, an occupational hazard of many earlier popular music books. These photographs present other aspects of the lives of the stars: recording, writing songs, traveling on the bus, waiting backstage, relaxing at home—moments away from the performance mode. I think you will agree that there is a great deal of variety to be found.

Since this is a book about the popular music written or recorded in Nashville, it lacks detailed discussion of the music made elsewhere during this period, country or otherwise. Bakersfield, California, made so many contributions to the country music charts in the 1960s that it was referred to for a time as "Nashville West," but these achievements, and the many fine records made in Muscle Shoals, Alabama, fall beyond the scope of this book. At times this was a painful decision; for instance, there was no way to claim either "Islands in the Strea[illegible] or "To All the Girls I've Loved Before" as a part of Nashville's contribution to popular music even though Dolly Parton, Kenny Rogers, and Willie Nelson have all been Nashville residents (Dolly still claims she lives here). The Parton-Rogers duet was written by the Gibb Brothers (the Bee Gees) and recorded in Miami, while the Nelson outing with Julio Iglesias, "To All the Girls I've Loved Before," was likewise written and recorded in other cities.

Though it is hard to be completely analytical about an art form as subjective as music (producer Fred Foster once told me, "If it pleases *you,* it's good"), the charts published by the music trade papers do provide a basis for comparison. For the purposes of this book I have chosen to focus only upon the charts published by *Billboard,* a weekly that has been primarily concerned with the music business since 1905. Whatever the merits of the competing trade papers, none has been in publication for so long and none approaches *Billboard* in terms of

Hank Williams, Jr., fiddles up a storm during a performance. (Photo: Jed DeKalb)

Above, left: *Fireworks light up the Parthenon in Centennial Park.* (Photo: Bob Schatz)
Above, right: *Dolly Parton obliges with an autograph.* (Photo: Steve Harbison)
Right: *Alabama whoops it up on "Hee Haw."* (Photo: Dean Dixon)

Left: *Nashvillians gather at Legislative Plaza to celebrate Century III as the city enters its third century. (Photo: Bob Schatz)*
Below: *A bluegrass group puts on a show at Fan Fair. (Photo: Steve Harbison)*

Above: *Barbara Mandrell reacts to the announcement that she is CMA's Entertainer of the Year in 1981. (Photo: Melodie Gimple)*
Below, left: *Loretta Lynn has some last-minute adjustments made prior to a TV taping. (Photo: Robin Hood)*
Below, right: *Ryman Auditorium, home to the "Grand Ole Opry" from 1931 to 1974. (Photo: Dean Dixon)*
Opposite: *None of the pornographic shops of today litter this 1970 picture of Broadway in the days before the Ryman moved to Opryland. Among the businesses pictured, only Friedman remains. (Photo: Bud Lee)*

BUCKLEY'S
RECORD SHOP
ROY ACUFF
EXHIBITS
Friedman
MUSIC &
RECORD

Top: *A television production—one of many—is taped at the Cannery in Nashville. (Photo: Dean Dixon)*
Above: *Music isn't limited to Nashville. This group in Murfreesboro, a town thirty miles from Music City, finds entertainment right at home. (Photo: Steve Harbison)*
Right: *Historic Fort Nashborough, Nashville's original settlement. (Photo: Jim Brown)*

Above, left: *Riding to hounds before the Annual Iroquois Steeplechase in Percy Warner Park. (Photo: Bob Schatz)*
Above, right: *A Rolls-Royce pulls up at the Hermitage, a luxury hotel in Nashville. (Photo: Dean Dixon)*
Left: *Kirkland Hall in Vanderbilt University, one of several major colleges in Nashville. (Photo: Bob Schatz)*

influence in the music world. *Billboard* also was the first publication to publish a weekly list of the top records in the nation, beginning in 1940.

Billboard was also selected as a basic reference tool because of a man named Joel Whitburn from Menomenee Falls, Wisconsin. Mr. Whitburn has computerized and indexed the charts published by *Billboard* since they began. These compilations have saved researchers in popular music thousands of hours that otherwise would have been spent gingerly turning the crinkly, tattered plates of aged bound copies of the magazine. None of the lists that appear in the back of *Music City U S A* would have been easily done without Mr. Whitburn and his various *Record Research Reports.*

I hope that the lovers of numbers and data will find pleasure in the many lists and charts at the back of the book. Much of the information has never been published before or presented in this manner. In the case of "The Ultimate Country Chart," the statistics represent the most concentrated collection of pertinent numerical data ever presented about country artists. It is anticipated that this information will also be of interest to casual readers, fans of particular artists, and scholars.

Since this is a book planned for mass appeal there are no footnotes implanted. The knowledge dispensed has come from standard sources, interviews with over three hundred people in the Nashville music industry, and twelve years of my own experience in various parts of Nashville's music community. Healthy doses of opinion also abound.

I have tried to steer clear of long, technical discussion best left to books concerned with teaching people about music as a career, "making it" in Nashville, or how to write songs, information that is readily available in many books. *Music City U S A* is my attempt to bring the reader insight into what makes Nashville tick and to mention many of the highlights that Nashville has furnished to America's, and the world's, music lovers along the way. I strove to give a strong sense of what it is like to live in Music City, of how the creative process works when it is exposed to the business of music, and what it's like to lead the life of a Nashville music star.

Nashville is a city that still seems to think of itself as a large town. Despite the presence of a music industry that brings several billion dollars into the city's coffers annually, people in the business are still viewed with some suspicion by the citizenry at large. In many ways, it seems as if the city is collectively holding its breath, fully expecting this unexpected goose that lays golden eggs to gather up its component parts and head for a more glamorous location. It is significant that Music Row was established not in the downtown business district but several miles south, in a once-proud neighborhood that may well have ended up as an inner-city ghetto were it not for the transformation wrought by the music industry.

And music connections are everywhere in Nashville. The city's mayor, Richard L. Fulton, was billed as "The Singing Senator" during the days when he combined careers as a state senator and an RCA recording artist. Tennessee's governor, Lamar Alexander, has treated many public and private gatherings during his tenure as chief executive to his own stylings at the piano. As if a singing mayor and a piano-playing governor weren't enough, flip on the TV set and there's a man named George Jones giving the news on WNGE.

How important is music to Nashville's economy? It's said by the Chamber of Commerce to be the fifth-largest industry here. Tourism, the fourth-largest business, is counted separately, as if music and tourism were as unrelated as insurance and religious publishing, two of the other leading industries. (I suppose the 7.5 million tourists that the Chamber estimates visit here annually come to look at the buildings where religious books are printed.) If the incomes from tourism and music were combined, the total would challenge manufacturing as the leading contributor to the city's economy.

The over two billion dollars Nashville's music industry generates for the city is largely created, in the beginning, by a handful of songwriters. A few hundred—less than five hundredths of one percent of Nashville's residents—write most of the hits you hear on the country radio stations of this land. So many here have so few to thank for so much!

"Skull" Shulman owns several nightclubs in Nashville's famed Printers Alley section of downtown clubs. (Photo: John Carnes)

And the songwriters are the heart and soul of Nashville. The singers may get all the headlines, the record labels, agents, managers, and publishers may get most of the money, but the songwriters start the process with the one thing that the industry must have in order to survive: a hit song.

Sometimes it seems that everyone in Nashville is, or wants to be, a songwriter. A famous record producer who once came here remarked, "The cab driver pitched me a song on the way in from the airport, the girl at the front desk handed me a tune along with my room key, and then, when I went out for a walk, the guy parking cars in the garage laid a cassette on me." And, if the truth were known, all three supplicants may well have handed the producer some pretty good songs. Don Williams pulled into his favorite gas station one day in 1974. The attendant filled up his car, then handed him a tape. Don left with his first No. 1 song, "I Wouldn't Want to Live If You Didn't Love Me."

Nashville is that kind of place, a city where a bit of magic seems to hang in the air. Walk down the streets of Music Row and you can almost *feel* the creativity crackling all around you, for the area features the most concentrated gathering of musical talent on the face of our planet.

MUSICAL NASHVILLE

Above: *Aerial shot of Webb Pierce's ill-fated guitar-shaped pool. The offices of Tree Music are above the pool; the Spence Manor luxury hotel is next door. The two pools in the foreground belong to the Country Music Hall of Fame and Museum. (Photo: John Carnes)*
Top, right: *In the countryside near Nashville, a couple of natives relax in the bucolic atmosphere. (Photo: Bob Schatz)*
Above, right: *The* Cumberland Princess *takes sightseers on a tour of Old Hickory Lake. (Photo: Jim Brown)*
Right: *Alabama works out at Cajun's Wharf, a Nashville nightspot. (Photo: Steve Harbison)*

Above, left: *Combine Music—home to the copyrights of Kris Kristofferson, Billy Swan, Larry Gatlin, Tony Joe White, Lee Clayton, John Scott Sherrill, Bob Morrison, and Johnny "Peanuts" McRae. (Photo: Jim McGuire)*
Above, right: *The State Capitol Building in Nashville. (Photo: Jim Brown)*
Overleaf: *Loretta Lynn's Country Western Store. (Photo: Jim Brown)*

No 10
Bon

Right: *At sunset the Tennessee Waltz ride looks as if it jumped straight out of a sci-fi flick.*
Below: *Opryland's antique carousel was discovered in 5,000 unmarked pieces in Copenhagen and rebuilt from a photograph on a postcard.*
Bottom: *The Grizzly River Rampage is one of the many attractions Opryland has to offer. (Photo: Dean Dixon)*
Center: *Minnie Pearl and Roy Acuff entertain an Opry full house. (Photo: Jim McGuire)*

Left: *One of the park's many musical revues in full swing.*
Below: *Many other programs besides the Opry take place at the Grand Ole Opry House, as this wide-angle shot of an "In Concert" taping attests. (Photo: Alan Mayor)*
Bottom: *These spectacular murals depicting turn-of-the-century Nashville are a highlight of the Opryland Hotel.*

Opposite: *Donna Butler, one of the many Opryland performers to graduate to the big time, is now with Loretta Lynn's group.*
Above, left: *Barbara Mandrell and WSM's Skip Woolwine prepare for the 1982 All-American Country Games at Vanderbilt University's Dudley Stadium. (Photo: John Carnes)*

Above, right: *Alabama's lead singer, Randy Owen, tries out a dobro on the Fan Fair crowd. (Photo: Robin Hood)*
Below, left: *Byron and Slim Whitman (left) entertain at Fan Fair. (Photo: John Carnes)*
Below, right: *Fan Fair autograph-hunters on duty.*

Preceding pages: *Twitty City at Christmas is a spectacular site.*
Above, left: *For her museum, Barbara Mandrell re-created her bedroom down to her bedtime snack of cola and crackers.*
Above, right: *Cheekwood functions as the Tennessee Botanical Center. (Photo: Bob Schatz)*
Below, left: *A National Historic Landmark, the Hermitage was home to Andrew Jackson, seventh president of the United States. (Photo: Bob Schatz)*
Below, right: *Belle Meade Mansion, one of the South's finest antebellum estates. (Photo: Bob Schatz)*

Above: *Oak Ridge Boy William Lee Golden at home. (Photo: Beth Gwinn)*
Below: *Tammy Wynette enjoys a rare serene moment in the home she and George Jones shared at the time. (Photo: Marshall Fallwell, Jr.)*

Above: *Ballet dancers in full sway at the new (1980) Tennessee Performing Arts Center, a three-stage complex. (Photo: John Carnes)*
Center: *The world's only full-scale replica of the Parthenon.*
Below: *High culture does exist in Music City—here's the symphony hard at it. Many string players moonlight as session players. (Photo: John Carnes)*
Overleaf: *Ricky Skaggs lets go with his custom-built "Mandocaster." (Photo: John Carnes)*

Nashville Today

Nashville in 1985 is a city much more diverse than its worldwide music reputation would indicate. Few people are aware that Music City USA is home to mammoth insurance companies, two medical colleges (including Meharry, the oldest black medical institution in the nation), a thriving artists' colony which predates the turn of the century, and so many colleges and universities (fourteen) that the city is sometimes referred to as the "Athens of the South." In addition, Nashville is the world headquarters for several major Protestant religions with large followings (Baptist, Methodist, Church of Christ). Their publishing concerns also form a vital part of the city's economy, helping mightily toward yet a third nickname for Nashville: "the buckle of the Bible Belt."

These considerations should be balanced against some conceptions of Nashville as a sleepy outpost inhabited by country singers, writers, and steel guitarists who spend most of their time drinking to excess, taking as much dope as they can introduce into their systems, and chasing any woman still breathing. Many outsiders also imagine a citizenry that communicates by exchanging punch lines from "Hee Haw." At the same time, they visualize the upper-class cotton barons seated on the verandas in their white suits and string ties, sipping mint juleps while cursing the "uppity" darkies and scheming up new ways to augment their vast landholdings.

The common perception of Nashville as simply a town where music and little else is made may be partially dispelled by a glance at population figures, which show that Nashville's population exceeds that of Atlanta, Buffalo, Cincinnati, Kansas City, Miami, Minneapolis, Pittsburgh, and St. Louis. Actually, with a total population of 455,651, Nashville is the twenty-sixth-largest city in the United States, which should lead one to deduce that it isn't such a sleepy place after all.

Though Nashville's population may not seem impressive, you have to travel 200 miles west (Memphis), 300 miles north (Indianapolis), 500 miles south (New Orleans, Jacksonville), and 650 miles east (Washington, D.C.) to find larger settlements.

In truth, Nashville is a magnet to thousands who come here from smaller settlements in the surrounding region to sample the latest in newfangled gadgets, seek work, or enjoy the other delights of a large urban center.

The first permanent settlement of what is now Nashville was established on Christmas Day of 1779, when a party of four hundred men led by James Robertson, an experienced backwoodsman, crossed the frozen Cumberland River after a three-hundred-mile overland trek from North Carolina. The settlers erected Fort Nashborough, in a near-three-quarter-acre compound perched on a bluff overlooking the river. (A scaled-down re-creation of Fort Nashborough stands on the spot today, less than a half-mile from the county courthouse.)

Robertson's band arrived without loss of life on the two-month journey. A second party, led by John Donelson, an overweight politician, had a much tougher time. This group, which included women, children, and elderly men, faced constant danger on the four-month voyage, which covered a thousand miles up and down four different river systems. About one-third of the members were lost to raging waters, marauding Indians, and disease. The eighty-five survivors were greeted warmly when they finally poled into view late in April of 1780.

The Indians who hunted and fished in the area did not take kindly to their new neighbors. The land had been set aside by the red man as a hunting preserve and no tribe was permitted permanent occupation. A series of attacks and skirmishes ensued between the two groups. In

RICKY SKAGGS *(Epic)*

Born and raised in rural Kentucky, Ricky arrived "out of the blue" in 1982 with three No. 1 singles. Still under thirty, Skaggs has had over twenty years of professional experience with a wide variety of musicians from Ralph Stanley and Bill Monroe to Emmylou Harris and Dolly Parton. After collecting an extensive dossier of recordings on independent labels, his first three major label LPs were certified gold. Ricky is married to Sharon White, of the group the Whites, which he produces. CMA winner in 1982 as Best New Artist and Male Vocalist, he plays anything stringed. He created a unique fusion music with jazz, traditional country, and bluegrass elements. Potential Hall of Fame selection, but should monitor the growth of his ego: when his band won CMA honors as Instrumental Group of the Year for the second consecutive year in 1984, Ricky accepted the award, ignoring the five musicians standing behind him.

the most notable encounter in 1781, the climactic Battle of the Bluff, the settlers prevailed only after they turned their dogs loose upon the attacking tribesmen. Despite this fortuitous canine intervention, no monument stands to commemorate Nashville's timely assistance by man's best friend.

The new settlement prospered as a frontier town largely because of the access the Cumberland afforded to the Mississippi, Ohio, and Tennessee rivers. Keelboats, barges, then steam-powered vessels plied the waterways and a flourishing trade with New Orleans soon developed. Tennessee joined the Union in 1796; Nashville's incorporation came eight years later. By 1810 nearly two thousand citizens were in residence.

The predominant figure in Nashville's first century was Andrew Jackson, a North Carolinian who came to the city in 1788 at the age of twenty-one. Jackson's political career began as district attorney here, and he eventually served two terms as the seventh president of the United States. Nicknamed "Old Hickory," he was perceived as the hero of the common man, though his closest friends were rather well-heeled. His route to the White House, masterminded by his Nashville associates, led to the foundation of the modern Democratic party. Though he was a peerless military leader who campaigned successfully against both the Indians and the British, Jackson received his only gunshot wounds in a duel and a brawl. His eight-year term in office might charitably be termed undistinguished.

A second Nashvillian, James K. Polk, known as "Young Hickory," served as the eleventh American president from 1844 to 1848. Although Polk, a far less colorful personality than Jackson, contributed little to the store of political folklore, he added over 1,200,000 square miles of territory to the United States, slightly over one-third of our current area. He was also the first "dark horse" candidate to emerge as a nominee from a political convention. Polk's expansionist policies were opposed during his tenure by Henry Clay, John C. Calhoun, and Daniel Webster, perhaps one reason why his administration wasn't as fondly remembered as those of men who accomplished less for the nation.

Nashville was an extremely important strategic city as well as a Confederate supply depot during the early months of the Civil War. The war itself was not favored by a majority of Nashvillians, many of whom had strong Union ties; historians agree that most in the city preferred a more moderate policy than secession. Tennessee was the last state to join the Confederacy. Union forces recognized Nashville's key value on the western front and seized the city in February 1862, shortly after Grant led the capture of Fort Donelson to the west. Despite its military importance, Nashville was never properly fortified by the Confederates. Nashville spent the next three and a half years as an occupied city, which helped it to emerge from the war with little physical damage. In truth, aside from the dead bodies of its soldiers, Nashville prospered during the war years. The presence of federal troops boosted the local economy, and immigrants from all directions swelled the population from seventeen to twenty-five thousand.

The remainder of the century saw Nashville prosper in business as well as education. The city became one of the major river and rail crossroads in the region and it also developed three major colleges—Vanderbilt, Fisk, and Meharry. Fisk University's Jubilee Singers, begun in 1871 as a way to raise funds for the fledgling black college, can justifiably be considered the first hit musical act to emerge from the city. They still perform today across the country, 115 years after their first national tour.

By the turn of the century Nashville had developed most of the parts in the balanced economy that characterizes the city today. The booming printing business, as well as the vast timber industry, laid the foundations for Nashville's current publishing business. In 1900 the city led the state in industrial output. Although it remains a significant center of manufacture—with factories that make clothing, airplane parts, trucks, and other items ranging from guitars and houseboats to plastics and religious artifacts—it contains no major refineries, steel plants, pulp mills, or other industrial behemoths to pollute the air.

Insurance, Nashville's second-largest industry, put roots down in the early years of the twentieth century. The two most important insurance concerns gave a leg up to the music and broadcasting industries by establishing radio stations in the mid-1920s. WSM became a child of National Life and Accident Insurance Company in 1925, while the Life and Casualty Insurance Company of Tennessee established WLAC the following year.

As the capital of Tennessee, Nashville has a thriving business in government. This factor helped the city to weather the Depression much better than most Southern cities. Also, Nashville's Joseph W. Byrns was Speaker of the House in 1935 and 1936, so perhaps it was no accident that the Tennessee Valley Authority and the Works Progress Administration became major sources of employment for many Nashvillians.

Other cornerstones of the local cash flow are banking, tourism, and medicine. Regardless of what one may think, music is not considered the leading contributor to Nashville's economy. Banking, manufacturing, and insurance bring in more money than does music, according to Chamber of Commerce figures.

Nashville sits in the north-central part of Tennessee, almost equidistant on Interstate 40 west of Knoxville and east of Memphis, Tennessee's most populous metropolis. The state's fourth-largest city, Chattanooga, sits 115 miles southeast down Interstate 24.

Through a freak of federal highway design Nashville is a nexus for three interstate routes: I-40 (east-west), I-65 (north-south), and I-24 (northwest-southeast). It's very unusual for a city to feature three separate interstates, a distinction shared only by Indianapolis, Chicago, Dallas, and Atlanta, cities whose metropolitan populations are much larger than that of our own.

This fortuitous interstate placement joins Music City to thirteen major cities within three hundred miles. To the west lie Memphis, St. Louis, and Indianapolis. Louisville, Lexington, and Cincinnati lie north and east, Knoxville and Asheville are within that radius to the east. Chattanooga, Birmingham, Huntsville, Montgomery, and Atlanta are within a five-hour drive to the south or southeast.

The practical aspect of this geography means that a singer can headquarter here and be within 300 miles of an audience of well over twelve million, just counting the number of people in the metropolitan areas of these thirteen cities. Extend the circle to 550 miles and even more territory is encompassed, particularly in the South and Midwest, the two major strongholds of country music audiences. Indeed, a 550-mile circle drawn with Nashville at the center touches twenty-two different states.

DOLLY PARTON *(RCA)*

Kenny may make more money, Willie may issue more albums, and Barbara Mandrell may win more awards, but Dolly is the biggest STAR in country music. Her background parallels that of Loretta Lynn—large family, tiny "town," Appalachian poverty—but while Lynn's life made a good movie, Dolly's *is* a movie. Her looks, voice, hair, personality, and breathtaking bosom are obvious Parton attributes, but her most important feature is less obvious: superlative intelligence. One of the finest *writers* in country history ("Coat of Many Colors," "The Bargain Store," "Jolene," "Love Is Like a Butterfly," "To Daddy," "I Will Always Love You," "Hollywood Potters," "9 to 5," to name but a few), Dolly is devastating in press conferences and overwhelming in a personal interview. Her 1980s pop/country records suffered from overproduction and the movies she starred in haven't been smash hits, but she'll be a star as long as there is electricity. Certain Hall of Famer.

Left: *The Sons of the Pioneers (left, in blue) and the Oak Ridge Boys exemplify the traditional and Western form and the modern, country-pop styles found in country music over the last 50 years. (Photo: John Carnes)*
Right: *Dolly Parton shows off the stained-glass windows in her brand-new bus. (Photo: Melodie Gimple)*

The area of this circle with a 550-mile radius equals about 950,000 square miles, slightly over 26 percent of the total area of the United States. This great circle covers 48 of the 179 cities in this country that have over one hundred thousand residents. When you add up the population of all of the South (save for the bottom 80 percent of Florida), most of the Midwest, and some of the mid-Atlantic area, along with parts of Pennsylvania, Kansas, Texas, and Missouri, you wind up with at least 80 million people located within 550 miles of Music City, about 38 percent of the total population of our nation, a percentage equal to and greater than similar circles around Manhattan and Los Angeles would enclose.

This is a classic case of having your own turf. Five hundred and fifty miles may seem like a lengthy junket to most, but it isn't an overly long hop if you're traveling in a $250,000 customized bus. Modern Silver Eagles, those unsung Boeings of the concrete, can gobble up 550 miles in eight to eleven hours, depending upon weather conditions, the urgency of the situation, and the skill of the driver. Inside, eight to twelve people can relax in a setting more luxurious than most apartments. Color television sets, video units, and tape decks help while away the hours between stopovers.

Country artists do most of their touring during the warmer months. No one books heavy travel during the holidays, and by January weather conditions are too severe to draw much of a crowd anyway. If you examined a country singer's logbook, you'd find that 90 percent of his or her appearances fall in the eight months from March through October. The stars use the colder months to write, record, make television appearances, polish their live shows, and spend time with their families.

Everyone within this huge circle is also within the coverage area of WSM radio, a 50,000-watt clear-channel station that carries the "Grand Ole Opry" and is the home base of the satellite-fed Music Country Network. Today these two programs blast over the radio waves six nights a week, carrying Nashville's message much as the famous Mexican border stations once boomed testimonials and music over a sizable portion of the central United States.

The diverse economy, temperate climate, clean air, tradition of Southern hospitality, moderate cost of living, and convenient geographic location are among the factors that have made Nashville an attractive place in which to live. These attributes and many others were evaluated in an exhaustive study published in 1983 under the title of *Places Rated Almanac.* That volume placed Nashville twelfth among 276 other United States metropolitan areas surveyed, which puts it in the top 5 percent.

Music Row

Nashville's population is listed as 455,651 in the *World Almanac.* That figure is misleading, because it is actually the population of Davidson County; city and county government here were merged in 1964. Those half-million folks are hardly squeezed together—the city occupies over 530 square miles, giving Nashville a population density of less than 1,000 per square mile, compared to New York City's 23,000 and Los Angeles's 6,500.

But the popular music made in Nashville doesn't come from all over the city. For the most part it is created, published, sung, recorded, mixed, mastered, marketed, and administrated in a twenty-four-square-block area just south of downtown known to one and all as Music Row.

The nickname is apt. This six-by-four-block section is home to most of Nashville's music business. All six major record labels have their offices on the Row, as do several hundred recording artists, publishers, producers, songwriters, agents, managers, publicists, and music executives. Few, if any, industries in the world have so many of their component parts as compactly located.

There are some exceptions to this cozy arrangement: about half the recording studios have opted for greater privacy by locating beyond the Row. The music publishing house of Acuff-Rose is situated some two miles south of Music Row, and several artists—the Oak Ridge Boys, Conway Twitty, and Johnny Cash among them—have established headquarters in Hendersonville, a suburb about twenty miles north. A small but thriving studio community has also sprung up in Berry Hill, a municipality enclosed by Nashville and located near a major shopping center three miles southeast of Music Row.

One might picture these thousands of people working in modern steel, glass, and concrete towers, a natural assumption considering the magnitude of the business conducted here. But the truth is that there are only two music business offices in the Row taller than three stories: the eight-story "United Artists" Tower and the six-story Financial Institution Services Incorporated edifice. Their owners have struggled for years to achieve 100 percent occupancy. Today fewer than half the tenants of the two structures derive their income from musical pursuits. Most of the companies and individuals work in renovated houses, relics of an earlier era when this part of the city was composed of fashionable residences.

How many people work in the Nashville music business? The author's own informal census reveals a figure of about five thousand. Add in those who work in outlying studios and offices and you'll see that less than 5,600, or 1¼ percent of Nashville's citizens, work in the business. This tiny part of Nashville is largely responsible for most of the $550 million in recorded country music sold annually in the United States alone.

Add the income generated by tourism, publishing companies, performance rights groups, booking and management companies, film and video concerns, and all of the other support services and you have some idea of the enormous economic impact this small band of music lovers has upon the other 98¾ percent of the Nashville citizenry.

If you think of Music Row as a separate town enclosed by a larger city it will give you a clearer idea of the relationship of Music Row to Nashville. People who work on the Row have little reason to travel into other parts of the city, save for commuting, shopping, dining, or serious banking transactions. Since all aspects of the industry are contained in the Music Row area, workers rarely venture downtown or to any other area of Nashville for business purposes. It's like a small version of the "garment district" or Wall Street in New York City—nearly self-contained.

Like any other small town, Music Row is a tightly knit community where everyone knows everyone else—and all their secrets as well. It has long been a Music Row axiom that if you sleep with anyone else in the business, male or female, it will become common knowledge by suppertime. And, as in any small town dominated by one industry, the business is clannish, suspicious of strangers, and riddled with nepotism. It has taken the people here many, many years of hard work to create this multibillion dollar industry, and they aren't wild about out-of-towners who wish to waltz in here to appropriate a share of the golden goose. Very few people can come here, regardless of their achievements in other music capitals, and make quick progress in the music industry. If you were to stick around five years or more, become involved in the community, and, if possible, marry into the clan, you *might* stand a chance. You can't make it on talent *alone* here without spending time learning the ground rules of the local music game and engaging in fraternizing and politicking with those in power.

This rather provincial aspect of Nashville can be greatly frustrating to newcomers with proven track records. They may feel that Music Row is a closed shop, open only to those born and bred within the system. While at first glance that may seem to be the case, it does not hold up under close scrutiny. Take a close look at the origins of the biggest record-sellers in Nashville's music history and you'll find only *one*—Brenda Lee—who even attended high school here. The same is largely true for studio players, producers, executives, and songwriters. A good track record may not gain newcomers quick accession to the top of the Nashville heap, but it does gain them entry into the game. Although the door here is not wide open, it isn't closed to those with talent, ambition, drive, and perseverance.

The fiction of Music Row's inaccessibility is spread partly by many of the thousands of people who come here annually without the skills to make it. On the surface, country music seems deceptively simple: the biggest stars are not supremely skilled vocalists or stunning instrumentalists. They do not dress that differently from their listeners and they sing about the everyday problems and concerns of ordinary people. They make it seem so easy that many dreamers see only the rewards their success has earned. So they head for the streets of Music Row faster than you can tune a steel guitar, convinced that the pot of gold at the end of the rainbow is waiting there for them to scoop it up.

Those who come here and fail have two things in common: too little talent and too little time. These same people would not dream of becoming a doctor in so little time or turning into an N.F.L. quarterback in a year, but they expect to make an impact on Music City and be well on their way to stardom in a ridiculously short time. What these people don't realize is that they stand a much better chance of making it in Nashville by staying home, practicing and performing or writing until they become so good that Nashville comes looking for *them*.

Charley Pride is a case in point: Red Sovine found him working days in a copper smelter and singing nights in a baseball stadium in Butte, Montana. Red urged him to come to Nashville and provided him with some introductions. Porter Wagoner was discovered singing in Springfield, Missouri. Alabama spent ten years playing all over the rural South and recording for tiny regional labels before their RCA contract helped accelerate their rise to stardom in 1980. Johnny Rodriguez was discovered by Tom T. Hall in Brackettville, Texas, shortly after he had spent a night in jail for goat theft. Red Stegall heard Reba McEntire sing the national anthem at a rodeo in Oklahoma and arranged the sessions that brought her a Mercury recording contract. To make it to the top in country music, you *will* have to come to Nashville—but why not wait until you're invited?

Of course, there are exceptions to this rule. Superstar Dolly Parton and award-winning songwriter Dean Dillon headed for Nashville as soon as they graduated from high school in East Tennessee. Eddie Rabbitt came to Music City from the lounges of East Orange, New Jersey, John Anderson from the scorching plains of Apopka, Florida. But those who single out these exceptions are overlooking the time factor in the equation. It took all four of the above artists at least five years of struggle in Nashville before they enjoyed even a small taste of success.

Three Music City hopefuls take a break from working up songs. (Photo: Marshall Fallwell, Jr.)

Another story may shed some light on the Nashville mystique. Kris Kristofferson spent many years here, trying to gain a foothold. For some time he was employed by Columbia Records as a janitor. In fact, he still held that job when he released his first album on Monument Records, a smaller company whose records were distributed by Columbia. Kris's record did well in the stores and gained rave reviews from the press. The head man at Columbia at the time began the usual Monday morning label meeting with a long diatribe about how good Kris's record was and wanted to know how the executives could have let him slip away to another label. One of the junior executives piped up, "But sir, he wasn't a very good janitor."

It would take fifty books of this size to detail 10 percent of the case histories of all those who have come here and failed, so a look at three particular acts will have to suffice. The Thompson Twins had a gimmick: they wore full-length fur coats and Russian Cossack hats. For several years, they strolled the streets of the Row, playing guitars and singing, attracting glances from the tourists and Music Row executives alike. They played the bars of Lower Broadway and were regulars at Tootsie's Orchid Lounge, a major industry hangout until the Grand Ole Opry moved from downtown to Opryland. Attention they got, but they just weren't good enough for a record deal. They haven't been seen in Nashville for several years.

JOHN ANDERSON
(Warner Bros.)

A native of Florida whose "hard-country" vocal phrasing has drawn comparison to Lefty Frizzell and Merle Haggard, John began charting in 1977 but did not reach the top until 1982, with "Wild and Blue." He followed it with "Swingin'," a Top-40 pop and No. 1 country success that helped bring him two CMA Awards in 1983. Anderson has an uncanny knack for unearthing superb original material; he also writes solid, if sometimes offbeat, songs with Lionel A. Delmore. Still under thirty, he is viewed as one of the top country discoveries of the 1980s. In live shows he likes to rock out; he does a fine version of the Rolling Stones' "Under My Thumb." If he keeps himself together he has a virtually unlimited future.

Miss Kimberly has spent almost four years parading her act for all Music Row to see. She dresses in a sort of "Heidi" outfit—midthigh shorts and suspenders—and sings and clogs to prerecorded music provided by a portable cassette player, usually on the steps of the United Artists Tower or in Music Square Park. She too got attention and quite a bit of media coverage for such antics as this, in her words, "Music Row Street Show," as well as for other stunts, such as plastering a sign next to producer Billy Sherrill's car urging him, in large letters, to record her song "The Streets of Music Row." But her songs aren't good enough, and she might be better off performing in the town she claims to be from: Horse Branch, Kentucky.

Charles Silver's songs were good enough to be recorded. One, in fact—"Standing Room Only"—became Barbara Mandrell's first major solo success in 1976. But Silver, a native of New York City and Baltimore, wouldn't or couldn't adapt to the accepted modes of behavior on the Row. He consistently pitched his songs while dressed in a coat and tie, exhibited the most rude and obnoxious conduct, refused to listen to those who tried to give him good advice, insinuated that those who didn't record his songs were idiots, bragged constantly about making Barbara Mandrell a star with his one song she had cut, and used filthy language around women in clubs when their dates were present—a habit that will get your face bashed in here as well as most anyplace else. Needless to say, few of his songs were recorded. One day he was found dead in his locked motel room, a gun nearby.

Apopka, Florida's gift to the country music world: John Anderson. His song "Swingin'" was one of the few "gold" country singles of the 1980s so far. (Photo: Cynthia Farah)

Opryland

The 406 acres of rolling hills that are home to Opryland USA showcase the most unique entertainment facility in the world. Sold in 1983 to Gaylord Broadcasting for a reported $270 million, the complex includes: a twelve-acre musical entertainment theme park, which hosts over two million people annually; the Grand Ole Opry House, home to the fifty-nine-year-old Opry; Opryland Hotel, a 1,070-room four-story hostelry that occupies thirty acres adjacent to the park; the Nashville Network, a national cable television programming source already available in over twenty million homes; and WSM-AM/FM, one of America's leading broadcast properties, the flagship station of the Music Country Network.

In addition, Opryland also houses a sightseeing company (Grand Ole Opry Sightseeing Tours), a package vacation concern (Opryland Travel), and a talent agency (Opryland Talent Agency), which books Opryland's shows, special acts, and individual performers for conventions, special events, and meetings nationally.

Nashville residents tend to be blasé about the hometown attractions—very few are among the visitors at the Opry—but a description of the activities at the entertainment complex draws superlatives even from locals.

For several years now I have referred to the collective facilities under the umbrella title of "O-Land," the "O" as in Oz, a fictional wonderland with no fewer surprises. "O" is also a fair description of the sound visitors make when first shown the sprawling hotel, spread over 1.25 million square feet in Southern plantation/Williamsburg splendor. Visitors have been lost for minutes in the seemingly endless corridors, where the rooms bear coded numbers like those on the offices in the Pentagon.

Opryland (the amusement park) is built around a theme of *musical* entertainment, and that music spans *all styles* of the music popular in our land. You will hear rock, country, blues, jazz, bluegrass, Dixieland, gospel, and pop music, as well as the mutant forms that borrow elements from several of the above. The park is capable of simultaneously mounting up to *fifteen shows* involving several hundred young singers, dancers, musicians, and stagehands. Opryland's many different theaters present the shows daily in the summer and weekends in late spring and early fall during the park's April to November season.

The park also presents twenty rides familiar to all who have attended similar theme parks like Six Flags, Freedomland, Busch Gardens, Astroworld, and Disneyland/Disneyworld. Opryland boasts a stunning carousel, built in Germany's Black Forest in the last century, then painstakingly reassembled after its five thousand pieces were located in storage. The park is also distinguished by more attractions designed for young children than can be found at comparable facilities. There is a marvelous petting zoo and a dozen rides made with the very young in mind. Tykes can also enjoy many of the "grown-up" rides like log rafts, a "Tin Lizzie," the park train (the Opryland Railroad, of course), and a sky ride.

But Opryland stands alone as a *musical* theme park, and music is what you will hear pouring from every corner of the grounds. The performers and technicians who stage the many musical activities are young people chosen each year in the winter months during Opryland's annual talent search. Every year the park's talent scouts visit thirty to fifty of America's largest cities, where they hold open auditions to fill the vacancies created by the natural turnover such an enterprise creates. Though the pay isn't munificent, the job does entail a paid summer vacation to Nashville and quite a lot of experience to those interested in careers in theater, music, or the technical professions involved in both endeavors. What the Opryland cast lacks in experience and expertise is more than balanced by exuberance and enthusiasm. Many of the

The "new wave" meets the "old guard": Lee Clayton and Hank Snow make desultory conversation before a Snow performance. (Photo: Bill Dibble)

performers have "graduated" from their Opryland days to become performers on the stages of Broadway and London. Songwriter-artist Dean Dillon and several others have gone on to fashion country careers, but none has yet become a country superstar.

Opryland is truly a world unto itself. The security staff rides around on horseback, there is an employee magazine for the workers, and one of the world's largest parking lots can accommodate anything on wheels. The hotel has the most complete convention facilities of any in this part of the nation. Open-air trams run continuously among the various park attractions.

In fact, Opryland is so full of interesting sights that plenty of time should be allocated to see them all. The gigantic mural—it covers thousands of square feet—at the end of the corridor between the reception desk and the Opryland Hotel's Presidential Ballroom is worth seeing even if you bypass the theme park next door. Painted by T. Max Hochstetler, the mural shows daily life in Nashville in 1880 in painstaking detail. Looking at it is a breathtaking and entertaining way to visit the past.

The hotel also houses some of the broadcast facilities of WSM Radio. Guests can stroll by in the morning to view the zany "Walking Crew Band," the only remaining live orchestra on radio, as they pump out songs and bad jokes Monday through Friday. In the evenings the studio hosts the Music Country Network, a satellite-fed country program delivered by WSM and the Associated Press to over one hundred stations nationally. As you pass by, you can wave to the legendary Charlie Douglas, who hosts the show until 1:00 A.M.

Just around the corner and down the hall from the hotel reception desk you'll find one of the most unusual rooms in America. Imagine a glass-topped space five-stories tall, surrounded by what appear to be exterior hotel walls and every type of vegetation imaginable. Catwalks thirty feet in the air traverse the structure on one level while walking paths wind through a most amazing collection of foliage below. This is the conservatory, added in 1983, and it encloses over two acres. Sparkling waterfalls dot the premises, and the paths wind around and between the amazing, near-tropical display, creating nooks and crannies where one can pause for conversation or simply to admire Tennessee's most unusual artificial environment.

The latest addition to Opryland's wonders is a 285-foot sternwheeler, *The General Jackson,* completed in the spring of 1985. The boat, nearly as large as *The Mississippi Queen,* can comfortably accommodate about 750 people for dinner excursions or entertain up to 1,000 for theatrical presentations. The ten-million-dollar vessel cruises the Cumberland River in the manner of sternwheelers of old from its moorings near the theme park. The boat's spring launch extended the Opryland touch over water as well as land—perhaps their next step will be to build a blimp to ferry visitors through the clouds as well.

Opryland has enjoyed many spectacular events, but no circumstance attracted a crowd as star-drenched as the grand opening of the brand new Grand Ole Opry House on Saturday, March 16, 1974. That night, the fifteen-million-dollar structure, of glittering glass, steel, brick, and wood, hosted a crowd that included President and Mrs. Nixon, both Tennessee senators, half a dozen governors, and an assortment of other celebrities.

Although the Opry cast, headed by Roy Acuff (in an outfit coordinated in red, white, and blue), was showcased in all its glory, the evening's most notable performer was Mr. Nixon. The president amused the crowd by aping Acuff's yoyo tricks; later he played the piano and sang "Happy Birthday," "My Wild Irish Rose," and "God Bless America," dedicating the songs to Pat.

In retrospect, this must have been Nixon's 1974 highlight as well as Opryland's. Less than five months later he resigned the presidency following impeachment proceedings by the House of Representatives Judiciary Committee, which cited him for abuse of power, obstruction of justice, and contempt of Congress. In this context Mr. Nixon's comments from the stage of the Opry House seem ironic, to say the least: "What country music is, is that it first comes from the heart of America, because this is the heart of America, out here in middle America. Country music, therefore, has those combinations which are so essential to America's character at a time when America needs character."

Bashful Brother Oswald of Roy Acuff's band was less florid in his summation of the evening: "I'll wear out a lot of overalls helping pay for this place."

Today the "Grand Ole Opry" continues to thrive as America's longest-lived radio entertainment program. The tourists still come by the busloads to view the performers, most of them far past their prime. As country music expanded and broadened its base beyond its rural Southern and Appalachian traditions, the power base built up around the Opry began to crumble. At one time the most important single factor in an artist's country music success, membership in the Opry today is not viewed as vital to career development.

It's in many ways like a living museum, packed full of exhibits that breathe, walk, tell jokes, and sing. Look, over there, isn't that Ernie Ashworth in the flashy suit with lips sewn all over the jacket? And there's Jan Howard, Minnie Pearl, Hank Snow, and Bill Monroe, all reliving their past glories every week. In a way, it's sad to see the Opry regulars as old-timers whose careers have seen better days. But, when viewed from another angle, it is a touching spectacle. It's as if country music is saying to its artists, "Now, we know you won't be a star forever. And when your days of stardom are over there will always be a place for you to come and sing."

A trip to the Opry House is a step back in time. The four thousand or so in attendance know they are going to receive a family show, so their ages vary from months to even a century. The show moves fast, divided into segments, each sponsored by a different purveyor. If you don't like the person onstage all you have to do is wait a few minutes for another act to take over. The performers are as comfortable on the stage as if they were relatives in your own living room.

In recent years the Opry has attempted to inject some youth into the program by inviting younger artists like Ricky Skaggs and the Whites, but the cast remains predominately aged. As of late 1984 only thirteen of the sixty acts on the Opry roster still held recording contracts with major record companies, and many of these thirteen—Dolly Parton, George Jones, Loretta Lynn, Barbara Mandrell, Ronnie Milsap, Dottie West, and Skaggs—are rarely seen on the Opry stage.

In the past the Opry *was* country music. Today it is only a small part of it, a backwater rather than the main current of the river that is the hybrid form of country music that today rules the radio. The "Grand Ole Opry" is a piece of America's bygone days kept alive for all who yearn for simpler times to come see and enjoy.

"Tricky Dicky" tells it like he thinks it is at the opening of the new Grand Ole Opry House in 1974. (Photo: Marshall Fallwell, Jr.)

Fan Fair

TAMMY WYNETTE *(Epic)*

Dolly will probably overtake her, but as of the end of 1984 Tammy had tallied more No. 1 singles than any other female country singer. She has survived it all—disastrous marriages, health problems due to stress, fatigue, and "abdominal disorders," and even a "kidnapping"—to claim her position as "The First Lady of Country Music." Her incredible upper register ("Stand By Your Man") sets Tammy apart from other women country singers. Her keen writing skills, combined with Billy Sherrill's production, carried her from nowhere to the top in 1967, beginning with "Your Good Girl's Gonna Go Bad." CMA Female Vocalist of the Year from 1968 to 1970 and a two-time Grammy winner, Tammy has also won thirteen BMI Awards. "Stand By Your Man," "Another Lonely Song," "'Til I Can Make It on My Own," and "Two Story House" stand out among her recordings. She's married to producer-arranger George Richey. Future Hall of Famer.

Fan Fair is where the buyers of country music come en masse to Music City to meet and mingle with the stars. For one glorious week in Nashville, the creators and sellers of country music play host to a swarm of the most single-minded individuals you will ever see. Try to imagine over 19,000 country music fanatics, all obsessed with getting a close look, a picture, and an autograph from their favorite country stars. Put all 19,000 of these zealots in Nashville during the second week in June and you have Fan Fair. There is no event remotely similar in any form of popular music in the world.

Here's how it works: for fifty-five dollars each registrant is entitled to see over fifteen different concerts featuring more than one hundred acts from every branch of country music—or over sixty-five hours of performances. The fee also includes three free meals, a ticket to Opryland, and a ticket to the Country Music Hall of Fame and Museum. You also receive free admission for four days to five exhibition halls crammed full of nearly four hundred booths offering every sort of country music gewgaw that can be sold or given away. In addition, you can meet and collect autographs from the singers and other stars who make periodic forays to their label or fan club booth to press the flesh and "interface" with the assembled multitude.

Serious dementia!

Fan Fair consists of four major activities: concerts or showcases, the exhibits themselves, autograph and picture gathering, and special events and sightseeing. From Wednesday through Saturday the exhibits area at the state fairgrounds is open. Registrants may browse at will through the hundreds of booths set up by record labels, fan clubs, country publications, individual artists, and associations. The sponsoring organization, the Country Music Association, employs a democratic approach to the allocation of booth space, so you'll find unknowns mixed indiscriminately with the biggest stars in the business.

As you mingle amid all this hubbub of confusion, conversation, and commercialization, you'll hear periodic announcements over the public address system urging you to come to booth 327 where Margo Smith is signing autographs or to booth 171 for Gene Winn or to booth 57 for Alabama at 2:30. The mass of humanity surges in one direction or another when the biggest names are broadcast.

The ultimate goal of this stampeding herd is an autograph, a photo, a moment with the object of their affection—a tired country singer standing at a table signing whatever is thrust before him or her at a mile-a-minute clip, all the while saying something like this: "How nice to meetcha, sure I remember Mason City, that was a great show, one of the best, where do you want me to sign, what'd you say your name was, how nice to have a chance to meet and chat with you."

And on they come, hundreds upon hundreds in any two-hour shift, which is about all the continuous exposure any artist can endure. All are grasping programs or autograph books, talking excitedly among themselves, waving paper fans, nudging one another back and forth, noisy and atwitter but polite.

They come from almost every state and over a dozen foreign countries. They are almost all over thirty and most are a decade or more beyond. There are at least 30 percent more women than men. They come from middle-class homes. For many of them, Fan Fair is their vacation. They come to Nashville every year without fail for this "crazed fiesta of the proletariat," as my colleague Bob Oermann, pop music editor for the morning Nashville paper, *The Tennessean,* terms the event.

The fans come to have fun and they do, for it is the one time each year when the record

Above, left: *Your dogs would wear sunglasses too if they had come to Fan Fair from Florida in a motorbike.*
Above: *Conway Twitty, "The Crown Prince of Country Soul," caught here in close touch with two of his loyal subjects. (Photo: Beth Gwinn)*
Left: *Tammy Wynette gears up to meet her public at Fan Fair 1982. (Photo Cynthia Farah)*

labels and the artists get together to throw a party for them. Label showcases are held in the 14,000-seat Nashville International Raceway adjacent to the exhibit halls. The major labels and some independents present package shows there, while smaller companies band together to put on mixed label shows or go in separate directions with showcases at nightspots and hotels scattered all over the city.

The shows at the raceway go on all day and through much of the night. A typical show will last one and a half to three hours and will feature up to a dozen artists. In addition to the label shows there are concerts presented around themes: bluegrass, Cajun, "New Faces," songwriters, old-timers, and international acts. During the three free lunches—two of which are catered by Odessa, Texas's barbecue specialists, the Chuck Wagon Gang—in an area of the fairgrounds normally used as a flea market or livestock holding area during the other fifty-one weeks of the year, you'll also be serenaded by lesser-known talents plugging away at "Rocky Top," "He Stopped Loving Her Today," or "Always on My Mind" while you munch on your barbecue.

One of my favorite moments of Fan Fair occurred as I ate barbecued beef under a huge tent while listening to Tammy Wynette's song "D-I-V-O-R-C-E" sung in Swedish.

Fan Fair was originally created because too many fans showed up uninvited at the annual Grand Ole Opry Birthday celebration in the second week in October, when the Country Music Awards show and many other activities are held. These events were supposedly limited to disc jockeys, so in 1972 a separate week in June was set aside for the fans. For the first ten years of its existence, Fan Fair was conducted at Nashville's aging Municipal Auditorium, a structure in dire need of serious renovation if not outright demolition. In 1981, when registration swelled to over fifteen thousand, the masses taxed the site's facilities to the limit; there were far too few bathrooms and too little room to accommodate those who wanted to attend the concerts held on the upper level of the building. Exhibits were placed on the lower level, giving the event a tidy compactness.

The decision was made then to transfer the festivities to the state fairgrounds, located south of the intersection of I-65 and I-40. The move, while offering a much larger site free from downtown traffic tangles, entailed splitting up the performances and the exhibits, themselves scattered among five adjacent buildings.

The shows are now held at the nearby raceway, a facility only partly protected from rain and the normally hot June sun. Given the age of many Fan Fair guests, this was not a totally popular solution. June temperatures in Nashville can reach over ninety degrees, and thundershowers are not uncommon. There were some complaints in 1982 when the new site debuted even though the weather was mild and dry that year. Fan Fair, like Topsy, "just growed"—if it grows much larger it will have to move again, and there is no site in Nashville capable at present of handling this size crowd.

Those who come to Fan Fair are not to be considered merely as fans but as *rabid* supporters. A person at a concert will spend from fifteen to forty dollars to see from one to four major acts and buy souvenirs in the course of a show lasting up to four hours. But coming to Fan Fair entails a commitment of a week, including travel time, and expenses can range from five hundred up to two thousand dollars per person, depending on the degree of luxury demanded and the amount of purchases made.

Bob Millard, formerly with the afternoon paper here, the *Nashville Banner,* conducted a random survey of one hundred 1983 visitors, slightly less than 1 percent of the total crowd that year. He found the average age to be forty-four and that the average fan had traveled 493 miles to take part. The average daily expenditure of those surveyed was more than one hundred dollars. With over 19,000 in attendance for the five-day event, this means that 1984's Fan Fair pumped in at least $9.5 million into the Music City economy.

Fan Fair visitors will gladly accept any free item or purchase just about any object purveyed by their favorite artist, but it is the collection of autographs that really gets their juices flowing. Fans began queuing up *four hours* before the arrival of the Oak Ridge Boys at their booth in 1983. They stood patiently in line, chatting with fellow participants and fanning themselves with the paper fans supplied by Tammy Wynette's booth, enduring the misery of the long wait just to get the signatures of William Lee Golden, Duane Allen, Richard Sterban, and Joe Bonsall on a program, a scrap of paper, or in some cases an arm or more intimate portion of the anatomy. "How can it be so hot with so many fans in here," Waylon Jennings once remarked. Similar throngs greeted the appearances of Alabama, Barbara Mandrell, and Loretta Lynn.

Fan Fair decals, signs, and bumper stickers can range from the ridiculous to the risqué. One that encompassed both areas of taste at the 1984 event proudly proclaimed "I love Peter."

My favorite item from Fan Fair was a tiny bar of soap from the Taft Hotel, given to me for purchasing a Jimmie Rodgers T-shirt at the 1981 Fan Fair. The deadpan concessionaire who doled out the soap hastened to tell me that the Taft was where Rodgers died from tuberculosis in 1933. The soap appeared to be of more recent vintage.

Here are some other of my favorite Fan Fair stories: A fan walked up to the tastefully decorated Jim Reeves booth. "Is Jim here?" she asked Mary Reeves Davis, widow of Reeves since his tragic death in a plane crash in 1964. "No, Jim isn't here," replied Mary, feeling no doubt that answer to be preferable to stating, "No, he's been dead for nineteen years." The disconsolate fan walked away slowly, muttering to her companion, "Yeah. And he wasn't here last year either."

Dr. Jim Matthews, "The Singing Surgeon," went all out in 1983. As usual, he came dressed in surgical scrubs, but this year his wife was turned out in a nursing outfit and his kids wore the garb of hospital orderlies. Dr. Matthews is from Meridian, Mississippi, and has recorded half a dozen albums of his renditions of country standards. One wonders if a discount on album purchases is available to his surgical customers.

James "Rebel" O'Leary and his daughter, Jammie Ann, are regular participants. Their double-sized booth offers perhaps the most varied and complete selection of all the merchants: vending glasses, rings, matches, towels, bumper stickers, pins, buttons, T-shirts, caps, key-chains, panties, and other delights. James is a dour individual from Pennsylvania who is given to wearing a turquoise necklace and turquoise rings on both thumbs and all eight fingers. Jammie Ann plays in the band led by her dad and usually looks like she'd rather be somewhere else.

Johnny Rodriguez certainly knows how to satisfy a Fan Fair crowd. At the 1983 CBS Showcase he worked the tip of the stage with a cordless microphone, shaking hands, hugging and kissing as many of his ardent female admirers as possible between verses, choruses, and in the instrumental passages. Label officials confided later that his legs were bruised from being grabbed and that he found three motel keys in his jacket pocket after the performance.

America may not have royalty but the expressions of rapture on the faces of the thousands assembled when a longtime superstar like Conway Twitty, Tammy Wynette, the Oak Ridge Boys, or Loretta Lynn performs reminds one of a regal tribute. Such blind adoration can be unsettling, but it seems to be a harmless passion. So much love pours out of the grandstands from the fans to the star that an almost palpable warmth can be felt.

Fan Fair's newest event is the All-American Country Games, a sort of country music version of TV's "Battle of the Network Stars," which finds three teams made up of country singers running, jumping, pushing giant balls around, and engaging in all manner of events usually associated with elementary school field days. Those who participate, invariably clad in scanty shorts, have a great time and give the proceeds to a good cause, the Special Olympics. The sight of such stars as Barbara Mandrell, Brenda Lee, Sylvia, Lee Greenwood, Gary Morris, Joe Bonsall, Karen Brooks, Michael Murphey, Gail Davies, Earl Thomas Conley, Kathy Mattea, Eddy Raven, and Larry Willoughby cavorting on the artificial greensward of Vanderbilt University's football field, Dudley Stadium, is one not soon forgotten.

Since Fan Fair is for the fans it's not surprising that fan club enterprises take up the lion's share of the booths to be found in the exhibit area. Almost every country artist of any renown has such an organization, usually run by an ardent fan. These groups range in size from a few dozen members to over 170,000, as is the case with Alabama. The Ernest Tubb Fan Club, run

SYLVIA *(RCA)*

She is proof positive that dreams of country stardom do come true. Born in Kokomo, Indiana, Sylvia was the staff artist for the Little Nashville Opry in her home state before she got a position in Music City as receptionist for producer Tom Collins. There she gained a vocalist audition and was taken on as a singer. Not long after that, she scored a No. 1 country hit with "Drifter," a Fleming-Morgan song, which sounded like Gogi Grant's "The Wayward Wind" recorded in 1956. Sylvia posted a large pop hit with "Nobody" in 1982. Chosen Female Vocalist of the Year by the Academy of Country Music (ACM) in 1983, Sylvia has made up for her limited vocal range with boundless energy, drive, and enthusiasm.

THE BELLAMY BROTHERS *(MCA-Curb)*

Florida boys, David and Howard Bellamy live and record on a farm near Tampa. They specialize in sometimes sappy love songs delivered in a white reggae style. In 1976, they had a big pop hit with "Let Your Love Flow." Later, they bailed out into country and caught fire with the punch-line song "If I Said You Had a Beautiful Body, Would You Hold It Against Me." Seven more No. 1s followed during the early 1980s, most of them written by David. In 1983, when research showed that they had scored more No. 1s than George and Tammy, Conway and Loretta, or Porter and Dolly, they laid claim to the title "most successful country duet."

Right: *There's fun for everyone at Fan Fair. (Photo: John Carnes)*
Below, left: *The Bellamy Brothers, Howard (left) and David, indoctrinate a young listener at Fan Fair.*
Below, right: *David Allan Coe supplies an autograph at Fan Fair. (Photo: John Carnes)*

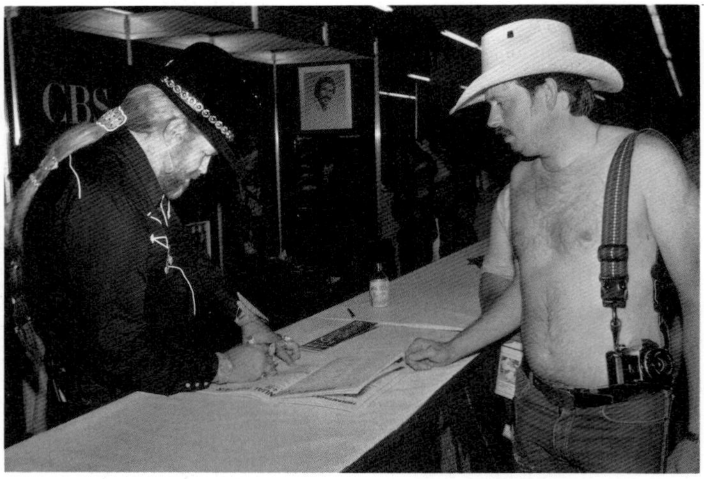

by Norma Barthel, has been in existence continuously since the early 1940s and has them all beat for longevity. Many of the clubs stage their own events during the week. Such events, limited to members only, include such gatherings as sisters Barbara and Louise Mandrell's formal banquet, Tubb's annual picnic at a large city park, Janie Fricke's breakfast, Susie Deveraux's yearly show at the Sheraton, a brunch with the Oak Ridge Boys, Helen Cornelius's dinner cruise on the river, Jeanne Pruett's fish fry and show, a T. G. Sheppard reception, Margo Smith's barbecue and performance at her own home, and countless informal club reunions.

Visitors can also have tons of fun by just circulating among the exhibits and eyeballing the different styles of presentation. The booths are rented bare, so each group is responsible for its own decoration. Contests are held for the "Best Booth," resulting in some very elaborate productions costing thousands of dollars amid many less ostentatious but touching expressions of devotion.

There are, in fact, so many fan clubs that there is an organization devoted entirely to monitoring them. IFCO, the International Fan Club Organization, is steered admirably by Loretta, Loudilla, and Kay Johnson, three single sisters who live in the unlikely spot of Wild Horse, Colorado. The Johnson sisters also direct Loretta Lynn's fan club (they were among her first supporters back in 1960) and are so well organized that they help the CMA by providing dozens of volunteers to aid in crowd control each June. IFCO also presents its own show during Fan Fair, and it is always packed with stars. The group publishes a semi-annual guide that rates each fan club according to the quantity, quality, and frequency of the material issued to members.

Fan Fair presents the best opportunity to see the bond that exists between country singers and their audience. The main thing country fans desire from the stars is *access*—and Fan Fair offers many chances to have that treasured time, even if it is only a moment, with the star of their choice. It's this personal touch that separates country singing stars from those in the other areas of popular music. Country singers aren't willing to give the fans a piece of their heart, but they do extend a bit of their time, and at Fan Fair you will see this practice in full operation.

RAY PRICE *(Viva)*

With over fifty Top 10s to his credit in a career still active after over thirty-one years, Price stands today as one of country's most enduring artists. Born in Perryville, Texas, and raised there and in Dallas, Price exemplifies the "modern" country sound of the 1960s, a sound that today would be dubbed "crossover." Back then, however, his change from honky-tonk stylings to a lush, orchestrated sound only won him wrath from purists who felt he had sold out and "gone pop." "Crazy Arms," "City Lights," and "For the Good Times" are his signature songs, along with "Danny Boy," the last a monster pop hit. Although his achievements merit inclusion in the Country Music Hall of Fame, Price probably will never be selected because of his outspokenness, his refusal to play Music City politics, and his long-time residence in Texas. Price lived for a while with Hank Williams in the early 1950s. Should Price ever decide to jot down his memoirs, the tale should be very juicy.

Ray Price applies the personal touch. (Photo: Cynthia Farah)

Visiting Stars at Home

JOE STAMPLEY *(Epic)*

Good ol' boys Joe Stampley and Moe Bandy have racked up numerous hits, both together and solo. Joe grew up in Springhill, Louisiana (where he lives today). As a boy, he idolized Hank Williams, and by the time the pair met, when Joe was seven, he had already learned every song Williams recorded. He shared CMA Duet honors with Bandy in 1980. The duo hit No. 1 with "Hey Joe (Hey Moe)" and in 1981 came out with the first country hit detailing transvestism in a honky-tonk, "Honky Tonk Queen." As a solo singer, Joe posted Top-10 hits annually from 1971 to 1982, including such memorable No. 1s as "Roll On, Big Mama," "All These Things," and "Soul Song." Several songs written by his son Tony ("I've Been Down," "Whiskey on Ice") were recorded by Hank Williams, Jr.—Joe's brother-in-law—on his *High Notes* LP. He and Bandy revived their duet partnership in 1984 with "Where's the Dress?," a clever swipe at both Boy George of Culture Club and the Wendy's hamburger commercials (which Tony also helped to write).

All the major country music stars have three types of homes. One is composed of countless motel rooms, another is defined by the boundaries of their tour bus, and the third is the more traditional stationary home like that most Americans occupy. It's interesting that motel rooms are still basic to the performing routine despite the use of the large, modern buses. In many cases the rooms are used as a staging point before the show. They also come in handy if several performers need to bathe and change clothes simultaneously. The shower facilities on the bus leave quite a bit to be desired.

The amount of time the top performers spend on the road can range up to three hundred days and nights a year. It's no wonder that when the stars do stop moving they usually opt for peaceful homesteads on large parcels of land.

The home is the artists' only refuge from public view, their only place to "be themselves" free from the scrutiny of fans, peers, and press. It's to be expected that some of the major artists jealously guard their privacy, a tack pursued by Dolly Parton, Eddie Rabbitt, Don Williams, Merle Haggard, and Hank Williams, Jr. Most of the rock stars of the day are likewise secretive about their residences; some employ guard dogs, security guards, and the latest devices to discourage intruders.

For the most part, though, country stars either make no effort to conceal their primary address or they go to extremes to call attention to it. The foremost example of this is Conway Twitty, whose Twitty City houses three generations of his family amid a museum and offices. For years Webb Pierce's mansion on a hill on Franklin Road was a popular attraction. The tour buses would stop in a specially built parking area, deposit their cargo, and wait for them to return, engines gently idling. The fans trooped up the driveway and were admitted to an area behind Pierce's house, the site of his guitar-shaped swimming pool. Pierce would then emerge from within to greet them, sign autographs, and sell copies of his old albums at more modern prices. The fans were enthralled at this process, which is similar to a piece in a museum

Opposite, left: *Opry star Skeeter Davis inspects one from her potpourri of pooches. (Photo: Marshall Fallwell, Jr.)*
Opposite, right: *Bobby and Jeannie Bare share a quiet moment at home with the kids. (Photo: Marshall Fallwell, Jr.)*
Above, left: *Joe Stampley and family at home in Spring Hill, Louisiana, in 1974. Son Tony (left) is now a successful songwriter.*
Above, center: *Star or not, there's still kids to raise and dinner to fix, as Connie Smith does here for two of her brood. (Photo: Marshall Fallwell, Jr.)*
Above, right: *The cows don't care if Reba McEntire is a superstar or not. (Photo: Mark Emmons)*
Left: *Brenda Lee relaxing at home. She has sold more records than anyone in Nashville. (Photo: Bud Lee)*

RONNIE MILSAP *(RCA)*

An entertainer deluxe, Milsap had mildly successful flings with rock and soul music before coming to Music City from Memphis in 1973. His third RCA single, Eddie Rabbitt's "Pure Love," hit No. 1 in 1974, and he added twenty-seven more hits by the end of 1984—more than anyone else racked up in the years from 1973 to 1984—and he did it all as a solo artist. CMA Entertainer of the Year in 1977, Ronnie has also won CMA kudos three times each for Best LP and Best Male Vocalist. He has also had hits in pop, rhythm 'n' blues, and a-c, and he received three Grammies. A ham radio operator who was born blind, he tells people he sees with his ears. (He has often been called a "white Ray Charles.") A shoo-in for future Hall of Fame honors.

Left: *Joyce, Ronnie, and Todd Milsap at work on Todd's piano lesson. (Photo: Marshall Fallwell, Jr.)*
Right: *Mr. and Mrs. George Jones and Tamala Georgette Jones in the mid-1970s. (Photo: Marshall Fallwell, Jr.)*

suddenly coming to life and chatting. (This charming practice ceased, however, when irate neighbors, among them Ray Stevens, complained of the noise and traffic disruption. A flurry of petitions and legal activity forced Pierce to close his "home office" to visitors and relocate on Music Row.)

What's most surprising about the country artists is the fact that so many of them do choose to live out in the open. Every day bus tours take thousands of tourists past the very houses occupied by such stars as Eddy Arnold, Waylon Jennings, Johnny Cash, Earl Scruggs, Hank Snow, Dottie West, Barbara Mandrell, Ronnie Milsap, T. G. Sheppard, Tom T. Hall, and countless others. The tour bus companies don't take too many pains to make sure that the star still lives in the home; it appears that all that is necessary is that the star *once* lived there.

Barbara Mandrell moved front and center in 1984 when she acquired control of a former museum on Music Row and "re-created" her home inside the building. Barbara spared no detail in the project: she even stayed up all night repainting a mural she had done for the children's room. Various Mandrell mementoes also are presented to spice up the surroundings. Needless to say, a gift shop is also on the premises. In the last few years, the creation of attractions centered around artists has become a separate cottage industry. These structures, featuring such stars as Marty Robbins, Ferlin Husky, Bill Monroe, Hank Williams, and Mickey Gilley, have begun to dot the areas around Music Row, Opryland, and Twitty City, Nashville's three main enclaves of commercialized country. The city also boasts not one but two country music star wax museums.

The willingness of the stars to allow fans to drive by for a look or a snapshot does not extend to more detailed interior inspections or tramping about the grounds. The following pages will permit the reader to peek into the homelife of several country stars.

Additional Attractions

There's never time to do everything during a visit to Music City, but fans of "The Crown Prince of Country Soul" will want to make a pilgrimage north of town to Hendersonville to view Twitty City, a "theme park" built around the glory that is Conway Twitty, one of country's most enduring stars and certainly the most famed personage ever to be raised in Friars Point, Mississippi.

The elegantly landscaped grounds contain museums devoted to Twitty, Marty Robbins, and Ferlin Husky, a souvenir shop, a theater, "Showcase of the Stars," Conway's offices, his palatial seven-thousand-plus-square-foot home, and the homes of all four of his children. Conway's mother and mother-in-law also live in the complex. (He wasn't kidding when he called it "Twitty City.")

Notwithstanding all these lures, Conway's many fans will receive an even bigger thrill if they are in attendance when he emerges from one of the buildings to stroll the grounds to another of his edifices. On such forays he will take the time to chat, pose for photos, or sign autographs. The best opportunity for a Twitty sighting is during the week; most weekends he goes out to make personal appearances. Twitty City makes Graceland, Elvis's home, look like a souvenir stand!

Across the street, Johnny and June Carter Cash have created a most intriguing museum stuffed with many of the items they have collected during Cash's fabulous career. The building once was home to the House of Cash, Johnny's recording studio, and it has a large collection of bric-a-brac ranging from antiques to guns to the one-of-a-kind Cadillac Cash sang about in his late 1970s hit "One Piece at a Time," which detailed the gradual theft of a Caddy from an assembly plant. Naturally, the facility includes a souvenir shop.

On your return visit you may well wish to stay on U.S. 31E (also known as Gallatin Road) all the way to town, a route that will lead you past the Jim Reeves Museum and the Willie Nelson Country Store, spots that will be of interest to fans of those two stars. The Reeves museum housed in Evergreen mansion gives a good glimpse into the life of "Gentleman Jim," and your host for this stop may well be his charming widow, Mary Reeves Davis. The Nelson store is run by Frank Oakley, a most convivial chap who'll possibly be willing to regale you with tales of Willie's life during the days before he became the superstar he is today.

Music City isn't all country music, and music isn't the only interesting diversion Nashville has to offer. The city also boasts many scenic, cultural, athletic, and educational attractions. Some of the most popular are discussed below while a more complete listing is carried in the back of the book.

Spectacular and interesting as the Opryland complex and the Country Music Hall of Fame and Museum are, other cities do boast theme parks and museums. No other city, however, plays host to a full-scale replica of the Parthenon. Built originally in 1879 for Tennessee's Centennial from plans supplied by the king of Greece, the Parthenon was rebuilt in the 1920s. The structure, the centerpiece of Centennial Park, houses an art gallery in its lower level. Copies of ancient statuary grace the ground-floor level.

Fort Nashborough, home to Nashville's original settlers over two hundred years ago, has been restored to look as it did more than two centuries ago. Suitably attired members of Historic Nashville, a group dedicated to preserving the skills of the pioneers, demonstrate to visitors how these pioneers lived, worked, and prepared their food.

The Nashville area is also home to a number of mansions and residences built in the previous century. Visitors with interests in the architecture, furniture, and way of life of the

1800s will enjoy visiting the Hermitage (Andrew Jackson's home), the Belmont Mansion, a huge building just above Music Row that is now part of Belmont College, and Belle Meade Mansion, considered by many to be "The Queen of Tennessee's antebellum estates." All have been restored and all offer fascinating glimpses of the way our ancestors lived.

Nashville and the surrounding area also offer several historic Civil War sites. Major battles occurred in Nashville as well as in nearby Franklin and Murfreesboro. There are many markers commemorating the bloody fighting at these locations and intrepid searchers may still find buttons, Minié balls, or other relics of the war in many parts of the countryside.

Nashville's Performing Arts Center provides culture on two levels. The State Museum, located in the basement, presents exhibits and re-creations of bygone times stretching back to the days when Indians roamed freely through the area. Upstairs, the Tennessee Performing Arts Center encloses three auditoriums where most of Nashville's "high-culture" events take place. The city's orchestra, touring symphonies, ballets, Broadway shows, plays, and foreign troupes perform here regularly. TPAC's Andrew Jackson Hall is the site of many televised country music specials.

The Cumberland Museum and Science Center is the city's other general museum. Privately owned, the Cumberland offers exhibits, live animal feedings, slide shows, a hands-on children's play area, laser shows, a planetarium, a nature trail, and many lectures and demonstrations.

Various sporting events also provide recreational entertainment for those in Nashville. In addition to a full slate of high school events, most of the area colleges field teams in the major sports. Vanderbilt is a member of the Southeastern Conference, one of the nation's premier athletic groups, while Tennessee State University has produced many notable black athletes in football, basketball, and track, most notably Wilma Rudolph, a triple gold medal-winner in the 1960 Olympics.

Fans of professional sports will enjoy baseball games at Greer Stadium, home of the Nashville Sounds, a class AAA team that competes in the American Association. The Sounds have been one of minor league baseball's most successful franchises since the club began operation in 1978. Over half a million people annually attend the team's seventy-one-game home season, attendance exceeded among minor league cities only by Louisville.

This box-office success led to Nashville's moving up a notch to AAA status in 1985, when the city assumed the Evansville, Indiana, franchise. Many local sports experts predict that the city is no more than ten years away from gaining a major league franchise, depending upon the big leagues' expansion plans.

The players, supplied through a farm-system agreement with the Detroit Tigers, are almost all nineteen to twenty-five years old, so the quality of play is less polished than in the majors. But they more than make up for any lack of skill by flashing the enthusiasm common to young men paid to play a kids' game. The talent is certainly there: in the first few years of operation the Sounds have "graduated" many players to the majors, including Frank Pastore, Don Mattingly, Steve Balboni, Pat Tabler, Joe Price, Dave Van Gorder, Paul Householder, and Bill Dawley.

If you get a chance, go on out and take in a game. Visitors from a city with major league ballclubs are doubly encouraged to attend to find out how much fun it is to see baseball in a more intimate setting. You'll be much closer to the action so rest assured that any loud remarks you make to players or umpires will be heard. You'll also enjoy the camaraderie among the spectators, the beauty of a grass field, and the low cost—the best box seats are under five dollars. And you just might catch a glimpse of Conway Twitty, Jerry Reed, or Richard Sterban of the Oak Ridge Boys—all are major stockholders in the franchise.

If you are a lover of the outdoors, then you're in the right place, for south of town lies Warner Park, a sprawling hilly area that encloses hiking trails along the Little Harpeth River as well as tougher paths cut through the brush to the tops of one thousand foothills. Tennessee's only wildlife sanctuary, Radnor Lake, lies about ten miles due south of town. It presents many splendid vistas from the hiking trails cut up and down its hills as well as the best and most

CONWAY TWITTY
(Warner Bros.)

Far from handsome, Conway nonetheless enjoys an almost religious hold on American middle-aged women. He has made a career from his understanding of women's feelings, voicing words women want to hear from men. He specializes in corny but subtly salacious sentiments delivered with an understated vocal elegance. He spent seven years onstage before speaking to his audience (he only opened his mouth to sing). He is currently vying with Charley Pride and Merle Haggard for the record number of No. 1 singles in music history. "The Crown Prince of Country Soul" erected for himself Twitty City, the most ambitious monument to a living musician's career ever built. His 1983 Yuletide LP, *Merry 'Twismas from Conway Twitty and the Twitty Bird,* is the most ambitious and costly children's album ever made by anyone: it required over 1,000 hours in the studio and cost over $250,000. One of the best at selecting material in country music, Twitty knows the business well and would make a superlative manager should he ever decide to stop thrilling housewives personally. Future Hall of Famer.

It took a big shovel to break ground for Twitty City in 1981. Conway and his wife, Mickey, didn't know what the future held at this point.
Overleaf: *Music Row tourist shops in front of the Nashville skyline. (Photo: Jim Brown)*

A Modest Proposal

Some years back Nashville suddenly changed the names of most of the streets in the Music Row area. One day I found I no longer toiled on Sixteenth Avenue South but on a street called Music Square East. Seventeenth Avenue South had metamorphosed into Music Square West, and other streets with perfectly good names like Grand, Hawkins, and South were given the unromantic new monickers Music Circle South, Music Square South, and Music Circle North.

No reason was ever announced for this municipal exercise. Music Row workers shrugged, ordered stationery with their new address, and continued referring to the streets by their old names.

Then, in 1981, the city changed the designation of Music Row North, a two-block connector, to Roy Acuff Place, surely a more fitting address for Music Row.

This practice should continue. Why not rename Sixteenth Avenue South (Music Square East) Hank Williams Boulevard and Seventeenth (Music Square West) Fred Rose Avenue? Other Nashville pioneers who brought the music industry here—Owen Bradley, Chet Atkins, Paul Cohen, Jim Denny, Don Law, Ernest Tubb, Red Foley, Art Satherly, Edwin Craig, Marty Robbins, Hank Snow, Frances Preston, Eddy Arnold, and Webb Pierce—could be honored by being immortalized on the town's green and white street signs, thus lending even more atmosphere to the most important two square miles in American popular music. If the pioneers of Nashville's musical development aren't honored here in Music City then who *will* honor them?

Any city can have numbered streets, circles, and squares, but Hank Williams Boulevard—now that's class!

varied birdwatching opportunities in the state. There has been a concerted effort in Tennessee to keep all parks in a condition as near to their original condition as is possible. Hikers on these trails need only use a little imagination to picture these areas as they were when Indians and wild animals were the land's only residents.

If you're here in the warm months you might well want to visit Hermitage Landing, a resort/amusement complex located just east of town on Old Hickory Lake. Hermitage Landing offers swimming, boating, tennis, miniature golf, a waterslide, and other recreational facilities. Cabins are available for rent or you can just pack a bathing suit and snacks to make a day of it.

All the above-listed attractions round out Nashville's entertainment picture for those whose interests extend beyond the Grand Ole Opry, Music Row, and the city's other music-related attractions. There's plenty to do here, so be prepared to do a little exploring when you arrive—you'll be glad you took the time to discover some of Music City's many additional delights.

One of Nashville's many emporiums dedicated to a country star.

NASHVILLE'S MUSIC

What Is Country Music?

JOHN CONLEE *(MCA)*

Raised on a four-hundred-acre farm in Kentucky, John was a farmer, embalmer, and rock DJ before he wrote "Rose Colored Glasses" (with George Baber), the song that put him on the map. His next chart record, "Lady Lay Down," hit No. 1, and the next release, his own "Backside of Thirty," also hit the top. His wonderfully rich voice is best suited to traditional country ballads. He also selects superb, *different* songs for singles: "Miss Emily's Picture," "I Don't Remember Loving You," "Friday Night Blues." The LPs he cuts are solid, and he doesn't play games with copyrights (that is, unlike several stars, he doesn't demand part of the publishing rights for cutting a song). He should become a major star in the 1980s.

Left: *Hank Williams (center) and the Drifting Cowboys (left to right, Don Helms, Bob McNett, Jerry Rivers, and Hillous Butrum) pose in this early 1950s promotional shot.*
Right: *"Common Man" John Conlee hasn't gone uptown; he still keeps in touch with his public. (Photo: Tim Naprestek)*

Country music is Hank Williams, Jr., singing "a country boy can survive" or Loretta Lynn telling her adversary that "you ain't woman enough to take my man." It's Lefty Frizzell, Merle Haggard, and John Anderson moaning a classic tale of blood, lust, and death in "Long Black Veil" or Kitty Wells stating that "it wasn't God who made honky-tonk angels." It's George Jones urging us to "step right in" as he takes us on "The Grand Tour" of the home where his heart was broken or Crystal Gayle defiantly proclaiming, "I'll get over you."

And it's songs that bring tears to your eyes: Dolly Parton recalling the "coat of many colors" from her childhood or Guy Clark's memories of his relationship with his grandfather—"I was grown and he was almost gone," surely one of the finest brief summations of youth and old age ever set on paper.

Or country music can be based on more pleasant themes: John Conlee declaring, "I'm only in it for the love and affection" or Donna Fargo merrily bubbling away about being "the happiest girl in the whole U.S.A."

Country tunes can be cloaked in mystery, leaving the listener to wonder just what has happened, as when Willie Nelson and Merle Haggard sing "the dust that Pauncho bit down South ended up in Lefty's mouth." Sixteen years later, listeners still aren't sure what transpired on the Tallahatchee Bridge as detailed in Bobby Gentry's "Ode to Billy Joe," a chilling tale of the death of one person—or was there a murdered newborn involved as well?

Country music songs are about fishing, drinking, living, working, dying, and about loving the right and wrong person. The one unifying characteristic is that the lyrics are grounded in human experience.

The lyrics of country songs, like those of folk music, must stand alone. Poetic or not, the country songs that stick in the minds of Americans contain hidden kernels of wisdom that wind up being assimilated into the spoken language: "Pick me up on your way down," "You've

Left: *Merle Haggard's songwriting and singing skills have overshadowed his instrumental prowess. (Photo: Cynthia Farah)*
Right: *Earl Thomas Conley during a tender moment in performance in 1982.*

got to know when to hold 'em, know when to fold 'em," "Your good girl's gonna go bad," "When you're hot, you're hot, when you're not, you're not," "I've got a tiger by the tail," "She got the gold mine, I got the shaft," and "Turn out the lights, the party's over."

Country songs can be wrapped in the dominant themes of literature, as in Bob McDill's "Good Ole Boys Like Me," a song that reveals McDill's interest in the great Southern novelists:

> Well, nothing makes a sound in the night like the wind does
> But you ain't afraid if you're washed in the blood like I was
> The smell of Cape Jasmine through the window screen
> John R. and the Wolfman kept me company
> By the light of the radio by my bed
> With Thomas Wolfe whisperin' in my head
>
> I still hear the soft Southern wind in the live oak trees
> Those Williams boys they still mean a lot to me
> Hank and Tennessee
> I guess we're all gonna be what we're gonna be
> So what do you do with good ole boys like me

Country can also encompass biting social comment, as in Jack Moran and Glenn D. Tubb's stinging tale of adult hypocrisy, "Skip a Rope":

> Listen to the children, how they play
> But it isn't very funny what the children say
> Skip-a-rope
> Cheat on your taxes, don't be a fool

EARL THOMAS CONLEY
(RCA)

A drifter, picker, artist, poet, and factory worker before his first hits in 1979, Earl left his Ohio home at fifteen. Well-read and self-educated, he writes some of the most sensitive and compelling songs in the field and delivers them in a vocal style that combines classic influences. In live shows, he can rock out as well as John Anderson but is quiet, even shy offstage. Recently, only he and Vern Gosdin managed to nab a No. 1 single on an independent label ("Fire and Smoke," 1981, Sunbird Records). Earl comes from a smoky, mysterious place all his own; he's a potential superstar.

JOHNNY CASH
(Columbia)

"The Man in Black" came from utter poverty in Kingsland, Arkansas, to become one of the greatest folk/country singers the world has yet seen. One of the most recorded singers in American music, Cash has helped dozens of songwriters, musicians, friends, and prisoners. Cash's stern visage masks a heart the size of a watermelon. He conquered personal problems with drugs and alcohol and has devoted years since that time to trying to help others combat their substance-abuse problems. Already a Hall of Fame selection, Cash has won five CMA Awards, four of those in 1969 alone.

What was that they said about the Golden Rule
Never mind the rules, just play to win
And hate your neighbor for the shade of his skin
Skip-a-rope

And country songs can eloquently fathom the wrenching sadness felt for a person and a place erased by time's inexorable march forward, as written by Sandy Pinkard and James Cowan in their spine-tingling song "Disappearing Farmer":

Now a modern two-lane blacktop runs across the old home place
The man that runs the graveyard didn't recognize my face
And the ground seems drier now than "My God when will it rain?"
It's pushing flowers up around my grandpa's grave
And it's a sad thing when the wind can blow a man's whole life away
Like it strips the topsoil from the ground where the corn grew yesterday
Makes him a disappearing farmer 'cause his dreams rode with that wind
Now all he's got is dominoes and some oh so wrinkled friends

The heartfelt emotion found in country music is expressed with remarkably few words. Most of the songs use less than one hundred and fifty words to tell a story, make a point, delve deeply into emotion, or explore social conditions. McDill calls country songs "three-minute movies" because of this lyric compression, a point to consider when listening to Tony Joe White tell of "Polk Salad Annie" and her unpleasant father: "Her daddy was mean and low-count. *Claimed* he had a bad back"—a thirteen-word sketch that forever brands Annie's pa as a person of little character.

Country music is an *amalgamation* of styles developed by singers, writers, and instrumentalists who have borrowed freely from every style of music that has interested them since they heard their first singer sing the first note. It is a form that is always evolving; each person in the field spent his or her early years absorbing country's heritage before combining these elements with their own contributions to form their version of modern country music. Rock 'n' roll is a fusion of black blues and white country, but country itself is an earlier fusion made up of musical elements from white European settlers blended with the African-derived music of blacks forcibly relocated in the American South. This mixture is evident in the music of such pioneers of country music as Jimmie Rodgers, Fred Rose, and Hank Williams, the first three men honored by selection into the Country Music Hall of Fame.

Today's country music has retained its lyric preoccupation but it has rhythmically broadened to become a field of music that offers flavors to suit the taste of almost any consumer. Purists can take heart in the arrival of such singers as Ricky Skaggs, John Anderson, John Conlee, George Strait, Reba McEntire, David Frizzell, Emmylou Harris, Gene Watson, the Judds, and the Whites as exponents of the more traditional elements that link modern country to its roots.

Fans who like their country seasoned by a rock beat can hearken to the sounds of Waylon Jennings, Charlie Daniels, Alabama, Hank Williams, Jr., and Earl Thomas Conley, or they can groove to the rockabilly stylings of Eddie Rabbitt and Steve Earle.

The hard-core purists who love only the old-time music can still go to see most of the stars of the past thirty years—Hank Snow, Kitty Wells, Roy Acuff, Webb Pierce, Hank Thompson—as well as their successors—Merle Haggard, George Jones, Loretta Lynn, Tammy Wynette, and Conway Twitty.

Those who like their country a bit softer and smoother can be palliated by the strains of Barbara Mandrell, Don Williams, T. G. Sheppard, Janie Fricke, and Rosanne Cash.

If you want pop touches in your country, then Kenny Rogers, Anne Murray, Ronnie Milsap, Crystal Gayle, and Lee Greenwood will satisfy that appetite.

Preceding page: *Johnny Cash has been a friend to talented but unheralded songwriters throughout his 30-year career. (Photo: Jim McGuire)*
Don Gibson is one of country's top songwriters. (Photo: Marshall Fallwell, Jr.)

STATLER BROTHERS
(PolyGram)

You might think that, with nine CMA Awards, a No. 2 million-selling pop single ("Flowers on the Wall"), and the admiration of Kurt Vonnegut, the Statlers by now would have to their credit more than two No. 1 singles on the country charts. But these four Virginians—brothers Don and Harold Reid, Phil Balsley, and Lew DeWitt (replaced by Jimmy Fortune in 1982)—don't think about it; they're happy to be out singing their tightly knit four-part harmonies and trotting out corn-pone humor for their fans. Besides, the quartet pulls in over $5 million a year from appearances. Their annual "Old-Fashioned Fourth of July Celebration" in their hometown of Staunton, Virginia, draws upwards of sixty thousand, making it the largest regularly scheduled annual country fest anywhere. Charts or no charts, the Statlers know their place is secure in the hearts of their fans. Practicing Christians, they still live in Staunton and maintain offices in their old elementary school. Possible Hall of Famers.

Above: *Jessi Colter in red and blue. (Photo: Bill Dibble)*
Below, left: *Owen Bradley (foreground) and Governor Jimmie Davis. (Photo: Bud Lee)*
Below, right: *You never know just who will turn up on "Hee Haw." Here co-host Roy Clark greets Sammy Davis, Jr. (Photo: Robin Hood)*
Overleaf: *The Statler Brothers and Roy Rogers, "The King of the Cowboys," at a TV taping. (Photo: John Carnes)*

Above: *Willie Nelson's Band takes a bow. (Photo: Dean Dixon)*
Right: *Three-time CMA Award-winner Charley Pride at the 1982 Fan Fair. (Photo: John Carnes)*

CHARLEY PRIDE *(RCA)*

A son of the Mississippi soil, Pride is the only black singer to post a solo Top-10 country hit. He grew up picking cotton, and he recalls listening to George Jones and Webb Pierce singing "Why Baby Why" and "More and More" on the radio while he worked in the fields by day. Almost three decades later, he made hits of these two songs all over again. He is one of the few country stars who have never written a hit song. He is astute in business, with substantial interests in music publishing, real estate, banking, cattle, and oil, all directed from his office in posh north Dallas. Chosen CMA Entertainer of the Year in 1971 and a two-time Male Vocalist winner, Pride will be in the Country Hall of Fame someday.

Above, left: *June Carter Cash (in shawl) and Loretta Lynn, two of country music's finest and most enduring women performers. (Photo: Robin Hood)*
Above, center: *Don Williams cranks up the bus for a short haul. (Photo: Jim McGuire)*
Above, right: *Rhonda "Kye" Fleming and Dennis W. Morgan were Music City's leading songwriters in the early 1980s. (Photo: John Carnes)*
Overleaf: *"The Killer"—Jerry Lee Lewis on the prowl. (Photo: Jim McGuire)*

JERRY LEE LEWIS *(MCA)*

Quite possibly the foremost rock-country-blues musician of the twentieth century, Lewis is also seriously tormented. One of the most charismatic performers to ever grace a stage or deface a piano, Jerry Lee has influenced every rock and country player who has ever sat behind a keyboard. He lives according to his own rules and, as a result, he has been continually at odds with women, alcohol, amphetamines, the police, and the IRS. He is probably the all-time leader in legal fees. When word leaked out of his marriage to his thirteen-year-old second cousin, Myra Gail, he was practically deported from England. Lewis spent ten years in social exile before making a comeback in 1968. See biographies by Nick Tosches and Robert Palmer and memoirs of Myra Gail for further details. Lewis belongs in the Hall of Fame but will never be selected.

Above: *A 1982 CMA Awards show production number featuring (left to right): Reba McEntire, Janie Fricke, Charly McClain, Mary Fielder, Pam Rose, Linda Moore (the last three are members of the group Calamity Jane), Terri Gibbs, and Sylvia. (Photo: Robin Hood)*
Below: *Sevierville, Tennessee's gift to the world: Dolly Parton.*

Patsy Cline, one of the earliest women country stars.

GAIL DAVIES *(RCA)*

Oklahoma-born and raised in the state of Washington, Gail is the only female triple-threat in Nashville besides Dolly Parton: she writes, sings, and produces her own music. While she keeps touch with traditional country roots, like Emmylou Harris, she is equally at home with more modern material. A sometimes turbulent personal life and a confused direction in her music have so far kept Gail from realizing her full potential, but when she sorts these out she should rise to the top. Her dynamic, energy-filled live performance makes her a natural for development via video. Another possible future superstar—given the critical acclaim that greeted her late 1984 RCA debut album, *What's a Woman to Do,* and that album's overall excellence—and it seems she could be one of the best.

LYNN ANDERSON

North Dakota–born and California-bred, Lynn was an award-winning horsewoman before becoming a country star in the late 1960s after several years as a regular on "The Lawrence Welk Show." Daughter of noted songwriter Liz Anderson ("My Friends Are Gonna Be Strangers"), Lynn won CMA Female Vocalist honors and a Grammy in 1971 for her performance of Joe South's "(I Never Promised You a) Rose Garden" and posted hits throughout the 1970s. Early in the 1980s, she took time off to fulfill familial duties, but returned in 1983 on the independent label Permian Records of Dallas before moving to MCA the following year.

Above: *"The Queen of Country Music"—Kitty Wells—performs on the "Grand Ole Opry."*
Below, left: *Writer-singer-producer Gail Davies, one of the few women country artists to produce all of her own records. (Photo: John Carnes)*
Below, right: *Lynn Anderson's pop-country smash "(I Never Promised You a) Rose Garden" earned her a Grammy and a CMA Award in 1970. (Photo: Dean Dixon)*
Opposite: *Glamorous Crystal Gayle is representative of the modern country sound. (Photo: John Carnes)*

Above: *The Frizzell-West Clan: left to right, Allen Frizzell, Shelly West, Dottie West, and David Frizzell. (Photo: Beth Gwinn)*
Right: *Larry Gatlin checks out some jockeys of a different color during a brief stopover in Lexington.*
Far right: *Jeannie Kendall and her father Royce (not pictured) came into prominence singing "Heaven's Just a Sin Away."*

Above: *"The Alabama Wildman," Jerry Reed, elucidates a point. (Photo: John Carnes)*
Left: *Porter Wagoner and Dolly Parton work one up circa 1971. Note fan interest. (Photo: Bud Lee)*
Far left: *Lee Greenwood performs on the Opry. (Photo: Steve Harbison)*

The 'Mickey Michelle' Country Show
'With the Best in Country Music'
Appearing at:
Date & Time:
Kermit Clarin
Phil Rainer
JUNIOR SAMPLES
Sterling
Tootsie's PRIVATE COLLECTION
The Loretta Lynn Classic
In Cooperation With THE CIVITAN CLUB OF NASHVILLE
WORLD
Municipal Auditorium
FRI. 8 P.M. – SAT. 8 P.M. – SUN. 2:30 P.M.
Tootsie's ORCHID LOUNGE
Jed Ford
Country and Western Star

You can also hear "Cajun-country" as performed by Jimmy C. Newman, Doug Kershaw, and Jo-El Sonnier. The wellspring of rhythm that is reggae hasn't been lost on the Bellamy Brothers or Jimmy Buffett; they've made a career of it. Chet Atkins has been passing off jazz licks as country for decades now, and Willie Nelson has always cited French jazz guitarist Django Reinhardt as a major influence on his style.

Country's string-band roots are intact today through the work of such masters of bluegrass as Bill Monroe, the Osborne Brothers, Jimmy Martin, Don Reno, the Country Gentlemen, and countless others. Bluegrass has also attracted a progressive element led by the Newgrass Revival, a quintet that feels the form should bow to rather than be stuck in the past.

In addition, there are elements of blues or "soul" music in the work of almost every serious country stylist, a fact underlined in 1984 when such black musical classics as "Hold On, I'm Coming," "Three Times a Lady," "Double Shot (Of My Baby's Love)," "Save the Last Dance For Me," "Knock on Wood," and "You Really Got a Hold on Me" advanced into the country Top 20 years after their initial success on the black charts. How far apart are George Jones and Bobby "Blue" Bland anyway when we define the "soul" and emotion that lie at the heart of each master's appeal? "Country music is the white man's blues, that's all it is," noted Hank Williams, Jr.

Today's country music means different sounds to different people. If you were to talk with twenty different folks in the business of making country music you'd likely get twenty different definitions of what is and isn't country music. Today's audiences are willing to accept a wide variety of sounds under the loose title of country music so the producers and artists in the field have felt free to ornament the songs in a variety of trappings. If, however, you want to get down to what makes a song "country," strip away the fancy production and evaluate the song. Chances are you'll find a lyrically strong tale built around the basics of human experience, usually detailing adventures drawn from the relationships between men and women.

DAVID ALLAN COE
(Columbia)

The first time Nashville noticed Coe was when he parked a hearse in front of Ryman Auditorium while pretending to be a country star. His first major national notice came when he claimed a murder while in prison. (Later research cast doubt upon that "achievement.") Coe has fashioned a very erratic chart career distinguished by only three Top 10s: "You Never Even Called Me by My Name" in 1975, "The Ride" in 1983, and "Mona Lisa Lost Her Smile" in 1984. His biggest successes have come from covers of his songs: "Would You Lay with Me (In a Field of Stone)" sung by Tanya Tucker and "Take This Job and Shove It" by Johnny Paycheck, both No. 1 hits. Coe is perhaps a bigger star in his own mind than in reality, a supposition reinforced by four books he wrote, which present his views on his life, religion, philosophy, and getting out of prison. He remains one of the most colorful of the country stars and is definitely the most tattooed. Although he can turn out achingly good songs, he seems to be unable to tell the difference between the sublime and the ridiculous in his own work.

U.S. PRE-RECORDED MUSIC SALES: 1921–83
(figures in millions)

1921	$106	1944	66	1967	1,051
1922	92	1945	109	1968	1,124
1923	79	1946	218	1969	1,170
1924	68	1947	224	1970	1,182
1925	59	1948	189	1971	1,251
1926	70	1949	173	1972	1,383
1927	70	1950	189	1973	1,436
1928	73	1951	199	1974	2,200
1929	75	1952	214	1975	2,360
1930	46	1953	219	1976	2,737
1931	18	1954	213	1977	3,500
1932	11	1955	277	1978	4,131
1933	6	1956	377	1979	3,676
1934	7	1957	460	1980	3,682
1935	9	1958	511	1981	3,626
1936	11	1959	603	1982	3,592
1937	13	1960	600	1983	3,815
1938	26	1961	640		
1939	44	1962	687		
1940	48	1963	698		
1941	51	1964	758		
1942	55	1965	862		
1943	66	1966	959		

Sources: National Association of Record Merchandisers (NARM). RIAA. *Billboard International Buyer's Guide.*

David Allan Coe has been many things in his life. Here he is when he was known as "The Mysterious Rhinestone Cowboy." (Photo: Al Clayton)

Below: *Handsome George Strait goes beltless in this 1981 shot.*
Bottom, left: *"I love her mind," sings Howard Bellamy as David looks on in disbelief. (Photo: Tim Naprestek)*
Bottom, right: *Gene Watson lays down a vocal track in 1981. (Photo: Melodie Gimple)*

WHERE THE MONEY GOES

Assume the artist is booked out at an average of $25,000 per night for 180 shows in one year. Assume also that the act nets $675,000 in the year off T-shirts and paraphernalia sales.

Thus, the act would gross $25,000 × 180 = $4,500,000 + 675,000 = $5,175,000

Expenses:		
Manager (15% of all gross)	$776,250	*15.0%*
Booking agent	675,000	*13.0*
*Salaries for road crew, pensions, employer's taxes, etc.	675,000	*13.0*
Cost of gas, oil, maintenance on 2 buses, 2 trucks	216,000	*4.2*
Food and lodging	300,000	*5.8*
Insurance	400,000	*7.7*
Bus payment/lease	108,000	*2.1*
Truck payment/lease	36,000	*0.7*
Accountant's and legal fees	85,000	*1.6*
Plane and pilot	150,000	*2.9*
Taxes	600,000	*11.6*
Overhead	250,000	*4.8*
	$4,271,250	
Net to artist	**$903,750**	*17.4%*

*Salaries figured at following weekly rate: Driver (2) one at $500/wk., one at $475. Band (6) $600/wk. Roadie (4) $300/wk. Road Mgr. $700/wk. Sound & light crew (10) $375/wk. Includes misc., relief driver, etc.

(Figures supplied by trade stories, research, guesswork, and industry insiders. Subject to change without notice as act's popularity waxes or wanes.)

Sources: Record World. 1972 Country Who's Who. Educated guessing.

Country Music's First Forty Years

It's hard to pinpoint an exact date for the beginning of country music. It is certain that songs similar in content to the ballads of today were sung on the streets of England years before the Pilgrims arrived at Plymouth Rock. Historians are in agreement, however, regarding the three major sources for the commercial country music that emerged in the 1920s: Anglo-American folk music, old-time religion, and elements of nineteenth-century American show business.

The folk music tradition has always been well represented in twentieth-century country music. Songs like "Black Jack Davy," "Greensleeves," and "Barbara Allen" crossed the ocean from England to join with songs from the American working class like "Tom Dooley," "Home on the Range," "The Wreck of the Old '97," and "Casey Jones." The melodies from countless tunes also journeyed westward, there to receive new titles. The emphasis on instrumental interplay, particularly among such unamplified instruments as guitar, fiddle, banjo, and mandolin, that can be heard on early recordings of country music stems from earlier English times as well. A different folk tradition, the African-derived blues music of the South, was another major influence on early country performers, most notably Jimmie Rodgers.

The music of the church was certainly a vital factor in the development of country music. In the days before electronic communication the houses of worship served as social centers to a much greater extent than they do today. People spent more time attending church and participating in church-related activities, which included singing in the choir. Traveling evangelists used music as part of their presentation. In those days there were few opportunities for the average citizen to hear music other than in church. Many of the harmonies and melodies of early twentieth-century country music came straight from the hymnals of the day; such songs as "Amazing Grace" and "Will the Circle Be Unbroken" remain popular in modern times. Many of country music's biggest contemporary stars have issued albums of gospel songs, affirming this link to the past.

Traveling shows, minstrel shows, and vaudeville also provided material and ideas for early country music. Cornball humor and novelty songs were vaudeville staples. Early country music shows utilized the staging and promotion methods developed by these troupes, be they based on minstrels, ministers, or medicine men. When country music artists began to make out-of-town trips to perform, it was only natural that they take along techniques developed by the early traveling shows.

Country's reliance on love ballads, or "heart" songs, as they were once called, can be traced to the show tunes turned out prolifically by the songwriters of Tin Pan Alley from the 1870s onward. Love songs remain the backbone of country lyrics today, as one brief exposure to modern country radio will quickly certify.

The creation of phonographs and records did not immediately start a huge new record business. For many years after their invention in 1877 record players were too expensive for anyone but the wealthy. The records of the time, made for this "highbrow" audience, reflected the taste of the upper class. By the second decade of this century the cost of manufacture had dropped to more affordable levels. As prices fell and more units were sold, the enlarged consumer base broadened the kinds of music offered for sale. Country and blues recordings began to be simultaneously available in the years after World War I.

The invention of radio was instrumental to the spread of country music and the growth of the recording industry. The first commercial station, KDKA in Pittsburgh, went on the air in 1920, and others quickly followed suit. Country programs featuring live music were offered on

GEORGE STRAIT *(MCA)*

He rode in to Nashville from a Texas ranch with a college degree and ten years of honky-tonk experience in his saddlebags. One of country's brightest discoveries—by former MCA promotion man Erv Woolsey (now his manager)—George has matinee-idol looks to go with a voice capable of handling "hard country" or mainstream a-c with equal ease. He began recording for Pappy Daily's D Records, the same label that introduced George Jones two decades earlier. When not out singing, George lives on a working ranch outside of San Marcos. The most handsome of Texas's many country singers, George would benefit from a revival of the rage for singing cowboy movies that were big in the 1930s and 1940s—he can outride, outrope, and outsing Hopalong, Gene Autry, or Roy Rogers. Strait has tremendous potential.

most of these stations, usually sponsored by a local merchant as a means of boosting sales. Before the decade was out, the "Barn Dance" concept (programs like today's "Grand Ole Opry"), first introduced in early 1923 on Fort Worth's WBAP, became common.

These programs, an actual Saturday night dance or a simulation of one, became very successful. Each offered a large cast of performers who played before an audience for the live radio transmission. The show was broken into segments, each with its own sponsor, which presented an artist who sang—between discourses on the delights of the sponsor's product. Chicago station WLS started its own "National Barn Dance" program in 1924; it was the most popular show of its type for many years until it was supplanted by WSM's "Grand Ole Opry" in the 1950s. The most popular and enduring of the competing shows were "The Louisiana Hayride" from Shreveport's KWKH and "The Wheeling Jamboree" from WWVA in Wheeling, West Virginia.

The "Barn Dance" idea is far less popular today, but at its zenith in the 1930s and 1940s such programs were aired in Cincinnati, Dallas, Des Moines, Fort Wayne, Kansas City, Minneapolis, New York City, Philadelphia, Richmond, St. Louis, Springfield, and Tulsa, in addition to the five programs already mentioned and lesser-known shows that emanated from smaller cities. The shows were carried by powerful stations whose signals penetrated to listeners for several hundred miles. Almost without exception, every major recording star of the period from 1930 to 1960 came to stardom following a stint on one of the many "Barn Dance" programs.

When the early country recordings of the 1920s sold better than the urban record executives expected (those recording pioneers actually called the music "hillbilly"), the music of such artists as Fiddlin' John Carson, Henry Whittier, Gid Tanner, Carl T. Sprague, Riley Puckett, Bradley Kincaid, and others became available on a fairly regular basis. At the time there were no record stores, so these discs were sold in department stores, groceries, music shops, and in whatever mercantile establishments the enterprising label salesmen could place them.

The best-known recording "star" of the first five years of country's recorded history was Marion Try Slaughter, a former Texan with aspirations of operatic stardom. He recorded an incredible array of material of all types under many pseudonyms. As Vernon Dalhart (a name furnished by two north Texas towns), he became country music's first million-seller with his 1924 disc "Wreck of the Old '97" and "The Prisoner's Song." None of his many later efforts sold nearly this well, and Dalhart eventually sought nonmusical employment. He died on the job as a night watchman.

The whole "Grand Ole Opry" cast poses in this early picture.

Far left: *Bill Monroe (second from left) and the Bluegrass Boys (left to right, Art Wooten, Billy Borum, and Jim Holmes) were early Opry regulars.*
Left: *Tex Ritter nuzzles his horse, White Flash.*

The honor of being the first true country star goes to Jimmie Rodgers, a Mississippian referred to as the "father of country music," who was discovered by Ralph Peer in 1927. Rodgers's music is a remarkable blend of black and white elements, which he drew from his experiences as a sometime railroad worker and near-full-time ne'er-do-well. Though he lived only six years after his discovery before tuberculosis cut him down, Rodgers sold records in quantities that would please record executives of the 1980s. Three of Rodgers's songs—"T For Texas (Blue Yodel #1)," "In the Jailhouse Now," and "Muleskinner Blues (Blue Yodel #8)"—are still vastly popular today.

The Carter Family, another 1927 Peer discovery, were also enormously popular artists. Their music stemmed mainly from the white Appalachian branch of country, which was a descendant of the English ballad tradition, and it included classic songs such as "Wildwood Flower," "Will the Circle Be Unbroken," and "Wabash Cannonball," all familiar numbers to today's audiences. Many historians feel that Mother Maybelle Carter's distinctive style of guitar playing was the major factor in changing it to a lead instrument; it was then mostly used as a source of rhythmic underpinning.

During this period, the rhythmic drive of string bands attracted a wide audience. Though such groups today have all but disappeared from the commercial end of country music in favor of a singer or singers backed by a band, the 1920s were filled with talented groups like the Stoneman Family, the East Texas Serenaders, the Skillet Lickers, and Charlie Poole's North Carolina Ramblers, all of whom featured fancy "picking" and group singing. This tradition lives on among the bluegrass contingent; otherwise, the main place to hear this influence today is in "breakdowns," hot instrumental passages between verses, from the bands fronted by many of the top stars.

The Depression years were grim ones for companies in the business of selling recorded music. Sales fell from a high of $75 million in 1929 to a low of only $6 million in 1933. (Today just one gold album generates almost $5 million at the retail counter.) But country music itself did remarkably well, primarily because the "Barn Dance" programs offered a free source of spirited entertainment to anyone with access to a radio.

At the same time country benefited from a national mania. The years leading up to World War II saw the United States "go Western" with a thoroughness unrivaled until the "urban cowboy" days of the late 1970s. Western movies featuring such singing cowboys as Gene Autry, Roy Rogers, Tex Ritter, Rex Allen, the Sons of the Pioneers, Eddie Dean, Ray Whitley, and Foy Willing's Riders of the Purple Sage ruled both the nation's airwaves and movie houses. As in the urban cowboy days, Western wear became all the rage, and many performers stood before their audiences dressed in full Western regalia as they warbled decidely non-Western tunes. The popularity of these singing cowboys and their movies grew to such a degree that the country field became known as "country & western," a sobriquet still used today by many misinformed pundits.

This period also saw the development of an entirely new form of music. Dubbed "western swing," the style was a mixture of country and jazz seasoned with a little Dixieland spice. As the country version of the popular "Big Bands" of the time, the western swing sound featured large ensemble playing with electric guitars, drums, several singers, and a horn section. This form emerged in Texas and Oklahoma. Its best-known artist, Bob Wills, exploited his musical fame to become a veteran of many Westerns. Wills's performances set attendance records all over his primarily Southwestern stomping ground. His two most popular songs, "San Antonio Rose" and "Faded Love," are included to this day in the repertoire of many touring country bands.

By the dawn of World War II country music had been a distinct part of the recorded music world for two decades. One of the most important subsequent developments was the field's attraction of a cadre of professional songwriters. Most of the early country material consisted of reworked hymns, ballads, folk songs, and traditional tunes, but by the late 1940s talented writers had moved into the genre and began to specialize. Blind Andy Jenkins, Carson Robison, Bob Miller, Fred Rose, Bob Nolan, Stuart Hamblen, and Cindy Walker were the cream of this crop, along with Billy Hill, a former Bostonian who traveled in the West before returning to New York City to compose many outstanding Western songs. The success of the above writers influenced many of the songwriters of the next generation to try country music rather than to delve into other forms.

Country music and songwriters were both helped immeasurably in 1940 by the founding of Broadcast Music Incorporated (BMI), a performance rights organization that became the only group to successfully challenge the American Society of Composers and Publishers (ASCAP). The two groups handle the collection of income due songwriters and publishers for the use of their music. Until BMI's existence, ASCAP was very exclusionary in its membership policies, snubbing country music, blues, and most jazz composers, who thus had no means of receiving compensation for the use of their songs in public broadcast. By providing a home and by collecting money for these songwriters deemed unfit for ASCAP acceptance, BMI opened the floodgates of American music to all composers.

The entire music explosion of the 1940s and 1950s, when country, blues, jazz, rhythm and blues, and rock 'n' roll flowed into the mainstream culture, can be traced to BMI's formation and eventual success through the tireless efforts of legal mastermind Sidney Kaye and visionary President Carl Haverlin, who ran the company from 1947 to 1964. Today the two groups remain bitter rivals, but the ASCAP membership policies were changed to embrace this "open door" philosophy many years ago, and most of the other practices begun by BMI were also adopted later by ASCAP. It is impossible to overvalue the vital contribution BMI made to American popular music by breaking the monopolistic creative logjam that ASCAP's narrow-minded attitude had caused.

The 1930s also saw the rise of several major country recording stars in addition to Wills and the singing cowboy posse led by Autry and Rogers (who was originally a member of the Sons of the Pioneers as Leonard Slye, his given name). One of the most popular stars of the Opry, past or present, Roy Acuff, was in his prime in the 1930s and 1940s. His popularity was such that he made several attempts to run for governor of Tennessee. In 1948 he actually won the Republican primary, but was not elected in the fall. Roy was one of the first country performers to take his show overseas to entertain the troops, venturing to Berlin during the airlift in 1949, to Korea during that "police action," and, at nearly seventy years of age, to Vietnam. Today, still known as "The King of Country Music," he remains a fixture on the Opry.

Jimmie Davis might have been elected governor of Louisiana without his massive country and pop success—but it's doubtful. As one of the country's biggest stars of the 1930s, with hits like "You Are My Sunshine" and "Nobody's Darling but Mine," Davis parlayed his great popularity into a brief Hollywood career. He was also an accomplished songwriter, furnishing songs for Gene Autry. In campaigning for the state's top office in 1944, Davis used country music heavily at his appearances; some would say that more time was spent singing country songs than in discussing campaign issues, a circumstance that would certainly enliven modern political campaigning. Davis won another term as governor in 1960.

In the 1940s, yet another distinct country offshoot came to the fore. Termed "folk music in overdrive" by musicologist Alan Lomax, bluegrass began through the efforts of Bill Monroe, whose band at the time included the talents of both Lester Flatt and Earl Scruggs. The combination of these three masters in one group was irresistible: Monroe is doubtless the finest mandolin player ever recorded, Scruggs developed his own distinctive method of picking banjo with several fingers (as opposed to the "claw-hammer" style then prevalent), and Flatt was uncommonly gifted as a singer and guitarist. Though bluegrass has never generated big bucks at the retail counter, it has managed to support several specialty labels, as well as its own festival circuit through hundreds of weekend events held all summer long. It has also given solid careers to a host of talented players like the Osborne Brothers, Jimmie Martin, Don Reno, and Mac Wiseman, and is a prominent ingredient in the music of such country singers as Ricky Skaggs and Emmylou Harris. The string-band tradition and some of the hottest instrumental interplay in the field of country music live on through this most exciting genre.

Country music's popularity has also grown over the years because of its ability to absorb elements of the music from different cultures. As pop music absorbed elements of reggae and disco music in the 1970s, so country music has absorbed such disparate influences as the accordion-dominated Cajun and polka forms, the folk songs of such artists as Woody Guthrie, Burl Ives, and Leadbelly, and the lively romantic sounds from south of the border that helped propel Marty Robbins to stardom.

Aside from the invention of the radio, World War II was probably the biggest single factor in the growth of country music. The war acted like a giant mixmaster on the citizens of America, scattering them all over the world. The young men of the urban centers in the northeast were thrown together in the service with many small-town sons of the South and Midwest who grew up on country music. Many of these lads brought a guitar and their love of country music with them, exposing others for the first time to country sounds. Soldiers stationed in the South and Midwest heard the music on the radio and in the barracks. Country music was even noticed in Japan; Tokyo Rose mentioned Ernest Tubb and Roy Acuff in her propaganda broadcasts. Armed Services radio programs included country selections in their repertoire of the music from back home.

Country music took yet another turning in the postwar years when honky-tonk music came barreling to the forefront. This brand of country, which relied heavily on electric guitars,

VERN GOSDIN *(Compleat)*

Born in Woodland, Alabama, in 1934, Gosdin was early influenced by bluegrass, gospel, and the Grand Ole Opry. Fame seemed near in the mid-1960s, when he teamed up with Chris Hillman in a folk-bluegrass combo, which yielded a superb LP, *Gene Clark with the Gosdin Brothers*. Various problems then combined to derail his career. In 1976 he was "rediscovered." Vern's "Hangin' On," a minor hit for him in 1967, was recut, and it rocketed to the Top 20. That association with Elektra yielded seven more Top 20s. Stints on Ovation and AMI preceded his current involvement with Compleat Records, a move that has produced a string of hits with strong songs like "Today My World Slipped Away," "If You're Gonna Do Me Wrong (Do It Right)," "Way Down Deep," and "I Can Tell by the Way You Dance." By 1983 he had fully developed his own sound, a soulful mixture laced with traces of the Louvin Brothers and George Jones. His emotive power and sincerity mark him as one of country's leading balladeers.

Lester Flatt and Earl Scruggs (second from right) prepare to hit the road.

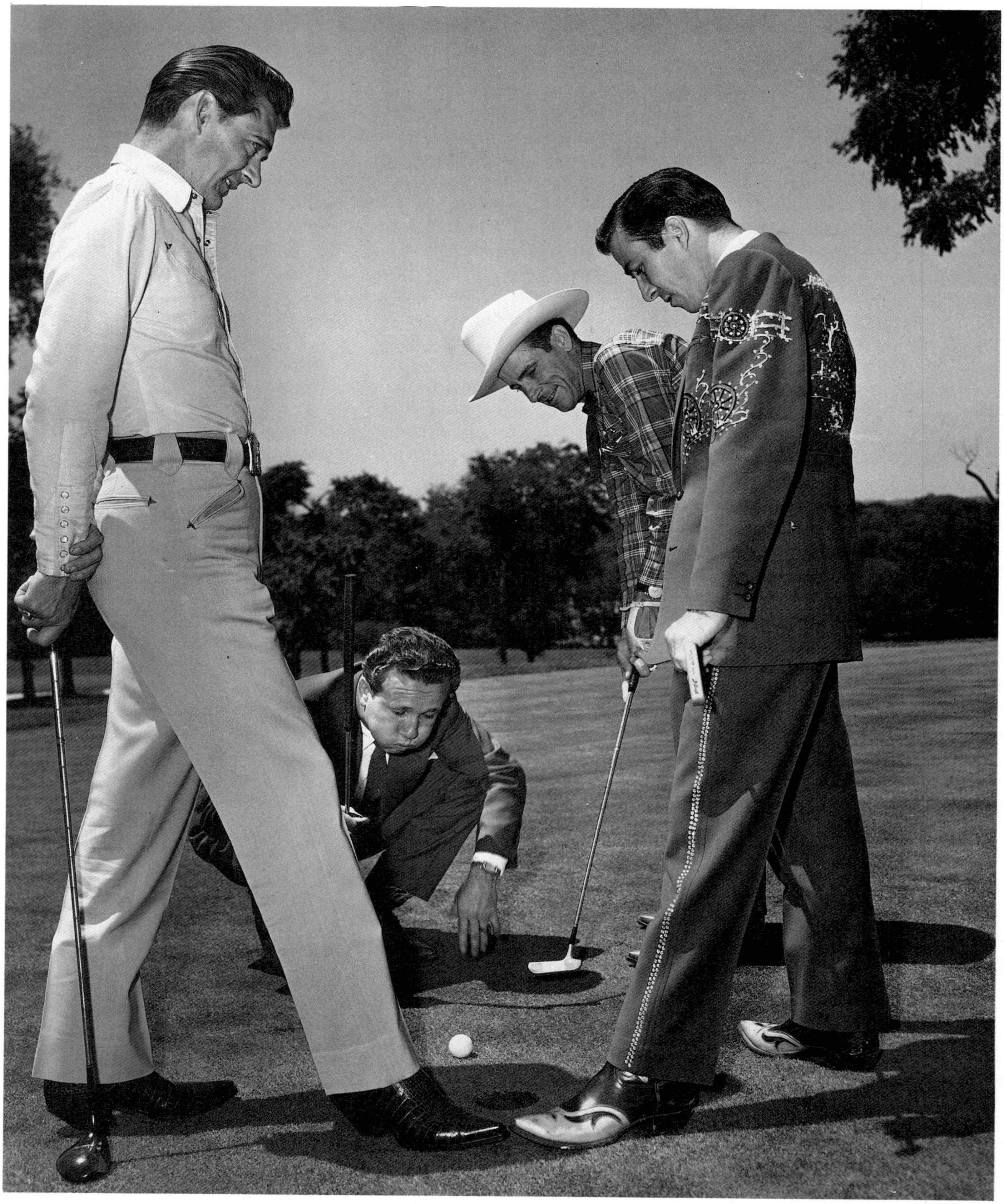

steel guitars, and drums, grew out of the taverns and roadhouses scattered along the increasingly traveled highways, no longer restricted by gasoline rationing. The honky-tonk sound featured more mature lyrics, which reflected the social changes of the times. The songs of the honky-tonks revolved more upon sensuality and the battle between the sexes than did earlier forms of country music. Although they dealt with the subject subtly, it was plain that they were talking about sex. Though honky-tonk music became popular nationally, almost all of the leading singers came from Texas, a list that includes Ernest Tubb, Lefty Frizzell, Ray Price, Al Dexter, Ted Daffan, and Floyd Tillman. In the years since, George Jones, Moe Bandy, Gene Watson, Freddy Fender, and George Strait have continued this tradition. Jones's mastery of the form is so complete that most country music followers acknowledge him as the greatest living singer in the field over the past thirty years.

But neither Jones nor any other Texas singer can lay claim to the title of being the best honky-tonk singer who ever lived. That honor belongs to Hank Williams, a tall, intense Alabaman who became country music's biggest postwar star. Though his career as a recording artist lasted but six years—the same span as Jimmie Rodgers's career—Williams, with his remarkable contributions, set high standards, which country music singers everywhere strive to emulate. Such songs as "I'm So Lonesome I Could Cry," "Jambalaya," "Your Cheatin' Heart," and "I Saw the Light" live on today and will likely continue to be country favorites as long as music is played where alcohol is served.

In the mid-1950s, rockabilly music, a blend of country and black music, was added to the country music stew. The style, initially fashioned at Sam Phillips's Sun Records studios in Memphis by such artists as Elvis Presley, Carl Perkins, Jerry Lee Lewis, Billy Lee Riley, and others, took off like a nitro-fueled dragster. The form eventually gained important contributions from the East Coast (Bill Haley, Gene Vincent), the Southwest (Buddy Holly, Wanda Jackson), and the West Coast (Eddie Cochran). Rockabilly was soon absorbed and eclipsed by rock 'n' roll, but it remains a vital and active form of music to this day, particularly in Europe.

As this new black-white fusion, rock 'n' roll, climbed in popularity, it sent country music into a tailspin. Almost overnight, the demand for country singers dropped dramatically, driving many of the day's country stars to try their hand with the new style. The results of these experiments were about as successful as Porter Wagoner's highly publicized attempt to "go disco" in the late 1970s. There was, however, one notable exception. Conway Twitty, who had been unable to fashion a hit as a country singer or a rockabilly artist, hit it big in the new field with "It's Only Make Believe" and several other tunes before returning to country in the mid-1960s, eventually to gain the title of "The Crown Prince of Country Soul."

Opposite: *Left to right, Carl Smith, Marty Robbins, Ernest Tubb, and Faron Young putter around. Note the "golf shoes."*

The civilians are, left to right, Rod Brasfield, Red Foley, Little Jimmy Dickens, Minnie Pearl, and Hank Williams, in Germany to entertain the soldiers.

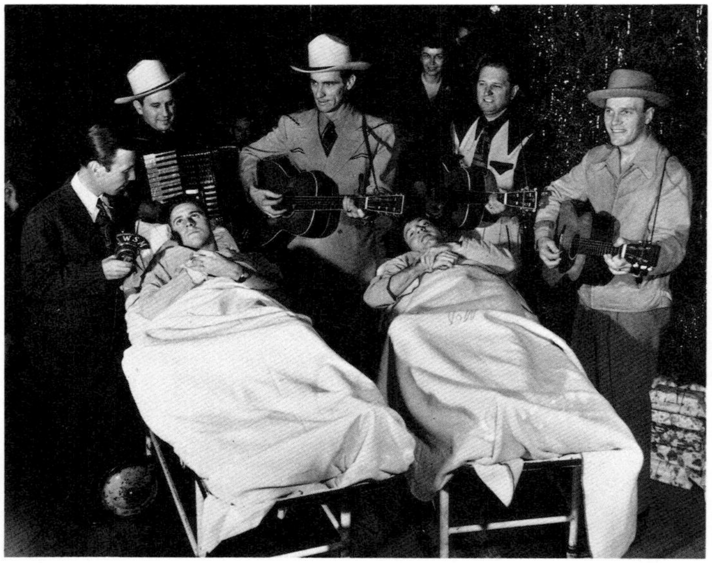

Left: *Pee Wee King (with accordion), Ernest Tubb (center), and Eddy Arnold (right) cheer the patients of the Veterans Hospital, Christmas 1946.*
Right: *Conway Twitty and Owen Bradley share a chuckle in the studio in 1970.*
Opposite, left: *CBS Nashville chief Rick Blackburn (left) enjoys a moment of levity with two legendary Blackburn signings, Ray Charles (center) and George Jones. (Photo: Clark Thomas)*
Opposite, right: *Eddy Arnold was the first country performer to host a regular network TV show. Over 50 when this picture was taken, he shows he's still got sex appeal. (Photo: Marshall Fallwell, Jr.)*

ROY CLARK
(Churchill/MCA)

In a career that dates back to the post-war 1940s, Clark has won five CMA Awards for his instrumental virtuosity, racked up country and pop hits as a singer, hosted "The Tonight Show" many times, headlined in Vegas, starred for fifteen years in "Hee Haw," performed at the Montreux Jazz Festival, and toured in Russia. He has also won CMA kudos as Entertainer of the Year and Best Comedian. He loves to relax by flying his own antique plane, which he keeps in his hometown of Tulsa, Oklahoma.

Music City's reaction to rock 'n' roll's predominance was to refine the sound of country music. This approach, pioneered by Chet Atkins, Owen Bradley, Floyd Cramer, Don Law, Anita Kerr, and others, came to be known as the Nashville Sound. The recordings were sweetened, taken "uptown" if you will, through the use of string sections (rather than one or two fiddles), fancy piano work, usually courtesy of Cramer and his "slip-note" style, and melodious background vocal touches provided by Kerr or the Jordanaires, a quartet that lay unchallenged claim to participation on more hit records than any other group or individual in music. Atkins dates the 1958 Don Gibson sessions that produced "Oh Lonesome Me" as the beginning of his efforts to consciously break the mold; not coincidentally, that song became Gibson's first country hit and a major pop smash as well.

In a nutshell, the Nashville Sound was a successful attempt to put more pop into the country music of the day. Such singers as Jim Reeves, the Browns, Sonny James, Eddy Arnold, and Patsy Cline enjoyed many country hits with this approach; all five also scored at least one pop smash with it as well. In the next few years almost every country singer either flirted with the Nashville Sound to some degree or fully adopted it. Soon it seemed that everyone in Music City was producing smooth-sounding records without any rough edges. However, a few staunch individualists, including such talented singers as Merle Haggard and Johnny Cash, forged fabulous careers without resorting to the "sweetening" process.

The "folk boom" from 1958 to 1962 did not pose a serious threat to country music. If anything, its success helped listeners in the nation to become more conscious of song lyrics, a development that also focused attention on country songs. Several of today's country stars broke into the national picture as folkies during this era, most notably Kenny Rogers (with the New Christy Minstrels), Don Williams (the Pozo Seco Singers), John Denver (the Chad Mitchell Trio), and Jim Ed Brown (the Browns). Juice Newton and Emmylou Harris began their careers in folk music as well, though neither achieved fame in the form. The national attention to folk songs was also a factor in the success of a brief flurry of "saga songs" that became country and pop hits, including "Big Bad John" (Jimmy Dean), "El Paso" (Marty Robbins), "Wolverton Mountain" (Claude King), and "Waterloo" (Stonewall Jackson). Though the four songs above were all huge hits, none came near the success of "The Battle of New Orleans," Johnny Horton's version of Jimmie Driftwood's account of the final battle of the War of 1812. The song was the No. 1 pop hit in America for six weeks in 1959, lasting longer at the top that year than any song except Bobby Darin's touching ode to "Mack the Knife." Horton went on to post several additional hits in this genre ("Sink the Bismarck," "North to Alaska") before tragically dying in a car crash.

As we shall later see, the period from 1957 to 1962 marked Nashville's Golden Age as a source of pop music hits. The biggest event to bridge the gap between pop and country music, however, came from a most unlikely source: Ray Charles, a blind, black singer. Charles confounded everyone in mid-1962 by releasing *Modern Sounds in Country & Western Music,* a collection of country standards backed up with big band arrangements. At the time, Charles was riding high on the rhythm 'n' blues charts. He had also made a successful crossover to popular music a few years prior and, at that point in his career, was establishing his reputation in blues and jazz circles.

The record, which featured some of the most heartfelt singing ever released on any disc, became an enormous success on the pop and black charts. Twenty-three years later it remains Charles's biggest seller. "I Can't Stop Loving You," Charles's version of Don Gibson's 1958 country chart-topper, hit No. 1 on the pop charts and won Charles his sixth Grammy Award, ironically for best rhythm 'n' blues recording. His follow-up disc, *Modern Sounds in Country & Western Music, Volume II,* released the next year, was also a big success and it won Charles another Grammy in the r 'n' b category—this time for his version of "Busted," a Harlan Howard song.

But the impact of the albums cut far deeper than sales, chart positions, or awards, for it brought country music for the first time to the young whites who were then confirmed rock 'n' rollers. They were willing to accept this music from a man widely known as "The Genius" who was then one of the biggest music stars in America, the same man already famous for such classic pop hits as "Hit the Road, Jack," "What'd I Say," "Georgia on My Mind," and "Let the Good Times Roll"—all songs that had established Charles as a "hip" act in the eyes of the young white rockers.

Ray Charles will never be inducted into the Country Music Hall of Fame but, like Gram Parsons, he made a lasting contribution to country music by pioneering its exposure to a broader-based audience. Today Charles is signed to Columbia Records out of Nashville and is seeking a comeback in the same field that he helped boost to glory.

Country music's success has also been aided mightily by the Country Music Association (CMA), a group of dedicated zealots who joined forces in 1958 to help get the form back on the radio following the rock 'n' roll attack. Its efforts have been so successful that the CMA has been termed "the world's most effective trade organization"; its membership now approaches 8,000—a respectable showing for a group that began with 233 members. Led for its entire history by Executive Director Jo Walker-Meador, the group has helped achieve country's im-

RAY CHARLES *(Columbia)*

They call him "The Genius," and for nearly forty years Ray Charles has been leaving his personal stamp upon the fields of country, jazz, rock, blues, and rhythm 'n' blues music in a career rivaled by no other American musician. A master of feeling, nuance, and that slippery quality called "soul," Charles signed with the Nashville branch of Columbia in 1982, returning to the country music he had heard as a child in rural Georgia.

Blind since early childhood, Charles has won more Grammy Awards (10) than anyone ever associated for any length of time with country music. His early 1960s recordings of *Modern Sounds of Country & Western Music* (Volumes I and II) exposed millions of urban listeners to the honesty and beauty of country music.

A reformed heroin addict, Charles, like George Jones, packs more emotion into a few words than other singers can deliver in an entire album. When he signed with Columbia and word circulated that he was considering cutting an album of duets, every artist on the label volunteered his or her services. His only flaw is his ego—but when you're Ray Charles, it's not hard to understand.

Right: *Surely you don't expect Porter Wagoner to appear on a talk show without his dogs? Host Dan Miller retains his composure. (Photo: Tim Naprestek)* Below: *Marty Robbins accepts the "Man of the Decade" Award, presented by Herb Alpert and Linda Crystal, from the Academy of Country Music at the 1970 awards show.*

pressive gains on radio. The number of full-time country radio stations has increased from about 80 in 1961 to over 2,250 in 1984, a jump of about 2,700 percent. In addition, country music has for many years enjoyed a nationally televised awards show, a museum, its own songwriters association, a hall of fame, and a resource facility for serious researchers. No other form of popular music of any kind in any nation has these attractions, and no other can offer any event remotely similar to Fan Fair, which is cosponsored by the CMA and the Grand Ole Opry.

Country music made several major strides toward acceptance on national television in the 1960s when such artists as Johnny Cash, Glen Campbell, Roger Miller, and Jerry Reed landed spots hosting weekly network variety shows, an honor that Eddy Arnold had first achieved a decade earlier. These shows opened the door for many country artists to gain their first national television exposure and also helped pave the way for the many syndicated country shows that poured out of Nashville in the 1970s. "Hee Haw," for example, which was hosted by Roy Clark and Buck Owens, debuted on national television in 1968 and was canceled by CBS after two seasons. But the program took its unique mix of fancy picking, country singers, gospel songs, cornpone humor, and buxom gals to the greener pastures of syndication, and is now in its seventeenth year of guffaws and gollys.

The popularity of country music over the years has risen and fallen as public tastes have changed and our social conditions have fluctuated. Like a professional ballclub or public corporation, country music has had good years and bad ones. When judged against the form's long historic background, the years from 1965 to 1968 weren't peak ones. Though many fortuitous events did occur—the Academy of Country Music and the Country Music Association began their televised awards shows amid growing membership, Roger Miller won eleven Grammies in 1964 and 1965, then gained an NBC network show, Bob Dylan first came to Nashville to record, the Country Music Hall of Fame and Museum opened its doors, and Jeannie C. Riley and Bobby Goldsboro posted No. 1 pop hits with the cynical "Harper Valley P.T.A." and the lachrymose "Honey" respectively—it was plain that country and Nashville-produced music were losing their grip on the national musical consciousness due to the new musical *group* format, which began to assert its dominance with the Beatles, the Rolling Stones, and other English bands beginning in 1964.

BOBBY GOLDSBORO

Florida-born, Goldsboro moved to Nashville after being hired to open shows with Roy Orbison's support band. He has gone on to achieve a fabulous career in both pop and a-c, with over twenty hits in each. His recording of Bobby Russell's "Honey" hit No. 1 on country, pop, and a-c lists in 1968. A strong writer, Bobby has won ten BMI Awards for his songwriting, and he established House of Gold Music, one of Nashville's top music publishing firms (it was sold to Warner Bros. in 1982). His last recordings were unsuccessful, but he remains a popular figure in clubs and on TV (he's a fast talker).

FREDDIE HART *(Sunbird)*

Alabama's Freddie Hart will always be remembered for "Easy Loving," a 1971 smash he wrote that *twice* won CMA Song of the Year honors. A rough-and-tumble youngster, Freddie was sent to join the Civilian Conservation Corps at age twelve. Three years later, he joined the Marines and saw combat action all over the Pacific for two years before the war ended. In 1952, he was signed to Capitol as a member of Lefty Frizzell's band. Nineteen years and several labels later, he finally reached the Top 10 with "Easy Loving," which kicked off six straight No. 1s and a dozen consecutive Top-5 hits from 1971 to 1976. Leave him alone, he knows karate.

Left: *Steve Sholes (at podium) and Chet Atkins guided RCA's Nashville operation from the 1940s into the 1970s.* Below: *Freddie Hart obliging autograph requests. (Photo: Marshall Fallwell, Jr.)*

At the same time, the Nashville Sound was wearing a bit thin, and the growth of country radio outlets began to show signs of retrograde motion. Country music wasn't producing a new breed of stars to replace the aging singers who had, in some cases, ruled the roost since the 1940s. Not coincidentally, the form was perceived as less and less valid in those turbulent times of youthful assertion, war protest, and social experimentation. Many of the same pioneers who helped form the CMA and inaugurate the Nashville Sound in 1958 had to be troubled by the view they saw of the future of country music and Nashville's place in popular music. In the eyes of the most farsighted and cynical, it looked as if country music was in serious danger of becoming a form like jazz, blues, or classical—revered and tolerated but relegated to a tiny percentage of the commercial music marketplace.

Nashville and country music desperately needed a savior; what they got was an acidhead kid from Florida who had dreams of a music he termed "American Country Cosmic."

TOP 10s AND NO. 1 RECORDS (1949–67)

TOP 10s

56	Eddy Arnold
45	Webb Pierce
36	Jim Reeves
34	Hank Snow
31	Red Foley
29	Johnny Cash
29	Ray Price
27	Hank Williams
27	Buck Owens
26	Kitty Wells
26	Carl Smith
24	Faron Young
23	George Jones
22	Marty Robbins
18	Hank Thompson
17	Ernest Tubb
14	Bill Anderson
13	Lefty Frizzell
13	Sonny James
13	Tennessee Ernie Ford
13	Don Gibson
12	Porter Wagoner
11	Loretta Lynn
10	Skeeter Davis, Roger Miller, Jimmy Wakely, Roy Drusky, Stonewall Jackson, Connie Smith
9	The Wilburn Brothers
8	Ernie Ashworth, Patsy Cline, George Hamilton IV, Johnny Horton, Hank Locklin, Warner Mack, Billy Walker
7	Bobby Bare, David Houston, Jimmy Dean, Jerry Lee Lewis, George Morgan, Jimmy C. Newman, Jean Shepherd, Margaret Whiting

Sources: Joel Whitburn's Record Research Reports. Billboard magazine

NO. 1s

15	Buck Owens
14	Eddy Arnold
10	Marty Robbins
9	Jim Reeves
8	Webb Pierce
7	Hank Williams
7	Sonny James
6	Elvis Presley
5	Johnny Cash
5	Hank Snow
4	Bill Anderson
4	Red Foley
4	David Houston
4	George Jones
4	Carl Smith
3	Lefty Frizzell
3	Merle Haggard
3	Ray Price
3	Johnny Horton

The Father of "Progressive Country"

Waylon Jennings and Willie Nelson have received most of the credit for creating "progressive country" out of thin air in the mid-1970s, but they were not the first to attempt to fuse country and rock elements. Three albums made in California for A & M Records late in the 1960s preceded those cut six years later by the two Texans.

Two of these albums have received scant recognition, and their creators fared little better, at least in terms of commercial success. Steve Young's *Rock Salt & Nails* and *The Dillard & Clark Expedition* recorded by Doug Dillard and Michael Clark represented two of these exceptional efforts. But when it comes to the successful mating of country and rock, the real unsung hero is the late Gram Parsons, a vastly talented, extremely troubled son of the South whose love of country music during the turbulent late 1960s brought him more derision than acclaim while he lived.

Parsons's name probably will never be inscribed on a bronze plaque hanging in the Country Music Hall of Fame in Nashville, but his influence on the course of country music exceeds the contributions of some artists and executives who have been so honored. Beginning with his 1967 International Submarine Band LP, *Safe at Home,* and in subsequent recordings with the Byrds *(Sweetheart of the Rodeo),* the Flying Burrito Brothers *(Gilded Palace of Sin),* and as a solo artist *(GP, Grievous Angel),* Parsons unveiled his love of country music. At a time when rock 'n' roll and acid rock ruled the airwaves, Parsons was determined to bring the purity and beauty of country music to the attention of his own generation, who perceived the form as the exclusive province of aging rednecks.

It must have been an awfully lonely task! Parsons's long hair and open drug use did not endear him to the country traditionalists whose music he so dearly loved. And his country stylings were decidedly unappealing to his generation. They were then enamored of the many electric and electronic rock experiments going on in what was called "progressive rock." These songs' lyrics were generally shrouded in abstruse symbolism; some were so mysterious that their meaning eluded their composers as well. The leading American bands of the day were the Jefferson Airplane, the Doors, Jimi Hendrix, Vanilla Fudge, Iron Butterfly, and the Grateful Dead. Even the Beatles and the Rolling Stones had become psychedelicized, as such discs as *Magical Mystery Tour* and *Their Satanic Majesties Request* plainly showed.

Parsons joined the Byrds in April of 1968 and quickly became the major influence in the group. "We set out to hire a piano player and we got George Jones in a sequined suit," the group's Chris Hillman later remarked. Their *Sweetheart of the Rodeo* disc, released late in 1968, can be considered the first recorded attempt by an important rock group to integrate country and rock styles. Alas, it did not do well at the retail counter. The Byrds' many fans, won by such "folk-rock" fusions as "Mr. Tambourine Man," "Eight Miles High," "Turn, Turn, Turn," and "So You Want to Be a Rock and Roll Star," weren't impressed when they heard the group perform country standards like "I Am a Pilgrim" and "You're Still on My Mind" or such gorgeous originals as Gram's "Hickory Wind," "One Hundred Years from Now," and "Blue Canadian Rockies."

Parsons moved on to form the Flying Burrito Brothers with Hillman, introducing rock fans to steel guitars and the handiwork of Nudie of Hollywood, the gaudy tailor to such country stars as Porter Wagoner and Hank Snow. *Gilded Palace of Sin,* which contained nine songs written or co-written by Parsons, sent the critics scurrying to the dictionary in search of superlatives. But it was a poor seller.

Above: *Gram Parson's vision of "cosmic American music" was a major influence on the Rolling Stones, the Eagles, Poco, and countless other artists. He had less than 7 months to live when these shots were snapped.*
Below: *Emmylou Harris onstage in 1982.*

EMMYLOU HARRIS
(Warner Bros.)

Beginning her career as a folk singer in the Washington, D.C., area, Emmylou got her first big break singing on Gram Parsons's gemlike solo albums. Two years after his tragic death, she returned as a solo artist. Her gorgeous "pure" country voice is used to best advantage on such classic chestnuts as "Beneath Still Waters," "If I Could Only Win Your Love," "Making Believe," and "To Daddy." But she also has a keen eye for fine new songs; she was the first to record Townes Van Zandt's "Pancho and Lefty," Karen Brooks and Hank DeVito's "Tennessee Rose," Delbert McClinton's "Two More Bottles of Wine," and over a dozen of Rodney Crowell's beauties. (Her band has served as a launching pad for the careers of Crowell and Ricky Skaggs.) CMA Female Vocalist of the Year in 1980, Emmylou will be a country star as long as she wants to sing. Hall of Fame potential.

A second Burritos album also failed commercially, then a third. By this time Hillman was the only original member left.

Undeterred, Parsons continued to pursue his dream of a rock-country fusion, a marriage he termed "cosmic American music" or "soul country cosmic," by launching a solo career with *GP,* a brilliant album featuring country standards—"The Streets of Baltimore," "We'll Sweep Out the Ashes in the Morning"—and his own gems, including "The New Soft Shoe," "She," and "Still Feeling Blue." *GP* also rescued Emmylou Harris from the Washington, D.C., area folk-bluegrass scene, where she was slowly going nowhere, and introduced her to mass audiences. The group built around the album took to the road early in 1973 for a honky-tonk tour, traveling in an old bus rather than by air, as was the rock custom in those heady times.

Alas, Parsons, nicknamed "The Crown Prince of Excess," succumbed to his bad habits that September, just after finishing his follow-up LP. He was twenty-six. He died alone at the Joshua Tree Inn, a drug overdose who passed away before ever seeing the hardy crops that were to grow from the seeds he had sown. His final recordings were issued posthumously on *Grievous Angel,* an album that surpassed even *GP.* The disc was once again a mixture of classic country tunes, including "Love Hurts," "Cash on the Barrelhead," and "I Can't Dance," and Parsons's new tunes, "Return of the Grievous Angel," "Las Vegas," and "Brass Buttons." The album closes with "In My Hour of Darkness," the only song Gram and Emmylou wrote together:

> In my hour of darkness, in my time of need
> Oh Lord, grant me vision, oh Lord, grant me speed

That song, like much of Gram's material, deserved to be recorded by top country artists. However, the Nashville producers were not searching for material from California country rockers. Few of them knew, or would have cared had they known, that Gram was raised in Georgia and Florida; when they looked at Parsons, all they saw was the dreaded association with rock 'n' roll and drugs. Gram's wild and woolly reputation was one of the reasons Merle Haggard backed away from producing *GP* after originally agreeing to the project.

Parsons's influence upon country artists lay in seeding the ground that the progressive country acts later harvested. Without his seminal work, it's doubtful that Waylon and Willie would have found such a ready audience for their own recordings several years later. These ushered in the "outlaw" phase of country music, which rescued the form from the sales doldrums and led it to new heights of success.

Gram paved a new road to success for rock acts as well. Poco made it big with—guess what?—a fusion of country and rock, complete with steel guitar. Crosby, Stills, Nash and Young, Jackson Browne, Linda Ronstadt, and the Eagles later incorporated country elements into their sound to win large-scale commercial success. Even the Grateful Dead went country: their *Workingman's Dead* and *American Beauty* albums presented an acoustic sound with a decided country flavor.

And Gram's vision can also be found as an influence upon the Rolling Stones. Following a tour of South Africa by the Byrds—which aborted due to Parsons's distaste for the country's apartheid policies—Gram stayed with Keith Richards in France. The Stones subsequently released several country-flavored songs: "Honky-Tonk Women," "Dead Flowers," and "Wild Horses," the last said to be dedicated to Gram.

Today, over ten years after Gram's death, his work still sounds as fresh as it did then. His approach was vindicated by the changes that overtook country music in the next few years. A scruffy group of rebellious country musicians changed the sound of the music by following the Parsons formula of mixing rock and country elements to create a new type of music. The critics immediately tagged it "progressive country" and hailed its chief stylists as "outlaws."

A moment of silence for Gram Parsons, please. May his soul find the peace that eluded his mind.

The Coming of the Outlaws

Nashville's influence on popular music has waxed and waned over the years, reaching peaks and suffering troughs much like the prices of stocks or commodities. In 1968, country music's popularity bottomed out as it had done eleven years earlier. As in 1957, rock 'n' roll was the main reason, only this time the perpetrators were not American but British. The "English Invasion," begun early in 1964 with the Beatles, the Animals, the Rolling Stones, the Dave Clark Five, and others, launched a steady stream of westward-bound British groups that endures to this day.

The American pop charts were almost exclusively the province of American performers until the reign of the English bands, which was kicked off by the Beatles anthem "I Want to Hold Your Hand." In the three years prior, the only foreign acts to top the American pop charts were (in order) Burt Kaempfert, the Tornadoes, Kyu Sakamoto, and the Singing Nun. Very few bands made the top of the charts in that era; folk groups, soundtracks, vocalists, vocal groups, and instrumental groups held sway. The only bands to score No. 1 singles in that same time span were the Hollywood Argyles, Joey Dee and the Starlighters, and Jimmy Gilmer and the Fireballs.

Jerry Lee Lewis and his daughter Linda Gail work out in this early 1970s appearance. (Photo: Marshall Fallwell, Jr.)

Three "outlaws"—Lee Clayton, Billy Joe Shaver, and Willie Nelson—relax outside Armadillo World Headquarters in Austin in 1973.

To be sure, vocal groups like the Drifters, the Shirelles, the Tokens, the Four Seasons, the Crystals, and the Chiffons were very popular, but these acts consisted of singers who did not play an instrument. They were backed up by interchangeable musicians, anonymous to the public because they were never credited for their recording work.

The idea of a band—four, five, or six people who wrote the material, played, and sang—was an unproven commercial concept before the Beatles came on the scene. Most records of the day were recorded with studio musicians backing up the star or stars. When the time came to tour to promote the record, a different road group was assembled to re-create the hits onstage.

So the Beatles weren't just a bunch of guys with long hair: they represented the *rock group* concept, which was to rule the charts for the next two decades. Britannia may have lost control of the oceans by then, but she has certainly ruled the waves of American radio since 1964.

Headed by the "Fab Four," English rock groups held the top spot on American charts for twenty-three weeks in 1964 and twenty-six weeks in 1965. By 1966 the concept had been adopted in the United States by such bands as the Byrds, the Young Rascals, the Lovin' Spoonful, the Buckinghams, the Box Tops, the Doors, and the Monkees, an American counteraction to the invasion that cut the English share of the No. 1 slot to twelve weeks in 1966.

Interestingly, the music presented in this English assault was a British regurgitation of American music. From the beginning, the Stones, the Yardbirds, the Animals, the Who, and the Moody Blues took their main inspiration from blues, soul, and rhythm and blues, the same sources that rock 'n' roll had mined. This clever reconstruction was transported back to America and publicized heavily as "new music," which the American public bought, "hook," line, and fishing pole.

The Beatles, who led the British incursion, took much of their inspiration from artists who had recorded in Nashville. The Everly Brothers, Buddy Holly, Elvis Presley, and Roy Orbison were major influences—and all save Holly recorded huge pop hits in Music City in the years prior to the Beatles' ascendancy. (Holly cut in Music City as well, but his Decca sessions

WILLIE NELSON
(Columbia)

Besides being a great singer, Nelson is also one of America's finest songwriters and a vastly underrated guitarist. His 1975 album *Red-Headed Stranger* was influential in reviving minimalist production methods and, not incidentally, got him his first big hit after thirteen years of misses. He and fellow Texas roustabout Waylon Jennings kicked off the "outlaw" movement (also known as "progressive country"), which attracted thousands of young music lovers to country music. The Fourth of July picnics Willie held in the mid-1970s attracted the biggest audiences of any country music gathering. So far, he has picked up seven CMA Awards and has been named Entertainer of the Year. He lives on the road or in homes he maintains in Texas, Colorado, California, and Hawaii, traveling back and forth by Lear jet. Despite the "outlaw" tag, Nelson carries an air of serenity about him and is one of the *kindest* men in show business. A certain future Hall of Fame choice.

with Owen Bradley did not produce any smash hits; for the most part, those were waxed in Clovis, New Mexico.)

There were legions of young people at just the right age to buy this "new" music. The end of World War II in 1945 had resulted in a dramatic rise in new American families. These kids, born in the years from 1945 to 1953, were eleven to nineteen years old when the Beatles came along. Many of them had first encountered rock 'n' roll in their early adolescence; the group at the older end of the spectrum was quick to embrace this new variation of rock. (The long hair gave the sounds just the right touch of rebellion, helping to make the music unpalatable to parents much as the beat and lascivious movements of Elvis had made rock unpopular with the parents of half a generation back.)

How did all of this affect country music and Nashville? As in 1957, country acts found it very hard to get work. Record sales fell along with demand for live country talent. Fewer country records made it into the pop charts, fewer artists landed network television exposure or achieved significant pop airplay. Radio stations shifted away from country formats in their haste to embrace this exciting new rock group concept. All over Nashville, record executives scratched their heads and wondered what was wrong.

What was wrong was that country music had little relevance to a rebellious generation that was spending the second half of the 1960s experimenting with social protest, drug use, and sexual freedom. In the eyes of the fifteen to twenty-five age group, country music was square because it appealed to old whites and rednecks, two lily-white groups with few redeeming virtues for the young of the period. It wasn't until 1975 that a country song recognized the social changes brought about by the pill—and Loretta Lynn was criticized even then for tackling the issue head-on. But the young women of the 1960s had learned that lesson years before Loretta sang of it. The heart and soul of country music—lyrics built around tender sexual yearning—were thus amusingly anachronistic to young folks actively engaged in their own sexual "liberation."

The late sixties also saw a tremendous struggle for racial equality. Many young whites participated directly in this struggle for black rights guaranteed by the Constitution and the Bill of Rights but ignored in reality. Many more whites supported this cause indirectly, and others came to realize that black people in this country must enjoy the same freedoms and privileges as whites or no one was free. Country artists made no special effort to embrace the cause during this period. No great songs dealing with racial inequality emerged. Perhaps the city and the industry felt beyond such matters. Black harmonica virtuoso Deford Bailey went on the Opry in the late 1920s, Charley Pride began having hits in 1966, and Nashville was desegregated by the early 1960s without serious incident.

By 1968 the most popular country singers had been stars for almost as long as Carter has had liver pills. Very little new blood had entered the country mainstream during the preceding decade. Any creative field will suffer without an influx of fresh talent—and country music had been led by the same singers, producers, and studio players for a full generation.

The audience for country music then consisted primarily of old people getting older. Clearly, something had to be done. Some new fans were being recruited, but they weren't entering as fast as the older ones were dying off. In the late 1950s country had pulled itself out of the mudhole by upgrading recording facilities and adapting techniques from pop music production. These tricks were employed again in 1968, but the most important reason for country's upswing at the box office was the development of a whole new generation of artists and producers. From 1967 to 1972, country harvested a bumper crop of talented, younger artists. Such singers as Glen Campbell, Lynn Anderson, Hank Williams, Jr., Tammy Wynette, Conway Twitty, Charley Pride, Dolly Parton, Merle Haggard, Mickey Gilley, Charlie Rich, Barbara Mandrell, Kenny Rogers, Loretta Lynn, Crystal Gayle, Tom T. Hall, David Frizzell, Anne Murray, Tanya Tucker, Don Williams, Donna Fargo, Freddie Hart, Jack Greene, David Houston, and Johnny Rodriguez either posted their first chart record or their first No. 1 during these six years.

JOHNNY RODRIGUEZ
(Epic)

Discovered by south Texas entrepreneur Happy Shahan and Tom T. Hall, Johnny is the most famous former goat thief in popular music. He got his first hit with "Pass Me By" in 1972, and then nabbed fifteen straight Top 10s within five years before getting colder than a frozen moon pie: only three Top 10s from 1978 through 1982. Johnny has an extremely warm and romantic voice, and he sings in Spanish as well as in English. In 1983, he began a comeback with "Foolin'," his first Top 5 since 1977. Johnny wrote two of his biggest hits—"Down on the Rio Grande" and "Ridin' My Thumb to Mexico." The death of his close friend and road manager in an automobile accident several years ago took a toll on his emotions, but he has recovered fully, and he could have many more years like his first five; he unquestionably has the talent, voice, looks, and stage charisma.

WAYLON JENNINGS
(RCA)

Out of west Texas by way of Arizona, Waylon is one of the finest stylists in country music, as well as a great guitarist and songwriter. He once possessed one of the "biggest" voices in popular music. A former member of Buddy Holly's band who had flopped as a singer on Brunswick and A & M before coming to RCA, Waylon changed the course of country music history with Willie Nelson, setting off the "outlaw" era. He has since won four CMA Awards. He is married to Jessi Colter. Jennings's menacing appearance belies a sensitive mind and a wry sense of humor. Future Hall of Famer.

A pensive Waylon Jennings before the hair grew all over his face. (Photo: Marshall Fallwell, Jr.)

The newer acts that broadened country's appeal and attracted millions of new listeners were also aided by older stars whose popularity waxed anew in the post-1968 era. Jerry Lee Lewis's transformation into a country stylist began in 1968, George Jones made one of his many comebacks (and also began recording with Tammy Wynette), while Ray Price and Marty Robbins once again returned to favor with record buyers by altering or "modernizing" their sound, upgrading their material, and working with younger producers.

Many artists were able to gain control over their own record production, a list that included Bobby Bare, Dolly Parton, Don Williams, Waylon Jennings, Conway Twitty, Merle Haggard, Eddie Rabbitt, Willie Nelson, and Gail Davies. As these and the other up-and-coming artists hit their stride and gained slots at the top of the pile, they dislodged the aging acts who had been around as long as dirt. These fading stars had worn out their welcome with all but the over-forty age group and were about as thrilling as a chaperoned date to the younger listeners country was desperate to reach. The grip on the public's ears of stars like Johnny Cash, Hank Snow, Ernest Tubb, Eddy Arnold, Sonny James, Ferlin Husky, Webb Pierce, Porter Wagoner, and others lessened; after 1972 the above group of artists collectively posted three No. 1s and about a dozen Top 10s, although many of them remained linked to major labels throughout the decade.

As these aging pioneers grudgingly yielded their positions to fresher talent, they gradually assumed the role of elder statesmen, some more gracefully than others. As the 1980s spin by, most of these stars of yesteryear are still out there on the road, singing and playing and signing autographs for the folks, making a living the only way they know how. Any visit to the Grand Ole Opry will present an opportunity to see many of them in action.

Along with the new crop of artists came a new crop of listeners, which helps to explain the explosion of interest in country music that developed in the 1970s. The 1944 to 1953 period may have been called the "Baby Boom" for many decades, but the years from 1954 to 1964 were the *real* boom years for births in America.

A look at the birth records for the years under scrutiny bears this out. There were over four million new births each year between 1954 and 1964, while the totals for the 1944 to 1953 period as well as for the years since 1968 added up to less than four million new babies. What this means to the record business is that more kids in this country became sixteen years old between 1970 and 1980 than reached that magical age in the previous decade. And this section of the population furnished the new young fans who boosted country music tremendously, beginning in the second half of the 1970s.

The artists most responsible for making country music more appealing to young listeners were two maverick outsiders from Texas who had gone through the 1960s with scant success. Willie Nelson and Waylon Jennings were two stylists widely acknowledged to have enormous talent but who had not, as of 1970, found a large market for their records.

If they had stopped to count matters up on New Year's Day of 1970, Willie and Waylon together would have tallied only eight Top-10 records. Neither man had enjoyed a No. 1 single. Anyone who had said then that these two scruffy singers would revolutionize the country industry, kick off an entirely "new" direction for the music, and become heroes to thousands of pot-smoking youngsters would have been directed to a room with padded walls and no windows.

The key to success for both men lay in gaining control over song selection and production, actually a battle quietly begun years earlier by Bobby Bare. Waylon and Willie justifiably felt that there was too much clutter—strings, backing vocalists, and extra instruments—between their music and the public. These two men were vocal stylists. However, instead of playing up to their unique quirks, producers and label executives had gone in the opposite direction and tried to bury them amid layers of extraneous sounds. What Jennings and Nelson did when they eventually gained artistic freedom was to strip their music down to the basics and emphasize their own peculiar phrasing and distinctive vocal approach. In the process they also uncovered their individual guitar styles; Waylon's snaky guitar lines and Willie's jazz-influenced licks surfaced in their recordings for the first time.

Below: *What a pair! Bobby Bare and grizzly bear at a TV taping in Germany.*
Bottom, left: *There weren't many checks in Willie Nelson's mailbox back in 1966.*
Bottom, right: *A rare belly laugh from "outlaw" Waylon Jennings, with his wife, Jessi Colter ("outlawess"?), looking on. (Photo: Tim Naprestek)*

For want of a better term, this music came to be labeled "progressive country," and its practitioners were called "outlaws." No one seemed to mind that these were hilarious misnomers, for the appellations stuck.

Of course, progressive country was neither progressive nor country. In fact, a case could be made for it to be called "regressive rock," for the form was created by adapting elements from rock music, reversing a tactic employed in the mid-1950s when rock music had been created from elements of black music and country by such fusion stylists as Bill Haley and Elvis Presley. The "outlaw" tag was a marketing ploy built more around the artists' long hair and blue jeans than from any actual problems with the law.

Though Waylon, once a sideman in rock pioneer Buddy Holly's band, had charted records for nine years with RCA (and had previous unsuccessful outings on Brunswick and A & M), his first No. 1 single didn't come until 1974, when the first album he produced himself (with Willie Nelson) came out. This was the title track from his *This Time* LP. His subsequent recordings followed in this minimalist vein from a production standpoint, and Waylon continued to rack up No. 1s throughout the decade. Though the years have taken their toll on Jennings's once robust voice, he seems likely to continue to exert his influence as a songwriter, producer, and live attraction.

Waylon at least was in a contending position before his breakthrough. Any glance at the recording career of Willie Nelson prior to 1974 would certify his position as a lower-echelon artist. During the previous twelve years Nelson had placed twenty-five records on the charts but only two reached Top 10: "Touch Me" and "Willingly" (a duet with Shirley Collie), both in 1962. Nelson had gained a well-earned reputation as a songwriter with "Hello Walls," "Crazy," "Funny (How Time Slips Away)," and "Good-Hearted Woman," but his recording career had already encompassed four major labels. Nelson's first chart discs were with Liberty. He then recorded with RCA for seven years, with Monument for a few months, and with Atlantic for two years before finally cracking into the winner's circle with Columbia in 1975, scoring a No. 1 country, No. 22 pop smash with his version of a Fred Rose chestnut, "Blue Eyes Crying in the Rain." In the years since, Nelson has recorded a staggering body of work drawn from sources as diverse as honky-tonk and Tin Pan Alley, jazz and traditional country, blues and rock, gospel and bluegrass, western swing and Eastern religion.

Nelson displays a better grasp of the nature of popular music than does Jennings. He apparently realizes that since it is pop rather than "serious" music then you should put as much product into the market as you can from as many angles as you can conjure up and not worry if each isn't a masterpiece. In 1979 alone Nelson released a greatest hits double LP, a "live" platter, a movie soundtrack, a gospel album, a (reissued) Christmas album, an acoustic, jazzy set of Tin Pan Alley standards (*Somewhere over the Rainbow*), a duet package with Webb Pierce, a Kris Kristofferson tribute LP, and a session with old friends Roger Miller and Ray Price. Jennings's only release that year was a greatest hits package.

Once they gained production control, Nelson and Jennings also began inserting their own band members in place of studio musicians for their recording sessions. This not only gave them a continuity of sound between recording and road dates, it also brought new players into the studios, long the province of a handful of extremely talented but rather tired sessionmen, a group of thirty to fifty musicians who played on most of the pre-1974 hits cut in country music. Today many artists integrate band members with session players.

In fact, Nelson was so serious about finding a new sound that he left Nashville entirely and retreated to Garland, Texas, where he, his band, and Texas engineer Phil York created his breakthrough album, the unified, narrative tale of the *Red-Headed Stranger,* country music's most effective concept album to date and the source of "Blue Eyes Crying in the Rain." The overall production on *Red-Headed Stranger* was so subtle and sparse that several Columbia executives, upon first hearing the record, snorted that the tracks were not really completed at all but were "demos."

Waylon and Willie also changed their images along with their music. Jennings abandoned his slicked-back hair and suits for long hair, jeans, boots, and his now-familiar black leather vest. Nelson, who once had a publicity photo taken in a Nehru jacket (and another in a turtleneck sweater), adopted jeans, let his hair grow out, attached an earring to one ear, and went without shaving for days at a time. Both also let it be known that they didn't consider smoking marijuana a serious sin. Whether *they* smoked pot or not was beside the point—they *looked* as if they did. Nashville may have considered Jennings and Nelson a pair of dirty hippies, but the two small-town Texas fellows (Nelson is from Abbott, Jennings from Littlefield) knew the move closely identified them with the audience they wanted to reach—the

Below: *Loretta Lynn at a benefit for the American Indians at the Kennedy Center in Washington, D.C. (Loretta is one-quarter Cherokee.)*
Bottom: *Producer/songwriter Larry Butler (left) tries out a new one on Ben Peters, one of Music City's top tunesmiths since 1968.*

Opposite: *The hands of Jerry Lee Lewis, 1982. (Photo: Robert K. Oermann)*
Left: *A younger, thinner, and drunker Kris Kristofferson flashes vintage outlaw form. (Photo: Al Clayton)*
Right: *Ken Nelson (right) was one of country's leading producers in the 1950s and 1960s, working with Merle Haggard (left), Sonny James, Buck Owens, and Gene Vincent. This photo was taken in 1969.*

young, "hip" crowd of twenty- to thirty-five-year-olds who were beginning to tire of rock music.

By being rebels or "outlaws" in their refusal to kowtow to the coat-and-tie Nashville executives, Willie and Waylon aligned themselves with this group of young people who had spent the late 1960s and early 1970s involved in their own personal rebellions. By adopting coloration similar to the audience they sought, both artists helped create a vast new audience for themselves and exposed many thousands of listeners to country music for the first time.

The Nashville establishment, no fools they, soon realized that the Jennings-Nelson approach, odious though it may have been to them personally, was ringing cash registers at a rapid clip. Blue jeans and longer hair began to sprout in the label offices like new clover after spring showers. More production and song selection responsibility was ceded to the artists, and attempts to cash in on the outlaws "trend" accelerated. RCA pulled the marketing coup of this era when Nashville boss Jerry Bradley put together a batch of existing tracks from Jennings, Nelson, Tompall Glaser, and Jessi Colter, tagged the package *Wanted! The Outlaws,* and notched country music's first officially certified platinum album. (Ironically, only Jennings was still on the label when *Wanted! The Outlaws* was released in 1976. Nelson had moved from RCA to Monument to Atlantic to Columbia, Glaser was on MGM, and Colter had strolled to Capitol.)

The cover design was built around an old-time "Wanted" poster; the three male participants were bearded (probably the first No. 1 country album with three bearded men on the cover) and they looked shady in the extreme. Aggressive marketing helped propel this package to the consumers along with such selections as "Good-Hearted Woman," the first duet match between Waylon and Willie, minor hits from Glaser and Nelson, a Colter-Jennings recycling of their 1970 duet of "Suspicious Minds," and Jennings's fine version of "My Heroes Have Always Been Cowboys," a song later released as a single by Nelson (No. 1 in 1980). It's interesting to note that the word "outlaw" does not appear in any of the song titles, an indication that the project may have been somewhat contrived. Nevertheless, the album was a smash, the outlaw concept caught fire with the public, and country suddenly gained a whole new group of listeners.

The change in direction was not without a humorous side. Many male country singers threw away their razors and began sporting every variety of facial hair design save for a Hitler moustache. Everyone took to wearing blue jeans and boots, while snap-button shirts came into

KRIS KRISTOFFERSON
(Monument)

If Texas-born Kris hasn't done it all by now he probably will before he's through; to start with, he won letters in two sports at college, received a Rhodes scholarship to Oxford, and piloted helicopters in Vietnam. He spent four years scratching to make headway in Nashville as a writer before getting Roger Miller to cut "Me and Bobby McGee." As of now, he has won thirty-two BMI Awards, three Grammies, and a CMA Award, for tunes like "Sunday Morning Coming Down," "For the Good Times," "Help Me Make It Through the Night," "Why Me, Lord," "Nobody Wins," and "Loving Her Was Easier (Than Anything I'll Ever Do Again)." In the 1970s he moved into films and has since starred in more motion pictures than anyone else in popular music. Possible Hall of Famer.

The man Elvis Presley introduced as "the greatest singer in the world": Roy Orbison, shown here in concert at Manhattan's Lone Star Cafe. (Photo: Charlyn Zlotnik)

such demand that real cowboys out West had trouble buying them even at the inflated prices attached to such "fashionable" clothes. Aging country singers experimented with marijuana and began hanging out with younger musicians. Even Lynn Anderson tried to become an outlaw—a tough assignment for someone who had spent years as a regular on "The Lawrence Welk Show." Whether her advanced pregnancy aided or detracted from her acceptance is inconclusive, but the fact remains that the public didn't swallow Lynn as a "criminal."

However, behind all the publicity blarney generated by the outlaw label was a battle over creative control of the music. Today it is clear that the artists won the struggle, for they now have far more input into all aspects of the process than they had ten years before, from the songs they record to the producers employed right down to approval of the album cover art. Record label staff producers, earlier the industry norm, are far less common today, and many artists now have the freedom to simply deliver their latest album to the label upon completion, a practice unheard of for even the biggest stars prior to the mid-1970s.

The late 1960s and early 1970s also saw a "changing of the guard" in the producer's chair. Don Law, Chet Atkins, Owen Bradley, and Ken Nelson began to yield to a "new wave" of producers whose experience was much broader in musical scope than those of their predecessors. Billy Sherrill assumed production control at CBS and began issuing a long string of hits with such artists as Tammy Wynette, George Jones, Charlie Rich, Tanya Tucker, and David Houston. Jack "Cowboy" Clement, another rising producer, who, like Sherrill, had been fired by Sam Phillips from the Sun Records staff in Memphis, moved to town and soon was producing Charley Pride, the Glaser Brothers, and others, gaining notoriety as the first independent producer to be hired by a major label along the way. Larry Butler, who produced the big Kenny Rogers hits of the late 1970s, gained producer status at Capitol in 1969 and began crafting hits with Ferlin Husky and Jean Shepherd. Bob Ferguson and Jerry Bradley began their RCA production work during this period, while Jerry Crutchfield (now Lee Greenwood's producer) traded an artist's for a producer's cap. Jerry Kennedy, Shelby Singleton, and Allen Reynolds had all earned their production spurs by the early 1970s, and they were later joined in the Music City production ranks by Jimmy Bowen, Chips Moman (another Memphis refugee), Norro Wilson, Jim Ed Norman, Tom Collins, Ron Chancey, and many others, all lured to town because Music City offered better career opportunities than they had enjoyed in their previous niches. It wouldn't also be out of the question to presume that these men were able to sense the upcoming changes in the popular music field.

By the end of the 1970s, when the "outlaw" yielded to the "urban cowboy," country music had grown from a forgotten backwater of the American popular music river to a $500 million annual current in the $3.5 billion domestic record market.

The outlaws weren't the only group of people to help blast country music into a higher orbit; the contributions of the fairer sex to this success merit enough elaboration to require a chapter to themselves.

CHARLIE RICH

A truly gifted keyboard master, Rich is equally compelling in country, blues, and jazz selections. While Charlie is known to most listeners for "Mohair Sam," "Lonely Weekends," "Behind Closed Doors," and "The Most Beautiful Girl," his albums contain undiscovered gems galore. "The Silver Fox" has compiled an enviable dossier of hits in pop, country, and a-c and has won five CMA Awards. He and Merle Haggard are the only artists to win the four major CMA solo singing awards: Entertainer, Single, Album, and Male/Female Vocalist of the Year. In 1975, however, he scandalized CMA when he appeared drunk as a presenter on the annual awards show, telecast live nationally. Rich climaxed his appearance when he set fire to the envelope upon announcing that the Entertainer of the Year is "my very good friend, John Denver." Glen Campbell and Charley Pride helped Rich from the stage. The Mose Allison of country music.

The Ladies Get to Play

The singing stars in country music's first thirty years of recorded history were almost exclusively male. Though Roba Stanley recorded in 1924, thus claiming the honor of becoming the first recorded woman in country music, the fairer sex was relegated to roles as harmony singers or comediennes until the 1950s. Even in a supporting role women were limited; the sight of a woman onstage performing with men was tolerated only if she was related to at least one of the performers by blood or marriage. Roy Acuff found out about this taboo in 1939 when he added Rachel Veach to his group in the twin roles of banjo player and comedienne. The fans were outraged until Acuff hastily announced that Rachel was actually the sister of Bashful Brother Oswald, another member of the group, ironically named the Smokey Mountain *Boys.* The uproar subsided when the fans learned that Rachel had an onstage chaperone.

The only other avenue open to women was through an all-girl band, a solution that Eva Davis and Samantha Baumgarner exploited in the 1920s. The duo, Samantha on fiddle and Eva on banjo, became one of the first "string bands" to be recorded. In the 1930s and 1940s the Coon Creek Girls, a quartet led by Lily Mae Ledford, became a very popular act.

The Carter Family, consisting of A. P. Carter, his wife, Sara, and his sister-in-law, Maybelle, were the most popular of the family groups during the 1920s and 1930s as well as one of the most important groups in the history of country music. They recorded together for fourteen years, outlasting even A. P. and Sara's marriage. Most of the country acts that recorded back in that early period (the Carters began making records in 1927) lasted but a few years,

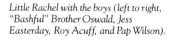

Little Rachel with the boys (left to right, "Bashful" Brother Oswald, Jess Easterday, Roy Acuff, and Pap Wilson).

Johnny and Jack Anglin, Kitty Wells, and the Tennessee Mountain Boys (Emory Martin, Paul Warren, and Ray Adkins) were all regulars on KWKH radio's "Louisiana Hayride" from 1949 to 1952.

making the Carter's longevity even more amazing. Of the over 250 songs included on these records, many were country standards or soon became standards following their "Carterization."

Duet teams were also popular during these times before the introduction of television when the barn dance shows ruled the radio waves. Lulu Belle and Scotty Wiseman were the best known; for twenty-five years they were fixtures on WLS Radio's "National Barn Dance" program, a stint that began in 1933 and included temporary visits to the Grand Ole Opry, the Boone County Jamboree, and Red Foley's Ozark Jamboree. Lulu Belle was voted America's Most Popular Radio Performer in the mid-thirties, a tremendous honor for a country artist, much less a woman. Though Curly Fox and Miss Texas Ruby were another important man and wife duet their popularity did not compare with that of Lulu Belle and Scotty.

As a member of the Prairie Ramblers, Patsy Montana became the first woman to enjoy a country million-seller in 1936 when her "I Want to Be a Cowboy's Sweetheart" became a national hit. The Ramblers, another of the groups featured on the "National Barn Dance," played a style of western swing that utilized piano, clarinet, and saxophone. Montana recorded for many years. She moved to California, and was still exhibiting her twin skills of singing and yodeling at festivals into the mid-1980s.

Besides Montana, the only other women to achieve significant "solo" careers in country music prior to the 1950s were Judy Canova and Minnie Pearl, both of whom took the much easier route of comedienne.

The obstacle to women country performers was not lack of interest on the part of the fans in hearing what they had to say or how they sang. What they faced were social barriers. Young ladies of the 1920s and 1930s were expected to marry and begin a family much earlier than they do today. Women could work if they wanted to be teachers or nurses. Under the mores of the time a single girl who traveled with a group of men was a walking scandal; a married woman on the road had obviously abandoned husband and/or family in favor of a career, a serious transgression of the social order of the day.

World War II changed many of the social attitudes of this country toward women, starting

Left: *For 27 years Jo Walker-Meador (right) has led the Country Music Association. BMI's Frances Preston (left) prepares to hand over a bouquet while CMA President Dick McCullough and BMI's Nancy Franklin observe.*
Right: *Patsy Cline with the Opry at Carnegie Hall, 1961.*

with the women themselves. It forced them to live independently; they entered the work force and, with the men away fighting, they learned out of necessity to make their own decisions. When the war ended and the men returned, they found their mates to be less subservient than in prewar days.

Developments in transportation and medicine also helped pave the way for women to find a place as solo artists in country music. Barbara Mandrell, the first two-time Entertainer of the Year in country music, adds her thoughts on the improvement in transportation: "The buses. They're glorified motor homes. I can be a full-time mother, have my children with me and have things very normal when I'm on the road."

The war gave women the freedom to work outside the home. Buses gave them the freedom to travel with their families. A third development, this one from a laboratory, gave them a means to plan those families, an option Loretta Lynn cannily summarized in her 1975 hit, "The Pill":

For several years, I've stayed at home while you had all the fun
And every year that came by, another baby's come
There's gonna be some changes made, right here on Nursery Hill
You've set this chicken your last time, 'cause now I've got the Pill

Now that the social obstacles had been removed, women might well have begun their years as country stars much sooner had it not been for the canard among record executives (all of whom were male) that "girl singers don't sell." Despite the success of Patsy Montana in 1936 and the years that followed, this became a Catch-22 in the industry that effectively blocked female country recording. Kitty Wells first questioned that article of faith in 1952 when she answered Hank Thompson's song "The Wild Side of Life" with "It Wasn't God Who Made Honky Tonk

Angels," the first No. 1 hit by a solo female. Wells was as surprised as anyone: "I was shocked. Women never had hit records in those days. Very few of them ever even recorded."

Wells's hit didn't exactly open the floodgates, but it did secure a foothold for women in general as well as a solid career for herself. Others followed in the next few years: Jean Shepherd, Bonnie Lou, and Goldie Hill, but only Shepherd was able to post consistent hits.

Patsy Cline opened the door a bit further for women with her 1957 country and pop smash, "Walkin' after Midnight." Even so it took her four more years to post a follow-up hit. Cline's early 1960s hits, "I Fall to Pieces," "Crazy," and "She's Got You," established her as a star until her tragic death in a plane crash in 1963. Had she lived she might well have wrested away Kitty Wells's sobriquet as "The Queen of Country Music" in addition to accelerating the arrival of women in greater numbers in the country music pantheon of stars. Country historians agree that she was well on her way to adding a new sexual depth to the recorded feelings of women at the time of her death.

Cline may have pioneered a new sexual depth, but it was Loretta Lynn who brought a feisty spirit to women's country recordings. While women's main reaction to male mistreatment up until then had been tearful acceptance, Loretta jumped into the fray espousing such sentiments as "The Home You're Tearing Down," "You Ain't Woman Enough (To Take My Man)," and "You've Stepped In (From Stepping Out on Me)."

Even though Loretta didn't come to Nashville until 1961, she still found many of the old attitudes intact. "When I got here there weren't hardly any women in country music. What women that was in the business tried to run me out of Nashville. They didn't want no competition. I had to prove myself. I had three hits before I was even allowed on the Opry. Things aren't so hard for women now. I think women's lib got a lot to do with it."

Wells, Cline, and Lynn were the postwar pioneers who blazed the trail for the many women who followed during the last twenty years. The fact that prior to 1964 the above trio represented the *only* female solo singers to enjoy a No. 1 hit in country music emphasizes the advance of women artists in the last two decades. Connie Smith added her only chart-topper

Left: *If grit, courage, and character could make the charts, Lacy J. Dalton would already be No. 1. As it is, this truly gifted singer/writer should not have to wait much longer. (Photo: Tim Naprestek)*
Right: *Deluxe road "mangler" Phil Kaufman gets down on boss Emmylou Harris's brogans. (Photo: Jim McGuire)*

LACY J. DALTON
(Columbia)

Born Jill Byrem in Bloomsburg, Pennsylvania, Lacy went to college in Wisconsin and Utah. Afterward, she settled on the West Coast, where she essayed folk, blues, and rock ventures before "Crazy Blue Eyes," which she wrote, caught the attention of Billy Sherrill. Widowed prior to her son's birth, Dalton raised Adam alone. A magnetic personality, Lacy has carved out a slot as the country answer to Janis Joplin. Her wide stylistic variety and writing skill make her a potential superstar. Equally at home with rowdy rockers or tender ballads, Dalton fits no mold but her own. Not only that, she's a *class* act. She'll be widely imitated in the future.

Billie Jo Spears dresses up as a carhop in this 1978 shot.

BARBARA MANDRELL
(MCA)

The first two-time CMA Entertainer of the Year, Texas-born, California-raised Barbara is one of the hardest workers in show business. She earns upwards of $300,000 per week for performing in Las Vegas and is one of America's most popular female TV entertainers. A tireless promoter of country music, Mandrell can play any instrument in the band. She lives in Hendersonville with her husband and children and maintains a $1.5 million-dollar ocean-going yacht on Nashville's Old Hickory Lake. She is managed by her father, Irby, and guided by her husband, Ken Dudney. In 1984, she opened a museum dedicated to her life in music, called Barbara Mandrell Country, and saw it become one of the top tourist attractions in a city filled with them. A serious automobile accident in the fall of 1984 took her off the touring circuit for some time, but no one doubted she'd return to live appearances. Probable Hall of Famer.

ROSANNE CASH
(Columbia)

She may be one of Johnny Cash's daughters, but Rosanne, like Hank Williams, Jr., and Crystal Gayle, has carved her own musical niche. "Seven Year Ache," which she wrote, dominated the airwaves in the spring of 1981, rising to No. 1. "My Baby Thinks He's a Train" and another of Rosanne's tunes, "Blue Moon with Heartache," also hit the top. Her husband, Rodney Crowell, produced these discs with lush textures, creating a sophisticated country-pop sound that outdoes Crystal Gayle. Her debut LP, recorded for Ariola Records in Germany, is now a collector's item. Although she is a determined musician, Rosanne puts her three children ahead of her career, thus limiting her road schedule. Before settling in Nashville she worked in London and studied acting in Hollywood. Bobby Bare says, "She has one of those *wet* voices."

in 1964, then Tammy Wynette signaled her arrival with the strident "I Don't Wanna Play House" in 1967. Dottie West gives a good example of the prevailing thinking during the late 1960s: "In those days record men would tell you a woman didn't sell, and on all the package shows, there'd be only one girl. And I think that was really because they didn't think of us as artists—they just thought they should have a girl on the show. Y'know, for looks."

Record executives have done an about-face in their attitudes toward women's sales power in country music in the intervening years. Between the beginning of 1968 and the end of 1984 Tammy and Loretta each posted well over a dozen No. 1 hits, and they have been joined by a long parade of talented and attractive hit artists such as Lynn Anderson, Melba Montgomery, West, Dolly Parton, Jeannie C. Riley, Sammi Smith, Billie Jo Spears, Barbara Fairchild, Crystal Gayle, Anne Murray, Barbara Mandrell, Jeanne Pruett, Tanya Tucker, Donna Fargo, Marie Osmond, Linda Ronstadt, Jessi Colter, Emmylou Harris, Janie Fricke, Margo Smith, Karen Brooks, Shelly West, Juice Newton, Charly McClain, Cristy Lane, Sylvia, Reba McEntire, and Rosanne Cash. These acts accounted for over 130 No. 1 singles during the sixteen years since 1968, leaving little doubt that the "cowgirls" have found a place in the corral of stars with the "cowboys."

Demographic studies have shown that the primary buyers of recorded country music remain female, so it must be assumed that distaff buyers in the last fifteen years have accepted the different viewpoint that has accompanied women's full entry into the field. In the 1970s women entered many occupations previously felt to be the exclusive domain of males; their inroads in country music parallel female achievements in society at large.

Women have also earned a place in the field of country songwriting. The three dominant female artists of the post-1968 period, Tammy Wynette, Loretta Lynn, and Dolly Parton, have demonstrated consistent writing talent equal to that exhibited by the males. Collectively, this trio of thrushes has accumulated forty-seven BMI Awards for their compositions. While many of Tammy's songs were co-written with men, very few of Dolly's and none of Loretta's received male assistance.

Indeed, women songwriters have made strides into what was previously nearly a male monopoly. Prior to 1968, Felice Bryant, JennyLou Carson, and Cindy Walker were the only female writers who had posted several major hits. They were joined first by Lynn, Parton, and Wynette, each of whom earned a niche in country songwriting by providing her own fresh perspective. As noted, Loretta's writing echoed female determination to keep her self-respect whether she kept her partner or not. Such songs as "Fist City," "Rated X," and "You Ain't Woman Enough" broadcast the fact that, at least as far as she was concerned, the days of woman's meek submission to everything hubby dished out were over. Tammy's viewpoint was somewhat more complex, perhaps because almost all of her hits were co-written with male writers, her producer, Billy Sherrill, being her most frequent collaborator. Though much of her material was set around the traditional suffering female outlook, such as "Stand By Your Man" and "Another Lonely Song," Tammy also delivered achingly beautiful works such as "'Til I Can Make It On My Own," a song about a woman's ultimate recovery from heartbreak, and "Two Story House," a devastating duet with George Jones about a disintegrated marriage.

It's ironic to note that although Loretta's songs usually were bellicose warnings to her man (or women who were eyeing him) and Tammy's were generally weepers built around staying together, it is Wynette who has been married five times while Lynn has remained in a union (albeit a stormy one) for over twenty-five years.

Dolly Parton's songs merit much lengthier study than this volume can afford because hers are the most varied of the three women stars as well as the most numerous. Though she shared the same Appalachian background as Lynn as well as the early poverty of both women, Dolly's songs range from the stunning evocation of love represented by a patchwork jacket in "Coat of Many Colors" to the urgent sexual yearning of the disco hit "Baby I'm Burning." She discusses the fear of losing her man in "Jolene," then tells us of a woman who just left when the kids were grown in "To Daddy." Frank Dycus, who oversaw her publishing company during her days with Porter Wagoner, spoke in awe of her output in the early 1970s: "She would come in off the road with literally dozens of new songs every time they'd take a trip." Already the most honored female country songwriter in history, Parton seems likely to add to her total of BMI Awards unless she leaves country forever behind in her quest for pop music and film stardom.

In the years after 1968 many women have penned country hits. By early 1985 a partial list of award-winning female writers included Susanna Clark, Gail Davies, Cindy Jordan, Wanda Mallett, Patti Ryan, Leona Williams, Janis Carnes, Linda Hargrove, Pam Rose, Lacy J. Dalton, Deborah Allen, Mary Sue Rice, Debbie Hupp, Mira Smith, Barbara Wyrick, Margaret Lewis, Patsy Bruce, and Rhonda "Kye" Fleming.

Special mention should be made here of Fleming, an Arkansas native who came to Nashville in the mid-1970s following several years as a solo performer, mainly on the folk circuit. Shortly after arriving in Music City she was teamed up with another young writer, Dennis W. Morgan, and the pair went on to become Nashville's most successful writing team of the early 1980s. As staff writers for Tom Collins at Pi-Gem and Collins Court Music (created following the sale of Pi-Gem), the duo has turned out hit after hit, mainly for such Collins-produced acts as Ronnie Milsap ("I Wouldn't Have Missed It for the World," "Smoky

TANYA TUCKER *(Arista)*

Out of Seminole, Texas, by way of Las Vegas, Tanya caught the eye of talent scouts at the age of twelve, signed with Columbia at thirteen, and had her first No. 1 single ("What's Your Mama's Name") at fourteen. A series of hits under Billy Sherrill's tutelage soon established her as one of country's leading thrushes; from 1972–77 she enjoyed consistent hits on Columbia and MCA. Success hasn't been as easy to obtain since she mounted an assault on the rock/pop charts; it not only failed to establish her in those fields but also caused her country popularity to decline (she's had only one Top-5 hit since 1979 and her last No. 1 was in 1976). Still only twenty-six, she has time for a comeback. A song she co-authored with Dean Dillon, Gary Stewart, and Hank Williams, Jr.—"Leave Them Boys Alone," a hit performed in 1983 by Hank Williams, Jr.—shows signs of her writing ability. Future Hall of Fame selection is a possibility if she regains top ranks and manages to stay there.

Left: *Barbara Mandrell was one of Billy Sherrill's early production customers as a solo and for her duets with David Houston.*
Center: *Dolly Parton in 1970 before she had posted any substantial hits.*
Right: *Tanya Tucker at 24. (Photo: Robert K. Oermann)*

Mountain Rain"), Barbara Mandrell ("I Was Country When Country Wasn't Cool," "In Times Like These"), Charley Pride ("Roll On Mississippi"), Sylvia ("Drifter," "Nobody"), and Steve Wariner ("All Roads Lead to You," "Kansas City Lights"). They were honored as Nashville's top songwriters by the Nashville Songwriter's Association for two years in a row, and they took home the amazing total of nineteen BMI Awards between 1979 and 1983. The partnership ended in 1983 when Fleming married and moved out of town.

They approached songwriting as a job and put in steady, "normal" hours at their craft. Both feel that the key to their success has been in constantly rewriting their songs until the finished work is as near perfection as it can be. They have shown that a male-female team opens more possibilities by presenting an opportunity to combine the viewpoints of both sexes. This approach was pioneered in country by Felice and Boudleaux Bryant, but, strangely, it was left fallow in the 1960s and 1970s. It hasn't been lost on other writers in modern times, however. Deborah Allen has had considerable success writing with her husband, Rafe Van Hoy, while the husband-and-wife teams of Ed and Patsy Bruce and Bill and Mary Sue Rice have contributed many outstanding songs.

Gail Davies also deserves special mention, for she has pioneered as a producer of her own albums, another field previously exclusively male. Though there are other female singers who take an active role in the preparation of their records as co-producer or executive producer, Davies is the only one who has succeeded in gaining complete production responsibility. She didn't accomplish this without a gutsy gamble, as Gail recalls: "I was working with a co-producer who was working all day with Don Williams cutting tracks and then all night with me till like two in the morning. After about three days he was really tired so I asked him if he thought I could do the album by myself and he said 'yes.' So I said, 'OK, I'll do that.' So I called up my label and said 'I'm going to finish the album by myself.' And they got real upset and said, 'Don't you go in the studio until I talk to you and I'm flying out there Monday.' I had booked time in Muscle Shoals so I went ahead and took the money I was going to buy my house with and cut the whole album. Monday I played the stuff for him and he thought it was great. I told him I had produced it. And he was a little ticked because he felt like I had pulled something. Then they paid me back all the money I had put into it. I bought the house, produced the album, just like a fairy-tale dream."

The ten Top-20 hits she posted between 1981 and 1985 have underlined her abilities in this area and have also proven to be an example to women in the music business everywhere. Gail's struggle for self-production followed a similar battle faced by male artists earlier in the decade.

The excellent work done by the above women and many others has forever opened the doors in country music to talented writers and performers of their sex. It's a safe bet that country music will never again be the province of men only, a kingdom of "male vocalists" and "girl singers."

Crossover to Consciousness

Oak Ridge Boys Duane Allen, Joe Bonsall, Richard Sterban, and William Lee Golden discuss hits with Reggie Jackson during his Yankee years.

THE OAK RIDGE BOYS (MCA)

This group, which formed in Oak Ridge, Tennessee, during World War II, was for years one of the top gospel quartets in the South. William Lee Golden celebrated his twentieth year with the group in 1984. Texan Duane Allen has been an Oak almost as long. The two above represent the Southern, rural half of the group, with bass singer Richard Sterban and tenor Joe Bonsall providing a northern, urban influence (both were raised in Philadelphia suburbs). They moved to country in 1976, on Columbia, without success. The next year, with ace booking agent/manager Jim Halsey, they regrouped on ABC and posted seventeen consecutive Top-10 singles by mid-1983. They also clicked big in pop with Dallas Frazier's "Elvira" (using Rodney Crowell's arrangement). One of the most exciting live acts in the business, they have won three CMA Awards and five Grammies, four for their gospel selections. Superb material and ace Ron Chancey production are two additional reasons for their tremendous success. They work tirelessly for children-related causes and raise hundreds of thousands of dollars at Dallas's annual "Stars for Children" benefit alone.

Country music is so much a part of the social fabric of our nation today that it's easy to forget that most of America scorned it for many years. The biggest country stars are now as omnipresent as the biggest names in rock or popular music. The great strides made in the mid-1970s through the "outlaw" movement and the rise of women to headline status helped to bring the form into public view in much the same fashion as the development of the Nashville Sound had picked country music up by its bootstraps in the late 1950s and early 1960s. But the events of the last five years have sent country music into an orbit almost equal to the stratospheric heights long enjoyed by artists in the rock/pop field.

The national print and electronic media, a film that fell far short of box-office expectations, and the fashion moguls of New York City have had as much to do with the huge success of country music in the last five years as the artists and label executives. In the years since 1979, country's profile in the national media has increased so dramatically that, if one were to judge from that factor alone, one would think that country artists had conquered the pop charts and put the rout to synth-pop groups, disco artists, movie soundtracks, rock bands, heavy metalloids, and mellow crooners. Such has not been the case; despite the frequency of country songs that echo from ever more radio stations, the sight of country artists emanating from an increasing number of television programs, and the exposure generated by unprecedented print media coverage, country's share of the Top 10 on the "Hot 100" has not increased dramatically. Country artists did not take over the album charts; in fact, only three country artists, Dolly Parton, Eddie Rabbitt, and Kenny Rogers, have nabbed No. 1 pop singles since 1975.

But in the early 1980s it sure looked as if country had become the leading force in American music! Magazines and newspapers from coast to coast heralded the times as "the age of the Urban Cowboy." General-interest magazines like *Time, Esquire,* and *Newsweek* ran

KENNY ROGERS *(RCA)*

Now in his fourth musical career, Rogers grew up poor in a tough inner-city section of Houston. After making a name as the bass player with the Bobby Doyle Trio, a cocktail jazz combo, he joined the New Christy Minstrels. He left this group to form the First Edition, which got a hit with Nashvillian Mickey Newbury's "Just Dropped in to See What Condition My Condition Was In" (No. 5 pop single in 1968). The First Edition stayed together until the mid-1970s. Then, with perfect timing, Rogers jumped to country. His first big hit was "Lucille," produced by Larry Butler. Rogers, one of the top five concert attractions in the Western Hemisphere, now transcends country. With his wife, the former Marianne Gordon ("Hee Haw"), and Christopher Cody Rogers, born late in 1981, he lives on an opulent "farm" outside Athens, Georgia. Extraordinarily intelligent, Kenny could be one of the world's best managers if he should ever hang up the microphone.

THE JUDDS *(RCA)*

Ambition, perseverance, and intelligence shine through the slim, dark good looks of Naomi Judd like klieg lights on a moonless night. Raised in deprived circumstances in rural Kentucky, she moved daughters Wynonna and Ashley to Hollywood in 1968 following the breakup of her marriage. There she landed several fringe jobs in films.

Disenchanted with the quality of life in Tinseltown, they went back to Kentucky before moving to Music City in 1979, where Naomi and oldest daughter Wynonna nabbed an RCA deal on the basis of a personal audition with label chief Joe Galante. Their debut effort cracked the Top 20; their next two, "Mama, He's Crazy" and "What about Me," hit No. 1, earning them a CMA Award in October 1984.

Their homespun harmonies, developed through years of singing and playing in their kitchen and on the back porch, recall the Carter Family and the Andrews Sisters. Brent Maher's understated production and Don Potter's sparkling acoustic guitar work appealed to country radio programmers at a time when overproduced schmaltz dominated the airwaves. As the only successful female duet team since the Davis Sisters in the early 1950s and the only successful mother-daughter team ever, the Judds have created a made-to-order screenplay for Hollywood scriptwriters.

spreads, the high-quality men's "skin" publications started to profile the leading artists, and such specialized publications as *Fortune* and *The Wall Street Journal* published lengthy articles on the financial aspects of this "new" life style. One wonders why *The National Geographic* failed to mount an expedition to explore this fascinating new terrain. Discos all over the nation packed up their 130-beat-per-minute platters in favor of wax by Kenny Rogers, Willie Nelson, and Waylon Jennings. Beards sprouted on men's faces like mushrooms on the floors of Oregon forests, and it seemed as though blue jeans and pickup trucks had just been invented.

Country was not just a kind of music—it was a way of life. Snap-button shirts, ten-gallon hats, engraved leather belts, and cowboy boots, previously found only in Western-wear stores, sprang up at Sears, J. C. Penney, Wal-Mart, and Target as well as in the trendiest of chic boutiques. Suddenly all the fashion designers in the world were marketing a brand of "designer jeans" with their name stitched prominently on the right rump pocket. Blue jeans, which had been selling steadily if not spectacularly for years at prices from eight to fifteen dollars a pair, suddenly began selling like hotcakes at forty dollars.

Behind all the frenzy was a young movie actor named John Travolta. Some years before, he had scored a huge cinematic hit with *Saturday Night Fever.* Besides raking in big profits, the film stamped disco with a seal of approval, making it more than just a fad. Travolta agreed to star in a picture based loosely on an Aaron Latham story that had appeared in *Esquire* about Gilley's club in Pasadena, Texas, a dingy establishment about the size of a factory that had been entertaining mostly blue-collar Texans for almost ten years. From that point on it was as if the five hundred most influential trend-setters, media kingpins, and fashion designers had met and agreed that the movie was going to be a box-office bonanza, that everyone in the United States would buy nothing but Western clothes, and that country music would take over America in much the same manner as a newly elected administration takes over the political process.

Amidst such a clamor no one seemed to notice or care that the movie, *Urban Cowboy,* was a box-office flop (although the soundtrack album did very well).

This mania of interest in country and things country was, of course, more illusory and fleeting than factual or permanent. Like all fashion fads, the "Western look" ran its course and

was replaced by a new fashion trend. The novelty of country stars on television wore off through overexposure. The country discos evolved into "dance" or "new music" clubs. The country music star's life style lost its allure for the masses after every major magazine ran a piece on "the magic and mystery of life on the road." (A seven-hundred-mile bus trip with eleven others in a forty-foot Silver Eagle loses its "magic" after about three hours.) The national media solemnly pronounced the "country music movement" to be "dead" and moved on to other unsuspecting fields to find a new candidate for elevation into the next major trend.

All of these grave pronouncements about the "death" of country music overlooked the fact that the corpse was not only twitching but was in robust good health. Radio was the reason. Sensing that country music was the wave of the future, American radio stations switched to the format in record numbers in 1980 and 1981. Suddenly radio stations with strong signals began to penetrate markets where country had not been heard before. By 1981 many other major markets that had made do with one country outlet for years gained several. The form spilled from its confines of the South and Midwest to become as truly national as rock, pop, or adult-contemporary. The number of country radio stations increased by more than even the most fervent booster of the form had ever dreamed possible: by 1983 nearly 25 percent of the 9,000 radio stations in the United States were full-time country outlets. In terms of impact, country music trailed only adult-contemporary music, according to a 1983 Simmons study of media and markets.

This unprecedented radio coverage translated into a major boost in sales of country music at the retail counters of record stores. Country's share of the $3.8 billion U.S. market for recorded music jumped from a single-digit number to around 15 percent, for a gross of just over $500 million annually.

Country music took a collective deep breath of this heady air and continued on as it has since the 1920s, presenting songs that expressed the feelings of people in ordinary life, described the problems inherent in male-female relationships, told of social conditions, and revealed the dramas of ordinary people.

How have the "outlaws" and the women who have only recently won their place in this

Opposite: *The Judds (Wynonna on the left, Naomi on the right) met RCA labelmate Kenny Rogers at a 1984 concert at the Salt Palace, Salt Lake City.*
Left: *Lester "Roadhog" Moran and the Cadillac Cowboys (a.k.a. the Statler Brothers) examine their first plywood LP, awarded "for sales in excess of 1,250 copies" of their parody disc, said to be a live recording from Johnny Mack Brown High School. (Photo: Alan Mayor)*

pantheon in the 1970s fared during all this? It's safe to say that the scruffy outlaws who helped initiate the movement are still with us, perhaps a little more grizzled (but financially much healthier). The women have consolidated the position they earned for themselves in the previous decade and are very much a part of the airplay picture, although no newcomer has yet demonstrated a level of talent equal to that of Dolly, Loretta, or Tammy. And country music is still very much a hybrid form that borrows elements from other types of music as freely as it looks to its own illustrious past.

Aside from its meteoric rise in popularity, country music hasn't yielded any major new trends as exciting as those of the previous decade. But there have been many changes in the way country music is created in the studio, broadcast to the listeners, administrated by the record companies, marketed by those labels, and in who we hear singing it.

A great debate has sprung up over the effects of crossover success. The rewards of landing on the "Hot 100" or the adult-contemporary play lists have tempted more and more country performers to aim for the greener grass on the other side of the fence. This trend has sent traditional country fans into paroxysms of rage, because they feel the form is "selling out" whatever is left of its soul. The supporters of crossover country maintain that this change is part of the natural evolution of the form, but this argument falls on deaf ears as far as the fans of traditional country are concerned.

One of the chief concerns of those who enjoy traditional country is that the modernization of the form has fostered changes in the instruments used in country recording. The steel guitar, staple of the sound during earlier years, has all but disappeared, replaced by various keyboards and even synthesizers. The distinctive sound of the dobro has also been all but dismissed from country sessions, and the role of acoustic guitars has likewise diminished. These changes parallel developments in pop and rock music of the 1980s, which saw the electric guitar grudgingly yield its dominant position to various keyboards, synthesizers, and electronic music. Today country sessions routinely employ brass instruments, full string sec-

Left: *For over ten years Maggie Cavender has directed the Nashville Songwriters Association under the motto "It all begins with a song." (Photo: Melodie Gimple)*
Right: *Roy Clark on the road in Russia, playing here at Riga in Latvia. Note the sign on the left; it says, "The Way Is Communism."*

tions, and many of the exotic new electronic devices, all of which draw the focus away from the vocalist, who has long been the primary figure. Should country go any further in this direction, it will soon become very difficult to distinguish it from rock or pop music.

A more positive benefit of country's pursuit of crossover success is the improvement in production values. Realizing that the sophisticated pop audience would be put off by a country platter that sounded as if it were recorded inside an oil drum, producers of country music, beginning with Jimmy Bowen in the late 1970s, fought for bigger production budgets. Although they have yet to reach those of pop or rock, which can cost from $100,000 to $500,000 per album, they have increased dramatically, with noticeable results.

It was certainly noticed by adult-contemporary radio, the format that reaches the most listeners by offering the blandest fare. Disco, "new wave" and its more strident predecessor, punk music, and the synth-pop discs were deemed a little too exciting for a-c, which relies on the softer sound of ballads. Through no accident, country came up with improved production techniques and an updated version of the Nashville Sound to fit the bill. Analysis of the adult-contemporary chart from its inception in 1961 to the present shows country's success in this area clearly: twenty-two country songs made it to the top of that chart between 1961 and 1976, and thirty-nine climbed to No. 1 in the following eight years. Nineteen country selections reached the apex of the adult-contemporary list between 1979 and 1983. Although this format does not boast as many stations as does country, most adult-contemporary outlets are found in major urban areas and are broadcast by stations with very powerful signals. According to the most recent statistics available, compiled by the Simmons 1983 study of media and markets, adult-contemporary stations account for an average daily audience of over 34,000,000 listeners aged eighteen and older. Country is next in line with over 28,000,000, while rock is in third place with just under 20,000,000, followed by beautiful music at nearly 13,000,000. Album-oriented rock (also called progressive) is next with just over 12,000,000. The news/talk format and nostalgia are in a dead heat for the sixth-place slot with about 9,000,000 each.

There's lots of ways to ride the range: Guy Clark (left) and Rodney Crowell try out new wooden ponies. (Photo: Jim McGuire)

These formats account for about 80 to 85 percent of what you hear on the radio.

The label rosters of the 1980s reflect the enlarged range of country. The labels balance their lineups by signing traditional country acts along with country-pop singers and the somewhat more adventurous who have forged their own synthesis of styles, like Steve Earle, Vince Gill, the Maines Brothers, and 1984's biggest success story, the Judds, a mother-daughter team that owes as much to the Andrews Sisters as to the Carter Family.

The duet has always been an integral element of country music, but in the past several years it has become even more pervasive. After hitting a low point in the late 1960s and early 1970s, the duet made a comeback when Moe Bandy and Joe Stampley joined forces in 1974. Waylon and Willie paired up the following year, and the race was on to explore every possible combination of country's leading men. In addition to his duets with Jennings, Nelson has ventured into the studio with a weird and wonderful array of singers, including Johnny Cash, George Jones, Merle Haggard, Faron Young, Webb Pierce, Roger Miller, Darrell McCall, Kris Kristofferson, Leon Russell, Neil Young, Carlos Santana, and Ray Charles. Never one to overlook the women, Willie has also shared musical credits with Dolly Parton, Brenda Lee, "Rattlesnake" Annie McGowan, and Tracy Nelson (no relation).

The duet explosion seems to be limited to male singers. Since the demise of the two most established male-female teams—Conway Twitty and Loretta Lynn and George Jones and Tammy Wynette—no established (and unrelated) men and women have emerged to replace them. David Frizzell and Shelly West, both related to famous stars (David is the late Lefty Frizzell's brother, Shelly is Dottie West's daughter), have been carrying on the family tradition, but with erratic results. Charly McClain and Mickey Gilley teamed up on the very successful hit "Paradise Tonight" in 1983, but their subsequent releases fell far short of their initial success. On the other hand, single hits resulted from the temporary pairing of such major stars as Don Williams and Emmylou Harris, Kenny Rogers and Dolly Parton, Rogers and Sheena Easton, T. G. Sheppard and Karen Brooks, Eddie Rabbitt and Crystal Gayle, and Rogers and Kim Carnes. To date the Kendalls have been the only successful father-daughter duet act, while Bobby Bare and his very young son enjoyed one big hit together.

The overwhelming success of the Judds in 1984 may have broken the ice for the all-female duet, but so far country music has yet to see another duet team made up of two distaff vocalists. (Loretta and Tammy have often spoken of joining forces. Dolly Parton and Brenda Lee did sing together on Monument Records's stunning 1982 LP *The Winning Hand,* but no singles resulted from that collaboration.)

If country music has no hit-singing sisters, that vacuum is at least partially offset by the plethora of vocalizing brothers. The Bellamy Brothers lead the way in this department; they have garnered more No. 1 hits than any duet team in any combination. Larry Gatlin and his two brothers have been the most successful trio of brothers, and the Maines Brothers have staked a claim as the only current major label country act consisting of *four* brothers. From here on it gets confusing—the Statler Brothers contain two brothers (named Reid) but they are a quartet; there are two Youngers in the Younger Brothers; the Thrasher Brothers, whose lineup has varied in size from four to nine, most recently included three Thrashers; Tompall and the Glaser Brothers comprised three Glasers until the youngest, Jim, went solo in 1981 (I assume they then should be correctly called Tompall and the Glaser Brother).

Enough of brothers and enough of duets. Country has so far survived without any duets involving the stars and their pets, but don't rule that possibility out. In November of 1984 *Country Rhythms* magazine announced a contest based around Willie Nelson's duet partners. With tongue firmly planted in cheek, the publication announced that Nelson had exhausted all possible duet combinations in the music world and was turning his attention to political partners. Readers were solicited to send suggestions for songs for Nelson to record with Margaret Thatcher, Geraldine Ferraro, and Princess Margaret.

The crossover game is certainly affecting the development of new artists. As the 1980s march onward, the new singers who receive the most concentrated "push" from the labels have

BOBBY BARE *(Capitol)*

After a tour of service duty around the time of the Korean war, easygoing and friendly Bobby Bare started his career as a pop singer on the West Coast. He was one of the first to press for control of his own production. He brought Waylon Jennings to Chet Atkins's attention and was among the first to record songs by Kris Kristofferson, Townes Van Zandt, Shel Silverstein, Billy Joe Shaver, Guy Clark, and Rodney Crowell. His only No. 1 single was "Marie Laveau" in 1974, but he is more characteristically known for humorous ditties like "Dropkick Me Jesus (Through the Goalposts of Life)," "Praise the Lord and Send Me the Money," "Tequila Sheila," "Numbers," and "The Jogger."

DAVID FRIZZELL *(Warner Bros.)*

While his brother Lefty nabbed his first No. 1 single at the age of twenty-two, David had to wait until he was thirty-nine, when "You're the Reason God Made Oklahoma" put him and his duet partner, Shelly West, on top of the charts. In 1982, he relaunched a solo career (first charted in 1968), scoring a No. 1 with his first release, "I'm Gonna Hire a Wino (To Decorate Our Home)," and followed it with "Lost My Baby Blues," another big hit. His tremendous, "pure" country voice has helped him and Shelly win two CMA Awards as Best Duet. His brother Allen, the youngest of the eleven Frizzell children, shows extraordinary promise.

Bobby Bare, Sr. and Jr., duetting on "Daddy, What If," a No. 2 single in 1972. (Photo: Alan Mayor)

RCA vice-president Joe Galante (left) looks happily at Alabama's 1982 harvest of gold and platinum. BMI vice-president Frances Preston is third from left, RCA's Jack Craigo is on the far right.

ALABAMA *(RCA)*

Three cousins from Fort Payne, Alabama—Jeff Cook, Teddy Gentry, and Randy Owen—enlisted South Carolina drummer Mark Herndon and became the hottest act in country music by 1981. Ten years of unrelenting struggle preceded their nine CMA Awards and two Grammies won between 1981 and 1984. As the first self-contained group in modern country music, they have opened the door of this "new" concept to many others. Alabama itself owes as much to such Southern rock groups as Lynyrd Skynyrd and Marshall Tucker as to Hank Williams or Jimmie Rodgers. Frontman/lead singer Owen is tops, and the group's harmonies are equal to any in music. Their first five RCA LPs have so far sold over ten million copies, a sales total that exceeds those of most American rock stars.

been mainly those who show the most promise in appealing to the country and adult-contemporary audience. In this respect, Alabama has been the biggest success story of the 1980s. Adopting the rock-group format pioneered by the Beatles and other English bands twenty years ago, Alabama (composed of cousins Randy Owen, Jeff Cook, and Teddy Gentry, and drummer Mark Herndon) has drawn together elements of country, gospel, and rock to create a sound that is exciting enough to capture younger fans but smooth enough to appeal to their parents. Their harmony singing and superb showmanship (the cousins played all over the South for ten years before their "discovery" in 1980) has made them an outstanding draw on the live-appearance circuit, and the quartet has won more CMA Entertainer of the Year Awards than anyone in history. Their success finally convinced label executives that the group concept was valid in the country field. Needless to say, each label now has at least one band that it hopes will be "the next Alabama."

Although two new artists with traditional styles came to the fore in the early 1980s—Ricky Skaggs, who has fused elements of bluegrass, old-time country, and gospel (with even a hint of jazz), and George Strait, another in the long line of Texan honky-tonk stylists—the emphasis in the middle of the decade shifted to artists like Lee Greenwood, Gary Morris, and Mark Gray, who excelled primarily on ballads. When they ventured into the studio, they dressed up their often sappy ballads in thousands of dollars worth of production so that the end result was long on pomp and circumstance but short on true emotion. Greenwood, who spent nearly twenty years in Las Vegas and who seemed to have based his vocal style on that of Kenny Rogers, proved to be the most successful.

Exile, a five-man group that bagged one huge rock hit in 1978 with "Kiss You All Over," switched to country in 1983 and began issuing a series of mid-tempo ballads that found immediate success among country radio programmers. The group strutted out its Kentucky roots and excellent harmonies to win over country audiences as well, becoming one of the form's top groups. Deborah Allen, a songstress with several songwriting successes to her credit, saw her recording career take off on a series of ballads, taking over territory her less gifted labelmate, Sylvia, had staked out a few years previously.

Left: *Deborah Allen appears to have enjoyed her first parachute jump. In 1983 her song "Baby I Lied" became a big pop, country, and a-c hit. (Photo: Larry Dixon)*
Right: *Handsome Gary Morris is one of country music's most promising new stars, versatile enough to sing opera with Linda Ronstadt or country duets with Lynn Anderson.*

Amid all these balladeers from the softer end of the musical spectrum, one could find other artists who, like Skaggs and Strait, achieved success by forging a style closer to the traditional country sound. Reba McEntire, a redheaded cowgirl from Oklahoma, has turned out a run of memorable hits in a more rootsy style, depending more on her own powerful voice than on overblown production. Earl Thomas Conley has fashioned a succession of stunning hit singles (most of which he wrote) that draw emotionally from George Jones and Merle Haggard but, in his hands, wind up sounding like solid rock 'n' roll. He has built his reputation by writing lyrics with considerably more depth and bite than those sung by many of the other newer stars, which gives him a better chance of leaving a lasting impression.

These are the newer artists who have established themselves in today's country music field, and they are likely to remain in the limelight for some years to come. Indeed, it looks like the beginning of a new cycle: just as the new crop of stars in the late 1960s and early 1970s pushed the aging singers out of the way, so this new group of stars has moved in to add some fresh blood to the circuit. But careers never end in country; the displaced stars, like those they pushed out before them, will simply take their place on the stage of the Grand Ole Opry.

While the pursuit of crossover success led to a higher quality album, the cost of making that album led to reduced output. In years past, it was not unusual to find two, three, or even four albums emerge from a single artist every year; today this is a luxury afforded to but a few of the superstars. New artists have to cool their heels awhile before they get to make their first album. The labels have also learned that each album issued must provide several hits rather than merely one or two hits and a lot of "filler" (cursorily produced second-rate material), which had long been accepted procedure.

At the same time, the labels are paying more attention to the marketing of their reduced album harvest. The development of marketing strategies, along with the addition of departments to handle them, has mushroomed in the field in the past ten years. Joe Galante and Rick Blackburn, of RCA and CBS, spearheaded this move. Not coincidentally, they both came to power from backgrounds in marketing rather than in record production, as had been the case in Music City for many years.

GARY MORRIS
(Warner Bros.)

Texas-born Gary credits Jimmy Carter and Denver, Colorado, as key elements in his career. Morris performed during many Carter fund-raisers during the 1976 campaign, and then refined his skills in the Mile-High City leading a group called Breakaway. He was discovered by ace writer-producer Norro Wilson, who recalled seeing him sing at the White House. A four-sport letterman in high school, Morris is a strapping lad who hunts with bow and arrow and skindives. His major successes so far have been with love songs that pay tribute to the glories of the "weaker sex": "The Love She Found in Me" and "The Wind Beneath My Wings." As one of the hottest discoveries of the 1980s, Morris appears to have a very bright future. If he continues to issue such powerful performances of stellar material, Morris seems destined to become a major country star by 1986. Late in 1984, he took time out from his country music career to sing a lead operatic role opposite Linda Ronstadt in *La Bohème*.

The strategy toward singles has also changed dramatically. Today the single is strictly a promotional tool for the album from which it is drawn. The 45s are expected not to make a profit but to lure the customer into making the bigger commitment of buying the album at eight or nine dollars. Although an occasional hit single like Kenny Rogers's and Dolly Parton's "Islands in the Stream" obviously is gladly welcomed, companies would much rather have a mildly successful album than several hit singles from an album that rings up unspectacular sales.

Meanwhile, women have contributed some changes of their own. The gains made by women in the marketplace in general have been paralleled in the Nashville music business. Ten years ago, BMI Vice-President Frances Preston and Jo Walker-Meador, executive director of the CMA, were the only women in positions of power. Today, all three of the performance-rights groups are led by females (Preston at BMI, Connie Bradley at ASCAP, and Dianne Petty at SESAC). In addition, women can be found in positions of authority at each of the six major labels here, particularly in the publicity, artist development, and A & R divisions. CBS Records became the first label here to move a woman, Mary Ann McCready, to vice-presidential level in 1983. The following year it conferred that status on Bonnie Garner. In between the CBS promotions, Warner Bros. elevated Martha Sharp and Janice Azrak to vice president. The other areas of the business have their fair share of the fairer sex in responsible positions.

Country's vast success in the past several years has not gone unnoticed by personalities from other forms of the entertainment industry. From 1981 onward a veritable parade of "ringers" has taken a shot at expanding their careers by embracing country. Pop stars whose careers have faded or those seeking even greater vistas for an already successful career have become ardent suitors of airplay on country stations. Members of this classification include Nancy Sinatra, the Eagles, Creedence Clearwater Revival, Dan Seals, Jose Feliciano, the Osmond

Left: *Ron and Dale Cornelius have been Nashvillians since 1979. Ron played guitar for Bob Dylan in the studio and for Leonard Cohen on tour. His wife, Dale, previously managed the New Riders of the Purple Sage. Since 1980 she has been executive director of the Nashville Music Association. (Photo: Beth Gwinn)*
Right: *ASCAP's Connie Bradley (left) and Terri Gibbs check out Braille songbooks given to Terri by ASCAP. (Photo: Melodie Gimple)*
Opposite, left: *Loretta Lynn and Sissy Spacek at the premiere of* Coal Miner's Daughter *in Nashville, 1980. (Photo: Melodie Gimple)*
Opposite, right: *Clint Eastwood's 1982 film* Honkytonk Man *was far from a brilliant success, but it put Porter Wagoner on the silver screen for the first time. It also gave Marty Robbins his last screen role.*

Brothers, Englebert Humperdinck, Petula Clark, Bob Seger, Julio Iglesias, Sheena Easton, Judy Collins, Lionel Richie, Bill Medley, and Roger Whittaker. Famed Irish flutist James Galway even jumped onto the bandwagon in 1983 when he joined Sylvia to record "The Wayward Wind," a moderately successful venture. Stars from films and television also took a shot; Clint Eastwood, Sissy Spacek, John Schneider, Pia Zadora, Tom Wopat, and Wayne Massey all fared well. Eastwood, who paired himself with established star T. G. Sheppard, did well with "Make My Day," a song written around a recurring piece of dialogue in his *Sudden Impact* actioner. Schneider, co-star with Wopat of "The Dukes of Hazzard," scored a huge hit late in 1984 with "I've Been Around Enough to Know."

The bedfellows country music attracted became even stranger: George Burns, Dean Martin, and Dallas Cowboys quarterback Danny White all released singles in the early 1980s. Perhaps the disc from the most unlikely source to chart on country lists was "The Night Dolly Parton Was Almost Mine," a selection from the cast album of the Broadway musical *Pump Boys and Dinettes.* At the rate these outsiders are trying their luck in the field it wouldn't surprise me a bit to find Ronald Reagan or Luciano Pavarotti mounting an attempt to cash in on the form's growing popularity.

The events of the past ten years have secured country music a full membership as one of America's most popular musical forms. Country, for years regarded as a regional form that looked backward for inspiration, has learned to gaze if not forward, at least sideways to see what elements it can borrow from other styles of music. Today, sixty-three years after Eck Robertson and Henry Gilliland talked their way into making the first country discs, country music has finally been fully accepted by the public. After standing outside the door of popular acceptance for six and a half decades, that door has finally swung open and country music has at last been invited into the party!

LORETTA LYNN *(MCA)*

Kitty Wells may be billed as "The Queen of Country Music," but Loretta's fifty-three Top-10 singles and sixteen No. 1s dwarf Wells's totals. She's the only country star besides Hank Williams and Willie Nelson to have had her life presented on movie screens. *Coal Miner's Daughter* was a huge box-office surprise in 1981, winning Sissy Spacek an Oscar for her portrayal of Loretta. An eight-time CMA Award–winner, Loretta has also earned nine BMI Awards for her songwriting (including "Fist City," "You Ain't Woman Enough," "Rated X," and "Coal Miner's Daughter"), a Grammy (for "After the Fire Is Gone," a duet with Conway Twitty), and twenty-four *Music City News* honors, voted by the fans. Her frankness about her intimate problems in life makes her an interviewer's dream. Certain future Hall of Famer.

ANNE MURRAY *(Capitol)*

Although she has relied heavily on Music City songs throughout her career, Canada's Anne Murray did not record in Nashville until 1981. She first hit the country charts in 1970, but it was in 1978 that she became a consistent country hitmaker. Since then, she has posted thirteen Top 10s, including the No. 1 hits "I Just Fall in Love Again," "Shadows in the Moonlight," "Broken-Hearted Me," "Could I Have This Dance," "Blessed Are the Believers," and "A Little Good News"—all penned by Nashville writers. She has enjoyed even greater success in pop, where she charted twenty-five singles, and a-c, with eight No. 1 hits. Fine material and excellent production by Jim Ed Norman have overcome her rather ordinary voice. So far she has won three Grammies, two CMA Awards, and sixteen Juno Awards, Canada's equivalent of the Grammy. For the past eight years, she has refused to be sucked into the show business whirlwind. She now lives in Toronto with her husband and two children.

COUNTRY ACTS ON MOR/A-C CHARTS 1961–84

Top-20 Records	Artist	Top-10 Records	No. 1 Records
37	Elvis Presley	31	7
30	Glen Campbell	20	6
26	Anne Murray	18	8
26	Kenny Rogers	19	7
23	John Denver	18	9
20	Bobby Goldsboro	12	2
19	Ray Charles	10	4
17	Brenda Lee	15	1
14	Eddy Arnold	6	2
14	Crystal Gayle	7	0
14	B. J. Thomas	11	4
12	Linda Ronstadt	8	2
11	Roger Miller	8	2
11	Ronnie Milsap	5	1
11	Dolly Parton	2	2
10	Eddie Rabbitt	6	1
10	Charlie Rich	6	4
9	Jimmy Dean	6	1
9	Ray Stevens	4	1
8	Johnny Cash	4	1
8	Willie Nelson	3	0
8	Juice Newton	4	2
6	Alabama	2	0
6	Jim Reeves	1	0
6	Marty Robbins	1	0
5	Michael Murphey	1	0
4	Mickey Gilley	1	0
4	Roy Orbison	4	0

Sources: Joel Whitburn's Record Research Reports. Billboard magazine.

MUSIC CITY
MUSIC BUSINESS

Nashville Goes Pop

A few days before June 30, 1922, officials of the Victor Talking Machine Company of New York City were startled by the unexpected appearance of two visitors: Henry C. Gilliland, then in his seventies, and Eck Robertson, some fifty years his junior. The two were dressed respectively in a Confederate uniform and the full regalia of a Texas cowboy, and they wanted to make guitar and fiddle recordings for the Victor company.

Perhaps the Victor employees decided it was easier to grant the odd-looking duo's request than to refuse but, for whatever reason they were made, their sessions, historians now believe, resulted in the first commercial recordings of country music. Today, the branch of the recorded music industry that Gilliland and Robertson inaugurated generates over $550 million in American sales alone.

At the time, the recording industry was in its infancy itself; none of the executives knew what sort of market, if any, existed for such music. Opera, classical, jazz, and religious music were selling well enough to generate over $100 million in revenues for this fledgling industry the year previous, so one might logically surmise that the Victor officials shrugged, looked at each other, and said, "Why not put the records out?"

It's intriguing to speculate upon the fate of the record business had they ignored country music during the next decades. The popularity of another new invention, radio, and its free exposure of music—in those days generally live performances—caused record sales to dwindle annually for the next four years, to $59 million in 1925. The following year saw them increase to $70 million, and by 1929 they had gradually climbed to $75 million. The Depression's arrival then kicked the record business in the teeth as it did most other retail endeavors; sales fell rapidly each year to a low of $6 million in 1933. Twelve more years were to pass before sales totals once again topped the $100 million mark. From 1923 through 1944 record sales amounted to $951 million in the United States. It would be interesting to know how much country records contributed to this total, for those years covered part or all of the careers of such artists as Vernon Dalhart, Carl T. Sprague, Carson Robison, Jimmie Rodgers, the Carter Family, Bob Wills, Roy Acuff, Tex Ritter, Jimmy Wakely, Elton Britt, Ernest Tubb, Gene Autry, the Sons of the Pioneers, and many others, all of whom sang material that today would be classified as country music.

The Gilliland-Robertson recordings of "Sally Goodin" and "The Arkansas Traveler," two popular guitar-fiddle instrumentals, were not big sellers, but by 1924 country music enjoyed what is now recognized as its first million-seller: Vernon Dalhart's "Wreck of The Old '97" and "The Prisoner's Song." After the commercial potential of the form was thus proven, talented country artists had little trouble attracting the attention of record label executives.

Although Nashville's first recording session was conducted in 1928, when the Victor company waxed several of the Grand Ole Opry singers, the story of Music City's climb to prominence as a worldwide recording capital does not begin until the 1940s. And the beginning of Nashville's rise to glory came because of a program on a radio station.

The "Grand Ole Opry" is a live radio show established by National Life and Accident Insurance Company, an insurance concern, in 1925 as a means of publicizing the low-cost insurance peddled by its agents, primarily in rural areas. The Opry, carried over radio station WSM, was originally known as "The WSM Barn Dance." It has become the most successful and most enduring program of its type (indeed, it is the longest-running regularly scheduled broadcast program of any kind in the world). The event was scheduled for Saturday night and it

Kenny Rogers with his wife, Marianne. (Photo: Dean Dixon)

Above: *Two-time CMA Entertainer of the Year Barbara Mandrell in full blossom at a Fan Fair showcase.* (Photo: Robin Hood)
Below: *The Statler Brothers hosted a star-studded lineup for their first TV special.* (Photo: Robin Hood)

B. J. Thomas, shown here at Fan Fair, is one of the most vocally gifted artists ever to sing country music. (Photo: John Carnes)

Above: Floyd Cramer—one of the chief architects of the Nashville Sound. (Photo: John Carnes)
Below, left: *Greg (above) and the late Duane Allman (not pictured) were born and raised in Music City.* (Photo: *John Carnes)*
Below, right: *Rock/soul sensation Delbert McClinton, seen here at 1982's "One for the Sun" benefit, has recorded often in Nashville studios.* (Photo: *John Carnes)*
Opposite: *Music Mill Studios (a. k. a. Fort Shedd), home of Alabama's producer Harold Shedd, hosted the recording of Alabama's LPs* The Closer You Get, Roll On, *and* 40-Hour Week.

Preceding pages: Moe Bandy *(foreground) listens as Jim Owen plays a Hank Williams number at Tootsie's Orchid Lounge. (Photo: Jim McGuire)* Above: *Alabama works out in the recording studio. (Photo: Dean Dixon)* Below: *Don Williams's band shows how traveling musicians work up songs and arrangements during the long hours on the bus. (Photo: Jim McGuire)* Opposite: *Willie Nelson and Leon Russell entertain Roy Acuff and Ernest Tubb during sessions for an as-yet-unreleased LP. (Photo: Jim McGuire)*

MOE BANDY *(Columbia)*

Born in Meridian, Mississippi, Bandy soon moved with his family to San Antonio. Moe made a living working part time as a rodeo rider and full time as a sheet-metal worker while singing in Texas taverns. In 1974, "I Just Started Hating Cheating Songs Today" on GRC Records catapulted him to Nashville recognition. Since then, he has carved a steady career as a solo singer and duet partner with Joe Stampley, picking up a CMA honor for best duet with Joe in 1980. Another fine Texas honky-tonk singer, Bandy is best when he sticks to traditional country ballads.

THE
CHARLIE

CHARLIE DANIELS *(Epic)*

Daniels has enjoyed more success on pop lists than in country, but his three CMA Awards (and a Grammy) in 1979 solidified his reputation as a country artist. Born in rural North Carolina, he left home in the late 1950s to pursue a career in music, playing first bluegrass, then rock. Proficient on guitar and fiddle, he moved to Nashville in the mid-1960s and became a session musician, backing Bob Dylan, Ringo Starr, Flatt and Scruggs, Pete Seeger, and Leonard Cohen. He formed the Charlie Daniels Band in the early 1970s and toured incessantly, particularly in the South and Midwest. His signature tunes are "The Devil Went Down to Georgia," "The South's Gonna Do It Again," and the patriotic "In America," songs that fuse the root forms of Southern music. His Volunteer Jam, held every January in Nashville, has become one of the top one-day music events in the United States. Outspoken but polite to a fault, Daniels is one of the most popular performers in music, both among fans and musicians. He told the Russians they can "go straight to hell" in his song "In America," long before the Korean Airlines 747 was shot down.

JOHN DENVER *(RCA)*

Denver has had almost as many careers as Kenny Rogers. Born John Henry Deutschendorf, Jr., John was an Air Force brat who lived all over the South and West before the family settled for a while in Fort Worth, Texas. Before striking it big in pop in 1971 with "Take Me Home Country Roads," he was a fine folk singer. The country-pop hits he posted in 1974–75 made him a star in both fields and brought him CMA Entertainer of the Year honors in 1975. He is a terrific live performer. Lately, he has had few pop hits, and his only Top-10 country single in the last nine years was Billy Joe Shaver's "Some Days Are Diamonds" in 1981—the only Denver hit waxed in Music City. His biggest country smashes were "Annie's Song," "Back Home Again," "I'm Sorry," and "Thank God I'm a Country Boy."

Charlie Daniels's Volunteer Jam is a special country music event. (Photo: Dean Dixon)
Overleaf: *The Whites, a traditional country trio, were discovered by Guy Clark and Emmylou Harris. (Photo: Jim McGuire)*

Opposite: *Janie Fricke, CMA Female Vocalist of the Year in 1982 and 1983, endured years of hovering in the background, singing jingles and session vocals, before achieving stardom. (Photo: Dean Dixon)*
Above, left: *Christmas comes to Warner Bros. Music. Karen Brooks is in the red sash; Gary Morris is behind her on the left. (Photo: Melodie Gimple)*
Above, right: *The scorpion isn't impressed that Bill Anderson has won 48 BMI Awards. "Whispering Bill" doesn't appear concerned, however. (Photo: Jim McGuire)*
Below, left: *Sylvia adds the vocals to the track in the studio. (Photo: Jim Brown)*
Below, right: *Songwriter Guy Clark relaxes on a bed of oysters. (Photo: Jim McGuire)*

&
Cowboy
Band

has been carried with 50,000 watts of clear-channel power since 1931. The strength of this signal, the clear-channel designation, and the then-uncluttered airwaves allowed the program to be tuned in from the Gulf of Mexico to the Canadian border, from the Rocky Mountains to the Atlantic Ocean. The program originated from several locations until 1931, when it was moved to the Ryman Auditorium, a cozy brick building in the heart of downtown Nashville just six blocks from the location of Fort Nashborough. Though the Ryman hosted musical, cultural, political, and religious events of all types, its association with the "Grand Ole Opry" for forty-three years earned it the nickname "The Mother Church of Country Music."

Aside from the magnetic pull of the Opry, there were several significant events that helped to establish the music industry in Nashville rather than in cities like Charlotte, Atlanta, Dallas, Cincinnati, Knoxville, San Antonio, or Bristol, where considerable field recording had taken place in the 1920s and 1930s. When Roy Acuff became disenchanted with his treatment by music publishers based in New York City and Chicago, he and Fred Rose formed Acuff-Rose Music in Nashville in 1942. Not long after, Julian and Gene Aberbach established Hill Music and Range Music (the two were later merged) to publish the songs popular in the genre that was then known as "hillbilly music." These two publishing concerns were cornerstones vital to the development of Nashville as a music capital.

The first two decades of country music recording were conducted under conditions very different from the modern process. In the 1920s, 1930s, and in the early 1940s the major recording concerns had studios in New York, Los Angeles, and Chicago. The records made with their hillbilly singers were usually made on location in many cities of the South. For instance, Jimmie Rodgers recorded in the second floor of a warehouse in Bristol, Virginia; in the Banquet Hall of the Jefferson Hotel in Dallas, Texas; at RCA's studios in Manhattan and in Hollywood; at the Women's Club in Atlanta; and in Louisville, San Antonio, and New Orleans. Studios were improvised in many locations during that time, which allowed many cities to claim at least some nationally famous recording for their area. Many cities enjoyed more early recording activity than did Nashville during this period.

Although Eddy Arnold recorded here in December of 1944, Paul Cohen of Decca Records is generally recognized as the first man to hold regular Music City sessions, an endeavor he launched in 1945. He used the WSM studios to record Ernest Tubb, Kitty Wells, and Red Foley, working around the WSM schedule, for the radio station was then the only local site to offer the proper recording equipment.

The backup musicians for these sessions were available. They had already come to Nashville to seek the employment opportunities offered by the stars of the Opry, who needed musicians for recording and touring purposes. In addition, WSM itself offered work for capable musicians, particularly after 1939, when the station first gained "network feed" status from the NBC Radio Network. From then on, WSM supplied many live music shows that were carried nationally.

Never one to miss a trick, WSM had established its Artist Service Bureau to book the Opry stars for outside appearances in 1934. As a result, the city began to develop experienced booking agents, another factor that put Nashville ahead of competing cities.

So by 1946, all the elements necessary for a music industry to flourish were in place: singing stars with a large national following, a weekly radio show to broadcast their voices over a substantial part of the United States, several different experienced booking agencies to schedule their personal appearances, a studio to record their latest efforts, musicians to accompany the stars, and publishing companies to sell the sheet music and arrangements of the songs written by such artists as Tubb, Acuff, Pee Wee King, and many others.

By being the first city in the South to bring these key elements together, Nashville was able to gain a tremendous head start on its competition. Indeed, by 1946 Nashville had slid quietly but snugly into fourth position as an American music center, directly behind New York City, Los Angeles, and Chicago.

Nineteen forty-six was the most important year for the development of Nashville as a

ED BRUCE *(RCA)*

Tall, weather-beaten, rugged, and quiet, Ed Bruce looks more at home on horseback than on a stage. After years of misses on RCA, Monument, United Artists, and Epic, Bruce finally began turning out consistent hits on MCA in 1980. In 1984, he returned to RCA. His wife, Patsy, is a leading TV and film casting expert who helped Ed land a supporting role in the television series "Bret Maverick" starring James Garner in 1981–82. Bruce is an excellent writer, with credits for "Mamas, Don't Let Your Babies Grow Up to Be Cowboys" and "When I Die Just Let Me Go to Texas," both co-written with Patsy. His Don Williams–type vocals are infused with a warm flavor.

Ed Bruce is the only current country star who has had a regular role in a prime-time TV series. (Photo: Robin Hood)

Right: *WSM's first studio.*
Below: *Hank Williams chats with a GI.*
Bottom: *No one will ever know how many hit songs Fred Rose helped others write or gave away. He remains the most accomplished musician ever to write country songs. He put the "music" in Music City.*

music center because of the efforts of three enterprising WSM engineers: Aaron Shelton, Carl Jenkins, and George Reynolds. The three men, who had been conducting recording sessions at WSM's studios, perceived the city's need for a full-time recording studio. The Castle Recording Company they established thus became the first commercial recording studio in Nashville. The trio took their name from WSM's slogan, "The Air Castle of the South," and built their early business around many of the stars of the station.

The establishment of Castle led to the creation of other studios just as the beginning of Acuff-Rose had encouraged other music publishers to locate in Nashville. By the late 1940s Nashville's fledgling music industry had attracted the interest of the major recording corporations. The companies realized that it made good economic sense to record their "hillbilly" artists (as country singers were then called) in Nashville rather than to bring them to New York, Chicago, or Los Angeles or to rely on makeshift facilities in scattered locations. Once this policy became established procedure, the next logical step was for the labels to establish offices in this new musical frontier.

Although Capitol Records was the first to hang out its shingle here, it was RCA, under the leadership of Steve Sholes and Chet Atkins, that took an even more important step by establishing the first major-label studio in Nashville. The company first located its operation downtown, then moved the facility into a permanent structure on Seventeenth Avenue South built to house both the recording operation and company offices. By locating there RCA pioneered in the development of the area now known as Music Row.

Hank Williams's enormous popularity also played a big part in establishing Nashville as a music center. His success encouraged many other country music hopefuls to test the Music City waters. In addition, Fred Rose, Williams's publisher, was able to generate considerable interest in Williams's songs with label executives in the pop field, most notably Mitch Miller, head of Artists and Repertoire (A & R) at Columbia Records. Such artists as Tony Bennett and Jo Stafford enjoyed big pop hits with Hank's material, and this helped all the local writers and publishers attract serious interest in Nashville as a source of songs.

The 1950s were boom years for Nashville's recording business as well as the American economy in general. Nashville continued to attract country artists and recording sessions, the American record business continued to prosper, and the "Grand Ole Opry" came to promi-

Three of rock's greatest pioneers, Chuck Berry, Bill Haley, and Bo Diddley, at a mid-1970s Nashville appearance. (Photo: Marshall Fallwell, Jr.)

nence as the most important music program on radio in the nation. Owen Bradley established his own studio in a surplus army building on Sixteenth Avenue South. Nicknamed the Quonset Hut, the facility became Nashville's second important studio; it was in place in time to host early sessions by Buddy Holly and Gene Vincent.

Several other cornerstones of the industry fell into place during the 1950s. Columbia and Decca Records (now MCA) joined RCA and Capitol by establishing permanent Nashville offices, the Music Row area became the location of choice for the new industry, and Broadcast Music Inc. built its regional office on Sixteenth Avenue, a move that truly cemented the area as the center for the city's music.

While Nashville boasted all the necessary ingredients for success in popular music by 1946, it lacked one essential element: a hit record. In 1947, however, a rather unlikely duo brought the city its first glory as a source for the recording of pop music hits: Kermit Goell and Francis Craig's song "Near You" was recorded by Craig's orchestra and the tune went to No. 1 on the national pop charts. It remained there for twelve weeks and spawned covers (different versions of the same song) by the Andrews Sisters, Elliott Lawrence, and Larry Green, all of which hit the Top 5 on the national pop lists.

It's ironic that the first hit record produced by the city now known as the country music capital of the United States was a *pop* hit; this, however, lends credence to Nashville's other claim, as "Music City U.S.A." An even more ironic twist was added in 1977 when George Jones and Tammy Wynette reached No. 1 on the country charts with that same song, "Near You."

Increased competition is good for any creative field because it normally raises everyone's standards of excellence. As Nashville grew and as more musicians arrived from different parts of the South and Midwest the overall "feel" and approach to music changed. Part of this change in music came from the basic urge to survive. But the innovation and skill came from the minds and souls of the musicians and writers. As the years went by, country music and Nashville broadened from a tree with but a few limbs to one with musical branches shooting in many directions.

Nineteen forty-eight became another milestone year for Nashville because the city enjoyed its first hit recorded by a visiting pop star. The Dinning Sisters came to town, and one of

GEORGE JONES *(Epic)*

The hands-down favorite as country's greatest living singer, Jones has a phrase-bending vocal technique that wrenches every ounce of emotion from a lyric. He conveys deep sadness, despair, and pathos better than any American singer ever has except perhaps for Billie Holliday. He is also a bad, bad boy whose conduct threatened to eventually overwhelm his career. Consistently in trouble with women, the law, alcohol, and/or drugs until 1983, George seemed determined to see how close he could come to self-destruction. In the personal appearance business, Jones is known as a "chancy booking." Jones found happiness in 1983 thanks to his latest wife, the former Nancy Sepulveda. He then moved to Colmesneil, Texas, near his birthplace, opened his own country music park, and cleaned up his personal life. Born in Texas, he charted his first hit in 1955 and is still racking them up thirty years later. Future Hall of Famer.

the songs they cut, "Buttons and Bows," reached No. 7 on the "Hot 100."

Two songs based in Tennessee brought Nashville the most fame it had yet received as a source of pop music hits in 1950: Pee Wee King and Redd Stewart's "Tennessee Waltz," sung by Patti Page, and Jack Stapp and Henry Stone's "Chattanoogie Shoeshine Boy," sung by Red Foley. Each went to No. 1 on the pop charts, and Foley's success marked the first time a country artist had ever topped that list. Other versions of these songs abounded; Bing Crosby took "Chattanoogie Shoeshine Boy" to the Top 10 while Guy Lombardo and the duo of Les Paul and Mary Ford reached the same level with their versions of "Tennessee Waltz."

It should be pointed out that "Tennessee Waltz" is one of the most popular songs of all time. Six versions of the song charted pop within four months of the Page release, activity no other pop song of any kind has matched. And interest in "Tennessee Waltz" does not appear to be waning; Lacy J. Dalton scored a country hit with it in 1980, and the tune is part of the live shows of many artists to this day.

Nashville and country music claimed the city's first true music superstar in the first years of the 1950s. Hank Williams came out of the Alabama backwoods to Nashville in the late 1940s and formed an association with Fred Rose through a songwriting contract with Acuff-Rose. Rose engineered a contract for Williams with MGM Records, and Hank had his first hit in 1949 with "Lovesick Blues," a song first associated with Al Jolson. Hank became such a favorite with country fans that he posted twenty-seven Top-10 hits in the years between 1949 and 1953.

However, Williams's most important contribution to country music lies not in the enormous impact his music made upon country fans but in the acceptance his songs found with pop artists and on the popular music charts. His songs were recorded by such pop stalwarts as Tony Bennett, Joni James, and Jo Stafford, a highly unusual occurrence for a country writer during the early 1950s. The general wisdom of the time held that country songs were about as important to the pop charts as Ukrainian folk ballads. Columbia Records's Mitch Miller, prodded doubtless by Fred Rose, proved that axiom dead wrong when Bennett's version of "Cold, Cold Heart," Stafford's rendition of "Jambalaya," and James's cover of "Your Cheatin' Heart" all made it to the top echelon of the *Billboard* pop lists. In all, fourteen of Williams's songs have been recorded over one hundred different times, and seven of them have logged over one million radio performances, totals that surpass those of all country writers before or since.

Williams's massive success propelled Nashville into the national spotlight, and the city's musical forces wasted little time in opening the door once this opportunity knocked. Some of the most exciting and turbulent years in American popular music history loomed ahead, and Nashville was the site of much of the action. In the ten years from 1956 through 1965, the city helped to launch the careers of more legendary singers than could be found in any other American city, a roster of musical glory that includes Elvis Presley, Gene Vincent, Buddy Holly, the Everly Brothers, Brenda Lee, and Roy Orbison.

Although these artists today might be considered "country," in the late 1950s there were fewer radio formats than there are today. Any artist with the slightest hint of broad-based appeal was given a shot in the pop market. There were at most only a few hundred radio stations playing country music at the time, so many companies chose to ignore that small market completely in favor of concentration upon the far larger and more lucrative "Hot 100" charts, where sales of a hit record could easily be twenty times greater than a hit limited to country. For the most part the audiences were completely different: the young listened to the rock 'n' roll of the "Hot 100" while their parents tuned in to country.

The three years immediately preceding 1956 were dull years for popular music in general, sort of a lull period before the storm that was rock 'n' roll hit with Bill Haley's "Rock Around the Clock" in 1955. Maudlin ballads were the order of the day in the pop field, an arena ruled by such crooners as Bing Crosby, Patti Page, Perry Como, Eddie Fisher, Kitty Kallen, Johnny Ray, Rosemary Clooney, the McGuire Sisters, and the Crew Cuts. As a sign of just how empty of stirring music those years were, one has only to note that "Doggie in the Window" spent eight weeks at No. 1 and "Theme from Moulin Rouge" by Percy Faith's Orchestra topped the pop list for ten weeks.

After being fed the aural equivalent of watercress for years it didn't take the young ears of America long to recognize an entree when it was served. "Rock Around the Clock" was the first fresh-sounding music that mainstream radio had played in years. Eight months later, Elvis's "Heartbreak Hotel" hit No. 1, and the sounds of American popular music changed forever. Four more Presley songs hit No. 1 in 1956; of the last thirty-seven weeks of that year, Presley held the top position on the charts for twenty-five.

"Heartbreak Hotel" was written by Florida tunesmiths Mae Boren Axton and Tommy Durden (with Presley credited as co-writer, a not uncommon inducement to get a song recorded in those days). The song was recorded at RCA's Nashville facility with such country stalwarts as Chet Atkins and Owen Bradley playing on the session. About half of Elvis's pre-1962 hits were made at that facility, now a museum operated by the Country Music Foundation.

The success of "Heartbreak Hotel," which led to Presley's electrifying television appearances, left no doubt that Presley had arrived as a major force in American popular music. "I Want You, I Need You, I Love You," a No. 1 pop hit in 1956, was a Music City Presley effort as well. After 1962 Elvis went into near-seclusion at Graceland, his Memphis home, and his records were made either there or in Hollywood when he traveled there to make films. Though Presley was universally touted as "The King of Rock 'n' Roll" throughout the 1960s, his singles recording success dropped dramatically after 1962; seven and a half years passed between his first and last No. 1 hits of the 1960s, "Good Luck Charm," which was cut in Nashville, and "Suspicious Minds," in 1969.

Gene Vincent was another rock legend who enjoyed recording success in Nashville when in 1956 "Be Bop A Lula" became his first and only smash hit. Gene was viewed by Capitol Records as possibly "the next Elvis." Ken Nelson, who was later to gain fame as producer for a

ELVIS PRESLEY *(RCA)*

There's been too much written about him already. Nothing matters now except for his recordings—that's why he's still a legend. His first success was in country music and, although he went on to fame as "The King of Rock 'n' Roll" and as a movie star, he remained the epitome of a Southern version of a Beverly Hillbilly. His personal life was a disaster, but he was undeniably one of the finest singers in the world.

Left: *Elvis in 1956. Check out those brogans!*
Right: *A still from a Presley film featuring the Jordanaires, the vocal group that often accompanied Elvis in recording sessions.*

Left: *"Little Miss Dynamite"—Brenda Lee—has sold over 70 million records worldwide, more than any other solo female singer.*
Right: *Phil (left) and Don Everly scored 15 Top-10 pop singles between 1957 and 1962, more than any other Nashville act, then or today.*

THE EVERLY BROTHERS *(PolyGram)*

The most successful duet act ever to emerge from Nashville, the Everlys—like Brenda Lee, Roy Orbison, and Elvis—were so big that they were claimed by the pop audience before country fans could say, "Hey, no fair, we found them first!" Sons of the superb country guitarist Ike Everly (an influence on Chet Atkins), Don and Phil posted four country No. 1s in 1957 and 1958, gaining the country summit for the first time in the summer of 1957 with "Bye Bye Love," a year before "All I Have to Do Is Dream" topped both country and pop charts. A major influence on the Beatles, the Everly Brothers were Opry members before country was popular. Felice and Boudleaux Bryant supplied most of their million-selling early hits, but Phil wrote "When Will I Be Loved" and Don penned "Till I Kissed You." Professionally separated for many years, the Everlys reunited in 1984 and scored a crossover hit with "On the Wings of a Nightingale," which was crafted for them by Paul McCartney.

long list of country stars including Merle Haggard, Hank Thompson, Sonny James, Wanda Jackson, and Buck Owens, produced the Vincent sessions at Owen Bradley's studio. "Woman Love," a song deemed very salacious for the times, was also among the Vincent sides created in Music City during those sessions. Quite a few Nashville guitarists hung around the studios during those recordings, listening through the walls to Cliff Gallup's lead guitar work in an attempt to get a handle on this new rock 'n' roll style. Though Vincent's popularity at home failed to equal that of many of the other legends of the time, he became a major figure in England; his influence is especially noticeable today in the guitar stylings of Brian Setzer of the Stray Cats.

Buddy Holly was yet another rock 'n' roll legend who visited Nashville to record in the spring of 1956. Though the sessions with Decca executive Paul Cohen (who labeled Holly "the biggest no-talent I have ever worked with") did not yield any hits, it was Holly's first experience with a large record company and his first venture into a music capitol. "That'll Be the Day" was first recorded at these sessions; a different version released sixteen months later on Coral Records (he was unceremoniously dropped by Decca) became Holly's first hit, and it launched his career spectacularly. By all accounts Holly was a very quick study, so it's probable that his Nashville sojourn constituted an important learning experience for the Texas rocker.

No one could have blamed the Nashville music community if it had held a gigantic party on New Year's Eve in 1956, for the city had never enjoyed such success outside the country market. It would have *really* been a party had the Nashvillians known then that those 1956 hits were to kick off a ten-year period of pop hit-making never since equaled or even approached. During this period, known as Nashville's "Golden Age," 118 songs written or recorded in Nashville made the pop Top 10. Twenty-seven of these went to No. 1. Though the city was already known as "The Country Music Capital of the USA," this enormous amount of pop activity proves that whoever attached that sobriquet to the city was a very short-sighted individual indeed, for Nashville could have staked a claim as a pop capital in view of such accomplishments.

The Everly Brothers became Nashville's first "home-grown" act to enjoy consistent pop hits. Their parents, Ike and Margaret Everly, were well-known country and gospel singers throughout the South in the 1930s and 1940s, and Ike was an early influence on Chet Atkins. Don and Phil both learned to sing and play musical instruments about the time they learned to write; both sang professionally before they were ten. In 1956 they signed with Columbia Records, but the association bore no fruit. By 1957 they were looking for another label. During their search for material to record they visited Acuff-Rose, where they were introduced to Felice and Boudleaux Bryant, a husband-and-wife team that had penned a few hits, most notably Carl Smith's "Hey Joe." Newly signed to Cadence Records, the Everlys hit it big in 1957, scoring a No. 1 with "Wake Up Little Susie" and a No. 2 with "Bye, Bye Love," both written by the Bryants.

They got even hotter in 1958, posting four Top-10 pop hits on "All I Have to Do Is Dream," "Bird Dog" (both No. 1), "Problems" (2), and "Devoted to You" (10). The two young lads were as hot as a pop act could get at that time, and their work was to become a major influence upon the next decade's biggest stars: the Beatles. The Everlys' 1984 comeback underlined just how enduring an act they are.

Most historians date the beginning of the Nashville Sound to Don Gibson's 1958 hit, "Oh Lonesome Me," one of Chet Atkins's very finest productions. As Atkins later explained, the Nashville Sound was created from necessity rather than from any desire to change or experiment for the sake of musical creativity. "I wasn't trying to move country music uptown or anything like that. I was just trying to keep my job; I knew I had to make records that would sell." Nevertheless, the more polished "feel" that distinguished this and subsequent discs did represent an "uptown" move for Nashville records, in an attempt to gain back an audience following the start of the rock 'n' roll era.

The biggest story of Nashville's impact on the pop charts in 1960 came from its smallest recording artist: sixteen-year-old Brenda Lee. She went on to become one of the best-selling female solo artists in the history of recorded music. Today Brenda is struggling to notch her first No. 1 country single, an ironic twist in view of her enormous pop success in the 1960s.

Brenda came to Nashville from Atlanta, a precocious youngster who began singing soon after learning to walk. Before she was ten she was the primary breadwinner in her family—her father had died tragically in an accident. She scored a minor country hit in 1957 with "One Step at a Time," but had been unable to follow it up. By 1960 she must have been wondering if she was in the right profession. By the end of the year no one had any doubts: Brenda racked up two No. 1 pop singles, "I'm Sorry" and "I Want to Be Wanted," and hit No. 5 with "Sweet Nothin's." She became an international sensation. During a visit to England, she attained massive popularity and was given Princess Margaret's Rolls Royce to use as her tour vehicle. The Emperor of Japan attended her performance in that country, a most rare public appearance for him. A minor scandal erupted in France when the press accused her of being a midget, stating that no sixteen-year-old could sing of love with such a mature voice and outlook. The French would have been even more amazed had they known that Lee also selected her own material.

Lee notched six more Top 10s over the next few years, all under the tutelage of Owen Bradley, before she cooled off somewhat following the English invasion. Even so, she continued to post hits, which just fell shy of Top-10 status. She has maintained her international fame to this day with appearances in fifty-two foreign countries and has to date sold over eighty million records worldwide, which places her at or very near the top for any solo female artist in history.

Music City saw the creation of a second legendary singer in 1960 when Fred Foster began issuing his Roy Orbison productions on Monument Records, a company originally established in Baltimore two years earlier. Orbison had been knocking around without a great deal of success, even during a stay at Sun Records. As Jack "Cowboy" Clement, who worked the board for Roy's only Sun hit, "Ooby Dooby" (No. 59 in 1956) recalls, "I don't think we had the facilities at the time to record him the way he wanted to sound. One track was all we had."

In 1960 Orbison moved east to Nashville, to a staff writing job at Acuff-Rose. Wesley Rose, son of the late Fred Rose, talked Foster into working with Roy on Monument after nothing had emerged from Orbison's stay with Chet Atkins at RCA. Foster had to agree to an arrangement to cut several songs Rose had in mind. Foster later recalled: "Well, three sides in an artist's career, if there's going to be one, is not that bad." "Only the Lonely" and "Blue Angel" were the first productive fruit from this association, reaching No. 2 and No. 9 re-

Johnny Horton sang historic sagas better than anyone ever has. His tragic death in 1960 left a still-vacant void in country music.

spectively. Each was written by Orbison and Joe Melson; none of the songs suggested by Rose was successful.

In all, Nashville accounted for seven No. 1 singles in 1960, the most ever for Music City. Nashville held the No. 1 position on the pop singles chart for twenty-eight weeks during that heady year. Three Presley hits, plus chart-toppers by Marty Robbins ("El Paso") and the Everlys ("Cathy's Clown") joined the Lee hits at the top. In addition to Orbison's hits, smashes were posted by Johnny Horton and Jim Reeves; the latter selection, "He'll Have to Go," featured Floyd Cramer's "slip-note" piano in a classic example of the Nashville Sound in full maturity.

Nineteen sixty-one became an even more prolific year for music written or recorded in Nashville. Although the city gained fewer No. 1 hits, it produced more Top-5 and Top-10 hits than in any other year in its history. Twenty-two discs hit the pop Top-10 and sixteen of those advanced to the Top-5. The stalwarts mentioned above were still churning out hits, and they were joined by Floyd Cramer, who became a solo artist long enough to fashion three instrumental hits: "Last Date," "On the Rebound," and "San Antonio Rose." The music business in Nashville was reminded of just how big a hit "Last Date" was when it was announced that the song was a favorite of Michael Jackson's mother. In due course, Cramer received an invitation to perform in 1984 at a very private party for Mrs. Jackson in California. The Nashville Sound works in strange and wondrous ways, does it not?

The parade of Nashville hits continued the following year, punctuated by several unusual out-of-town visitors like Burl Ives and Tommy Roe. Roe's "Sheila," brown eyes, ponytail, and all, went to No. 1. That year also marked the appearance of Ray Stevens on the national hit charts, with the zany tale of "Ahab the Arab" and his camel, Clyde. To this day Stevens remains Nashville's master of the novelty song, having scored hits from such unlikely sources as a gorilla ("Harry, the Hairy Ape"), unexpected public nudity ("The Streak"), and men in funny hats turned loose on the populace ("Shriner's Convention").

The same year was also notable for Nashville's discovery by black artists as a source of hit material. Although Ray Charles's forays into the form were recorded in New York and Los

Angeles, his *Modern Sounds in Country & Western Music* albums were drawn primarily from Nashville songwriters. That same year, rhythm 'n' blues stylist Esther Phillips scored with a remake of a country standard, Eddie Miller's "Release Me."

Nashville's reputation as a location for the recording of any type of music expanded in 1963 when the city hosted sessions that provided Music Row with its first major hits recorded by black musicians. Brook Benton's "Hotel Happiness" and the Dixiebelles' "Down at Poppa Joe's" both peaked in the pop Top 10 that year.

The Beatles exploded onto the American pop scene in January of 1964, which marked the beginning of the end of the glory years for Nashville-based music on the pop charts. The major bright spot for Music City in 1964 and 1965 came in the form of Roger Miller, a streetwise songwriter who had supported himself during the lean years as a bellhop in the Andrew Jackson Hotel. In those two years, Miller issued a string of massively successful and totally off-the-wall songs that captured the public's and the music industry's fancy to such a degree that he won the staggering total of eleven Grammy Awards for them. That achievement was so spectacular that it took nineteen years and Michael Jackson to establish new marks for the most Grammys won in any one- and two-year period. Miller's songs—"Dang Me," "Chug-a-Lug," "King of the Road," "England Swings," and "Engine, Engine #9"—remain as unusual now as they were then. However, they were the only big hits he was ever able to post on the pop charts.

As the English invasion gained strength, it was challenged by American bands. The Nashville Sound, all solo singers, and vocal groups suffered in favor of the band, or instrumental group, concept. Country crossovers became as rare as short-haired rock guitarists. Nashville was saved from a total shutout in 1966 only by two unusual sets of circumstances: Johnny Cash went to lunch and Bob Dylan came to town.

Cash's lunch is important because the Statler Brothers slipped into the studio (according to a prearranged plan) while he ate to surreptitiously record "Flowers on the Wall." Columbia executives were then so disgusted with the vocal group's lack of success that they had refused to advance them any more studio time. So Cash gave them the green light to "piggyback" in on

Left: *Jim Reeves had garnered 3 No. 1 singles before his death in a 1964 plane crash: he tallied 6 more posthumously and had a No. 5 "duet" hit with Patsy Cline as late as 1982.*
Right: *"The King of the Road"—Roger Miller strums in the street, 1968.*

his session, as Harold Reid of the Statlers recalled: "We had a banjo on it because there was a banjo player there. If there had been a lute player there I guess we would have had a lute on it." The song went to No. 4 for the quartet; needless to say, they had no more trouble getting recording funds out of Columbia after that.

No one is sure why Bob Dylan traveled to Nashville to make his first double album. Dylan has never been prone to overexplain his actions, and, in 1966, nobody went through his garbage. Bob Johnston had assumed the production reins on Dylan's previous LP, *Highway 61 Revisited,* and he had recorded successfully in Music City before. Charlie McCoy may also have played a role in Dylan's decision—he was the only Nashville player used on the *Highway 61* sessions.

In any case, Dylan ventured to Columbia's studio here, built over and around Owen Bradley's old Quonset Hut, and enlisted McCoy and fellow Music City sessionmen Wayne Moss, Kenny Buttrey, Hargus "Pig" Robbins, Jerry Kennedy, Joe South, and Henry Strzelecki. "Rainy Day Women #12 & 35" emerged from these sessions to become a No. 2 pop hit, tying it with "Like a Rolling Stone" as Dylan's most successful single. The album that resulted, *Blonde on Blonde,* was Dylan's first to use electric guitar; it created a storm of controversy among his outraged folkie followers. Dylan must have liked Nashville as a recording site; he returned three more times, to make *John Wesley Harding, Self-Portrait,* and *Nashville Skyline.*

That latest entry, *Nashville Skyline,* was the first time Dylan overtly called attention to his recording activities in Music City. The record also presented a historic collaboration between Dylan and Johnny Cash. Cash wrote the liner notes for the album and was featured as "guest

Kris Kristofferson has been a major influence on Nashville songwriters for 15 years. Here he strikes a Brandoesque pose.

Freddy Fender (left) at a jail concert in Austin, Texas. Fender served 3 years in Angola State Prison in Louisiana in the early 1960s for marijuana possession. (Photo: Charlyn Zlotnik)

artist," singing "Girl from the North Country" with Dylan. The hip, young writers from the rock press may not have noticed that Dylan had cut three previous discs here, but there was no way they could miss the source of *Nashville Skyline.* It remains the most country of Dylan's albums and even boasts an instrumental. "Lay, Lady Lay" cracked the Top 10 from these sessions; it was the last Top-10 single achieved by the enigmatic Mr. Zimmerman. (And it was the last time he recorded in a Nashville studio.)

The next major Music City breakthrough came in 1971, when Columbia Records's most famous janitor, Kris Kristofferson, enjoyed an incredible year. It is generally believed that this songwriter's success led to a more mature approach to song lyrics in Music City. Like Roger Miller before him, Kristofferson had worked many years in menial jobs, unable to get his songs cut. Ironically, Miller was the first to recognize his genius; he recorded Kristofferson's "Me and Bobby McGee" in 1969. Johnny Cash gained a big country hit the next year with "Sunday Morning Coming Down," but in 1971 two of Kris's tunes made the pop Top 10: a Janis Joplin cover of "Me and Bobby McGee" and Sammi Smith's version of "Help Me Make It Through the Night," a woman's plea for a temporary nocturnal partner. This song, considered rather risqué for the times, was turned down by several bigger stars. Soon after, Kris had his own record deal, and his days of pushing a broom vanished forever.

The next major flurry of Nashville-produced pop activity, beginning in the years 1974 and 1975, was set off by five memorable songs that blazed their way to No. 1 on the pop chart. Together, they illustrate the versatility of the city's musical cadre. Billy Swan's "I Can Help" was a simple production led by Swan's "roller-rink" organ. The song was set in a neo-rockabilly style and it carried a message of hope married to an irresistible melody. "I Can Help" followed up its American success by making it to No. 1 in many foreign markets. Ray Stevens's topical ditty, "The Streak," a perfect distillation of the ridiculous (and mercifully brief) craze of appearing naked at unexpected places, furthered the Nashville tradition of novelty records. Charlie Rich's wistful reading of Billy Sherrill, Norro Wilson, and Rory Bourke's "The Most Beautiful Girl" represented the Nashville Sound run amuck in search of the big bucks to be mined from crossover success, which it succeeded in attaining.

The 1975 hits were delivered by two Texans with extensive show-biz dossiers: Freddy Fender and B. J. Thomas. Fender scored with "Before the Next Teardrop Falls," a Ben Peters-Vivian Keith number that had been recorded many times before without making a dent even in the country charts. It is a weeper in the best tradition of heartbreak songs, which have always been a prominent part of Nashville's country base. Thomas had had a place in the

FREDDY FENDER

Baldemar Huerta (a.k.a. Freddy Fender) became an overnight sensation in 1975 with "Before the Next Teardrop Falls," which lifted him from the obscurity of south Texas Latin clubs to the stages of the world's concert halls. That song was No. 1 in country and pop, and also earned Fender a CMA honor for Single of the Year. He posted consistent hits until 1977; his last Top 20 was in 1978. A superb, romantic singer in Spanish or in English, Freddy badly needs a label and a producer. He spent time in a Louisiana prison for smoking pot long before marijuana was discovered by the middle class. Credit Doug Sahm for tirelessly promoting Fender in the pre-1975 era, and "the Crazy Cajun," Huey Meaux, for finding "Before the Next Teardrop Falls."

EDDIE RABBITT
(Warner Bros.)

New Jersey–born Rabbitt learned guitar while in the Boy Scouts. He moved to Nashville in the late 1960s, hoping to make it as a songwriter. After several years of struggling, he broke through with hit songs performed by Elvis Presley ("Kentucky Rain") and Ronnie Milsap ("Pure Love"). In 1974, he began performing, and scored his first No. 1 in 1976; by early 1985 he had a dozen more. Eddie co-writes virtually all of his material with producer David Malloy and his longtime collaborator, Even Stevens. In 1980, he became the first Nashville resident to lodge *two* pop Top-5 smashes—"I Love a Rainy Night" and "Drivin' My Life Away"—in one year since Brenda Lee in 1962. Tall, dark, and handsome, Eddie's a big favorite with the ladies.

CRYSTAL GAYLE
(Warner Bros.)

Fifteen years younger than her sister Loretta Lynn, Crystal grew up not in Butcher Hollow, Kentucky, but in the "big town" of Paintsville, Indiana. She has made her own name in the business on the strength of a truly exceptional voice, a keen eye for material, and excellent production by Allen Reynolds (plus Jimmy Bowen in 1983). Although she is strikingly beautiful, she has a wooden stage presence, her only major problem. A two-time CMA Female Vocalist of the Year (1977, 1978), Gayle had scored her fourteenth No. 1 single as of early 1985. She'll be a major country/pop star for years to come. Managed by her husband, Bill Gatzimos, she could benefit from more experienced assistance in this department.

Eddie Rabbitt and "aura." (Photo: Cynthia Farah)

limelight with several major pop hits dating back to 1966, but bad luck and personal problems had kept him from reaching the top. Then he came to Nashville and was matched with producer Larry Butler, co-author with Chips Moman of "(Hey, Won't You Play) Another Somebody Done Somebody Wrong Song," a selection easier to sing than to type. It updated what has been termed a "countrypolitan" approach to ballad singing. The "countrypolitan" monicker was first attached to Jim Reeves and Eddy Arnold to describe the way they used the Nashville Sound technique to smooth out the country approach to delivering a love song.

Today Kenny Rogers is a superstar who commands six-figure fees for his concert appearances. But in 1976 he was just another pop singer who had lost his audience. With his last major hit six years behind him, he came to Music City to see if his career could be revived, a perfect example of why Nashville has been termed "the Mayo Clinic for aging pop singers." His first comeback try was only modestly successful, but in 1977 Don Wayne's classic tale of a wife who left her husband at an inopportune time put Rogers back on the pop charts, made him a country star as well, and left American music lovers with a new "hook" line to sing: "You picked a fine time to leave me, Lucille." Rogers continued to record in Nashville until 1980, when he left to make discs in California with Lionel Richie. By 1983 he had bounced to Miami and a collaboration with the Bee Gees. Although the music that emerged from those sessions was decidedly pop, Rogers kept his country audience. Rogers may have left Nashville for good—unless his career sags in the future and he finds need for the town's musical surgery once again.

Late in the 1970s three of country music's top vocalists made determined efforts to invade the bigger pop field. All three—Dolly Parton, Eddie Rabbitt, and Crystal Gayle—were successful in scoring big pop hits without losing the country base that had brought them to fame in the first place. Dolly made her move first, in 1977, and galloped all the way to No. 3 on the pop lists with "Here You Come Again." She has since become a major show-business figure through starring roles in films *(9 to 5, Best Little Whorehouse in Texas, Rhinestone)* and two whopping pop and country hits: the title song from *9 to 5* and "Islands in the Stream," a duet with Kenny Rogers, which outsold all the singles of 1983, even those released by Michael Jackson.

Gayle, Loretta Lynn's youngest sister, enjoyed her biggest pop hit with "Don't It Make My Brown Eyes Blue," ironically among the most country of the songs and productions she has released. Her music turned in a more pop direction in the next few years. Although she did tally several fairly successful pop records, her quest for pop stardom has so far landed her in the adult-contemporary market rather than on the "Hot 100" chart.

Eddie Rabbitt came to Nashville from East Orange, New Jersey, and had built a solid country career before he aimed his music at a more mainstream audience. By 1980 he had notched six songs in the "Hot 100" with only moderate success—but "Drivin' My Life Away," a superb song of life on the road, drove all the way to No. 5. His follow-up, "I Love a Rainy Night," carried him to No. 1, and the next year "Step by Step" climbed to No. 5. The year after that he and Crystal teamed up on "You and I" to nab another pop Top-10 success. Rabbitt's country success has dwindled some in the last few years, but he doesn't seem to mind playing dates in Las Vegas and Atlantic City showrooms instead of in heartland honky-tonks.

Judging from all the hoopla over the film *Urban Cowboy,* one would have expected it to provide many spectacular pop hits. Such was not the case; Johnny Lee's "Lookin' for Love," one of the two songs heard repeatedly in the film, was the only song to achieve notable success on the "Hot 100," peaking at No. 5. "Could I Have This Dance," sung by Anne Murray, died just short of the Top 30. The film's soundtrack was a big hit among country fans, however: a record-shattering seven songs from the album scored high on the country charts in 1980 and 1981.

Willie Nelson's career was also helped by the silver screen. Although none of his movies—*Honeysuckle Rose, Electric Horseman, Barbarosa*—did great business (indeed, *Barbarosa,* though hailed by the critics, never gained release beyond a limited, regional scale), the theme song from *Honeysuckle Rose,* "On the Road Again," placed Nelson higher than he had

Left: *Billy Swan's "I Can Help" was one of the world's biggest hits in 1974–75.* Right: *Fred Foster and Wesley Rose congratulate each other on Roy Orbison's worldwide success.*

yet traveled on the "Hot 100," reaching No. 20. Two years later, in 1982, Nelson dusted off a Mark James-Johnny Christopher-Wayne Carson ballad, "Always on My Mind" (previously recorded by Elvis Presley and Brenda Lee), and took it to No. 5. The song won a Grammy for Nelson for "Best Country Vocal Performance" and snagged two Grammies for its composers when it was named Best Country Song and Best Pop Song of the year.

A year earlier, the Oak Ridge Boys had breathed new life into "Elvira," a 1966 Dallas Frazier chestnut about the girl who set her man's heart on "fire-ah," and found themselves with a Top-5 pop smash, which became one of the biggest songs of the summer of 1981. The quartet, composed of Duane Allen, Joe Bonsall, William Lee Golden, and Richard Sterban (the distinctive bass voice), followed up with "Bobbie Sue" and took another pop ride, all the way to No. 12.

Eddie Rabbitt and Crystal Gayle posted the only major pop hit for Nashville artists in 1983 with their first duet effort, "You and I." Two Nashville writers, Rodney Crowell and Danny Tate, posted major hits through pop singers—Bob Seger's version of Crowell's "Shame on the Moon" made it all the way to No. 2, and Rick Springfield's "Affair of the Heart" (co-written by Blaise Tosti) made the Top 10.

Despite the dwindling number of country crossovers, country songwriters never had it so good—over 20 percent of America's radio stations, which number over nine thousand, played country music full time during this period, and a good many more spun country platters at least part of their broadcast day. Thus, a substantial country hit could accumulate as much airplay as most pop hits of the period, even without crossing over to the adult-contemporary or pop charts. This was first borne out early in 1982 when Nashville writers won more pop awards from BMI than writers in New York City or Los Angeles combined. These awards are given according to the volume of radio performances logged during the preceding year, so it follows that by 1981 country music had attained enormous success as a key radio format.

In retrospect, it is ironic that Nashville enjoyed the greatest amount of success as a pop re-

BILLY SWAN

Another product of the Monument Records-Combine Music pipeline that produced Larry Gatlin and Kris Kristofferson, Billy was born and raised in Cape Giradeau, Missouri. He began his music career in the early 1960s by furnishing Clyde McPhatter with "Lover, Please," which Clyde took to the Top 10 on the pop chart in 1962. He has also produced Tony Joe White's "Polk Salad Annie." Billy played bass for Kris Kristofferson for many years and has also seen spot duty with bands headed by Billy Joe Shaver and Kinky Friedman. His "I Can Help" was one of the biggest worldwide hits ever recorded in Nashville. He wrote the song, produced the session, then watched as "I Can Help" went to No. 1 on the American pop, country, and a-c charts and those of eighteen foreign countries. This established Swan as a recording artist, but he has yet to follow it up.

cording center during the years from 1956 to 1964. During this time, first rock 'n' roll and then the English bands dominated the pop scene, and country music and Nashville were perceived as "square" and over the hill. The four dominant Nashville artists of the period, Elvis Presley, the Everly Brothers, Roy Orbison, and Brenda Lee, were distinctive, original stylists who *initiated* trends and offered a unique sound of their own making. Nashville executives seem to have forgotten this point as they chase pop dollars by attempting to imitate the "Hot 100" hits of the day with singers whose vocal chops are at best only average. A mediocre country singer can enjoy a very successful career in that field for many years, but the pop singers who post consistent hits must command more vocal range and finesse. (A case in point is Boy George of the British group Culture Club. Strip away the mascara and his penchant for cross-dressing and you'll find that he is a very gifted vocalist.)

Presley, Lee, the Everlys, and Orbison were all extraordinarily skilled vocalists who were capable of giving absolutely *riveting* live performances. (Lee, the Everlys, and Orbison are still out there, with almost all their range and finesse intact.) Modern country is littered with the collapsed careers of singers with limited talent and experience who rapidly lost the wind in their sails when they tried to jump too quickly into that big pop pond.

A look at the chronological list of pop hits with Nashville connections seems to show that the city "lost its touch" in the late 1960s. Fewer hits have emerged from Music City in recent years. Several factors have had considerable impact on all three major American recording centers. There are far more locations for recording now than existed twenty years ago, so no one city is able to dominate the pop charts as was the case prior to 1956. The English invasion brought serious competition from foreign shores for the first time. Since 1964, musicians from Sweden, Germany, France, Ireland, Scotland, Canada, Greece, South Africa, Jamaica, Brazil, Italy, Holland, and other countries, in addition to English acts, have tallied American pop hits.

Today, the songs that become the hits are written by tunesmiths all over the world and in every corner of the United States, a complete turnaround from the days when Tin Pan Alley, Hollywood films, and Broadway musicals furnished almost all of the hits. There are thousands more songwriters today than there were twenty years ago, all fighting for hits—and the number of spots on the "Hot 100" chart hasn't increased.

The group concept of the mid-1960s led to fragmentation of the sources of music. The stars of the day began to create their own songs rather than to depend on professional songwriters, to such a degree that artists who rely totally on outside material are now the exception rather than the rule.

In addition, recording artists today have a much broader choice of recording locales than existed in the past. Today a commercially successful band or singer can find a state-of-the-art studio in almost every state of the union and in most of the countries of the free world. A band that writes and plays its own material is like a turtle—it carries almost everything it needs along with it.

The growth of recording into a global industry ensures that Nashville probably will never be able to top that incredible year of 1960 when the city had the No. 1 single for twenty-eight of the fifty-one weeks charted by *Billboard.* It doesn't seem likely that any one city can ever again approach this degree of success.

Author Russell Sanjeck long ago noted that the formation of BMI marked "the democratization of American music" by opening the doors of remuneration to composers of all types of music rather than just to the lucky one thousand or so who belonged to ASCAP. The last two decades have brought about the "democratization" of much of the world's music through such technological developments as satellites, standardized equipment, and easily portable machinery. The largest recording corporations now have branches in many countries. They constantly are exploring ways to take hits from one country into the chart lists and sales totals of another. Instead of battling New York City and Los Angeles, Nashville today is fighting against the whole world for those top spots on the "Hot 100."

THE KENDALLS
(Mercury)

What is one to make of a father-daughter duet team that finally cracked into country and pop music hit lists singing "Heaven's Just a Sin Away"? Royce Kendall was a barber in St. Louis when he realized that the harmony singing he and daughter Jeannie produced could be good enough to parlay into a show business career. Several false starts preceded their initial success in 1977, and the pair has so far survived inconsistent production, a bankrupt record company (Ovation), and the early 1980s trend toward crossover records to forge a solid career built upon traditional country instrumentation, excellent harmonies, and consistently appealing stage performances.

For some years it seemed that the Kendalls were relying too heavily on songs of sexual straying— "It Don't Feel Like Sinnin' To Me," "You'd Make an Angel Wanna Cheat," "Teach Me to Cheat"—but in 1984 they snared their first No. 1 in many years with "Thank God for the Radio." Despite the rather risqué nature of their early hits, no hint of scandal has reared its head and, yes, Jeannie has been happily married for many years.

Ray Stevens prepares to duet with an unusual partner in this 1976 photo.

NASHVILLE ON THE POP CHARTS

Top-10 hits on the *Billboard* "Hot 100" singles chart that were written by Nashville writers (unmarked) and/or recorded in Music City studios (marked with an asterisk*).

1947	Near You	Francis Craig and his Orchestra*	No. 1
	"	Larry Green	3
	"	Andrews Sisters	4
	"	Elliott Lawrence	9
1948	Beg Your Pardon	Francis Craig Orch.*	4
	"	Frankie Carle	6
	Buttons and Bows	Dinning Sisters*	7
	Beg Your Pardon	Larry Green	8
1950	Rag Mop	Ames Brothers	1
	Tennessee Waltz	Patti Page	1
	Chattanoogie Shoeshine Boy	Red Foley*	1
	Bonaparte's Retreat	Kay Starr	5
	Tennessee Waltz	Guy Lombardo	6
	"	Les Paul/ Mary Ford	8
	Chattanoogie Shoeshine Boy	Bing Crosby	9
	Rag Mop	Johnnie Lee Wills*	10
	"	Lionel Hampton	10
	"	Ralph Flanagan	10
1951	Cold, Cold Heart	Tony Bennett	1
	Slow Poke	Pee Wee King*	3
	Down Yonder	Del Wood*	6
1952	Half as Much	Rosemary Clooney	2
	Jambalaya	Jo Stafford	3
1953	Your Cheatin' Heart	Joni James	7
1956	Singin' the Blues	Guy Mitchell	1
	Heartbreak Hotel	Elvis Presley*	1
	I Want You, I Need You, I Love You	" *	1
	Just Walkin' in the Rain	Johnny Ray	2
	Jingle Bell Rock	Bobby Helms*	6
	My Special Angel	" *	7
	Be Bop a Lula	Gene Vincent*	9
1957	Wake Up Little Susie	Everly Brothers*	1
	Bye, Bye Love	" *	2
	Young Love	Sonny James*	2
	A White Sport Coat	Marty Robbins*	2
	Gone	Ferlin Husky*	4
1958	Purple People Eater	Sheb Wooley*	1
	All I Have to Do Is Dream	Everly Bros.*	1
	Bird Dog	" *	1
	It's Only Make Believe	Conway Twitty*	1
	Problems	Everly Bros.*	2
	Oh Lonesome Me	Don Gibson*	7
	I Got Stung	Elvis Presley*	8
	Devoted to You	Everly Bros.*	10
1959	Heartaches by the Number	Guy Mitchell	1
	The Battle of New Orleans	Johnny Horton*	1
	Teen Angel	Mark Dinning*	1
	The Three Bells	The Browns*	1
	Big Hunk of Love	Elvis Presley*	1
	Fool Such as I	" *	2
	I Need Your Love Tonight	" *	4
	Waterloo	Stonewall Jackson*	4
	('Til) I Kissed You	Everly Bros.*	4
	Gotta Travel On	Billy Grammer*	4
	Danny Boy	Conway Twitty*	10
1960	El Paso	Marty Robbins*	1
	I'm Sorry	Brenda Lee*	1
	I Want to Be Wanted	" *	1
	Stuck on You	Elvis Presley*	1
	It's Now or Never	" *	1
	Are You Lonesome Tonight	" *	1
	Cathy's Clown	Everly Bros.*	1
	Only the Lonely	Roy Orbison*	2

	He'll Have to Go	Jim Reeves*	2
	Sink the Bismarck	Johnny Horton*	2
	Sweet Nothins	Brenda Lee*	4
	The Old Lamplighter	The Browns*	5
	Lonely Blue Boy	Conway Twitty*	6
	Let It Be Me	Everly Bros.*	7
	So Sad (To Watch Good Love Gone Bad)	" *	7
	Let's Think About Livin'	Bob Luman*	7
	Please Help Me I'm Fallin'	Hank Locklin*	8
	When Will I Be Loved	Everly Bros.*	8
	Blue Angel	Roy Orbison*	9
1961	Wooden Heart	Joe Dowell*	1
	Surrender	Elvis Presley*	1
	Big Bad John	Jimmy Dean*	1
	Running Scared	Roy Orbison*	1
	Cryin'	" *	2
	Don't Worry ('Bout Me)	Marty Robbins*	3
	Fool Number One	Brenda Lee*	3
	Last Date	Floyd Cramer*	3
	On the Rebound	" *	4
	Dum, Dum	Brenda Lee*	4
	North to Alaska	Johnny Horton*	4
	His Latest Flame	Elvis Presley*	4
	Little Sister	" *	5
	Walk on By	Leroy Van Dyke*	5
	Sad Movies	Sue Thompson*	5
	I Feel So Bad	Elvis Presley*	5
	You Can Depend on Me	Brenda Lee*	6
	Mexico	Bob Moore*	7
	Walk Right Back	Everly Bros.*	7
	Ebony Eyes	" *	8
	San Antonio Rose	Floyd Cramer*	8
	Crazy	Patsy Cline*	9
1962	Sheila	Tommy Roe*	1
	I Can't Stop Loving You	Ray Charles	1
	Good Luck Charm	Elvis Presley*	1
	You Don't Know Me	Ray Charles	2
	It Keeps Right on a Hurtin'	Johnny Tillotson*	3
	Norman	Sue Thompson*	3
	All Alone Am I	Brenda Lee*	4
	Break It to Me Gently	" *	4
	Dream Baby	Roy Orbison*	4
	Ahab, the Arab	Ray Stevens*	5
	She's Not You	Elvis Presley*	5
	Wolverton Mountain	Claude King*	6
	Everybody Loves Me but You	Brenda Lee*	6
	Crying in the Rain	Everly Bros.*	6
	P. T. 109	Jimmy Dean*	8
	Release Me	Esther Phillips	8
	That's Old-Fashioned	Everly Bros.*	9
	A Little Bitty Tear	Burl Ives*	9
	Funny Way of Laughing	" *	10
1963	The End of the World	Skeeter Davis*	2
	Devil in Disguise	Elvis Presley*	3
	Hotel Happiness	Brook Benton*	3
	Everybody	Tommy Roe*	3
	Busted	Ray Charles	4
	Mean Woman Blues	Roy Orbison*	5
	Losing You	Brenda Lee*	6
	Talk Back Trembling Lips	Johnny Tillotson	7
	In Dreams	Roy Orbison*	7
	Still	Bill Anderson*	8
	Take These Chains from My Heart	Ray Charles	8
	Down at Poppa Joe's	Dixiebelles*	9
	500 Miles	Bobby Bare*	10
1964	Oh, Pretty Woman	Roy Orbison*	1
	Bread & Butter	Newbeats*	2
	G.T.O.	Ronny & the Daytonas*	4
	I Can't Stay Mad at You	Skeeter Davis*	7
	Dang Me	Roger Miller*	7
	It's Over	Roy Orbison*	9
	Chug-a-Lug	Roger Miller*	9
	See the Funny Little Clown	Bobby Goldsboro*	9
1965	Crying Time	Ray Charles	4
	King of the Road	Roger Miller*	4
	Make the World Go Away	Eddy Arnold*	6
	Engine, Engine # 9	Roger Miller*	7
	England Swings	" *	8
1966	Rainy Day Women # 12 & 35	Bob Dylan*	2
	Flowers on the Wall	Statler Brothers*	4
1967	Woman, Woman	Gary Puckett/ Union Gap	4
	Release Me	Engelbert Humperdinck	4
	Then You Can Tell Me Goodbye	The Casinos	6
1968	Honey	Bobby Goldsboro*	1
	Harper Valley P.T.A.	Jeannie C. Riley*	1
	Little Green Apples	O. C. Smith	2
	Just Dropped in to See What Condition My Condition Was In	Kenny Rogers/ First Edition	5
1969	A Boy Named Sue	Johnny Cash*	2
	Ruby, Don't Take Your Love to Town	Kenny Rogers/ First Edition	6
	Lay, Lady Lay	Bob Dylan*	7
	Gitarzan	Ray Stevens*	8
	Polk Salad Annie	Tony Joe White*	8
1970	Everything Is Beautiful	Ray Stevens*	1
	Amos Moses	Jerry Reed*	8
1971	Me & Bobby McGee	Janis Joplin	1
	Rose Garden	Lynn Anderson*	3
	Help Me Make It Through the Night	Sammi Smith*	8
	When You're Hot, You're Hot	Jerry Reed*	9
1972	Heart of Gold	Neil Young*	1
	Funny Face	Donna Fargo*	5
	Sylvia's Mother	Dr. Hook	5
	The Cover of "Rolling Stone"	"	6
1973	Top of the World	The Carpenters	1
	Delta Dawn	Helen Reddy	1
	Burning Love	Elvis Presley	2
	Drift Away	Dobie Gray*	5
	Paper Roses	Marie Osmond*	5
	Uneasy Rider	Charlie Daniels*	9
1974	The Streak	Ray Stevens*	1
	I Can Help	Billy Swan*	1
	The Most Beautiful Girl	Charlie Rich*	1
	Please Come to Boston	Dave Loggins*	5
	Everlasting Love	Carl Carlton	6
1975	Another Somebody Done Somebody Wrong Song	B. J. Thomas*	1
	Before the Next Teardrop Falls	Freddy Fender	1
	When Will I Be Loved	Linda Ronstadt	2
	I'm Not Lisa	Jessie Colter*	4
	Love Hurts	Nazareth	5
	Get Down	Joe Simon*	8
1976	Misty Blue	Dorothy Moore	3
1977	Don't It Make My Brown Eyes Blue	Crystal Gayle*	2
	Blue Bayou	Linda Ronstadt	3
	Lucille	Kenny Rogers*	5
1978	You Needed Me	Anne Murray	1
	Dust in the Wind	Kansas*	6
1979	She Believes in Me	Kenny Rogers*	3
	Coward of the County	" *	3
	The Devil Went Down to Georgia	Charlie Daniels Band*	3
	When You're in Love with a Beautiful Woman	Dr. Hook	6
	You Decorated My Life	Kenny Rogers*	7
1980	9 to 5	Dolly Parton*	1
	I Love a Rainy Night	Eddie Rabbitt*	1
	Longer	Dan Fogelberg*	2
	Drivin' My Life Away	Eddie Rabbitt*	5
	Sexy Eyes	Dr. Hook*	5
	Lookin' for Love	Johnny Lee	5
1981	Slow Hand	Pointer Sisters	2
	Don't Fall in Love with a Dreamer	Kenny Rogers/ Kim Carnes*	4
	Step by Step	Eddie Rabbitt*	5
	Elvira	Oak Ridge Boys*	5
	(There's) No Gettin' Over Me	Ronnie Milsap*	5
	Crying	Don McLean*	5
	Same Old Lang Syne	Dan Fogelberg*	9
1982	Always on My Mind	Willie Nelson*	5
	Leader of the Band	Dan Fogelberg*	9
1983	Shame on the Moon	Bob Seger	2
	You and I	Eddie Rabbitt/ Crystal Gayle*	7

Note: Records are listed for the year in which they attained their peak performance, rather than the year in which they first charted, whenever possible. Records in which substantial overdubbing was done in Nashville are also listed as having been recorded in Nashville. Any additions to this list will be appreciated.

Pop Goes Nashville

Although the popular conception of Nashville is of a town devoted exclusively to the production of country music, considerable popular music history has been made in Music City. This other side of the Nashville recording coin has somehow escaped the attention of music journalists. When the Nashville Music Association (NMA) was established in 1980, a comprehensive list of noncountry artists who have recorded in Nashville studios was compiled. After months of research and three years of updating, this list now features hundreds of artists associated with all forms of American popular music. Here are a few of the best-known musicians who have recorded in Nashville:

Bob Dylan. Paul McCartney. REO Speedwagon. Gary Burton. Joe Tex. Ray Charles. Don McLean. Julie Andrews. Perry Como. Kansas. Dan Fogelberg. Little Richard. Dave Brubeck. Neil Young. Ringo Starr. Bobby "Blue" Bland. Patti Page. The Beau Brummels.

Ray Sawyer (left) and Dennis Locorriere (center) of Dr. Hook & The Medicine Show are here joined by Shel Silverstein for a vocal workout. (Photo: Alan Mayor)

Clint Eastwood. Joe Cocker. B. B. King. Rosemary Clooney. Elvis Costello. Pete Fountain. James Garner. Duane Eddy. Bill Haley. Dean Martin. Gordon Lightfoot. Joan Baez. Al Hirt. Earl Klugh. Gene Pitney. Andy Williams. Johnny Winter. Loudon Wainwright. Arthur Prysock. Paul Revere & the Raiders. Maurice Williams. Leon Russell. Twiggy. Gene Vincent. Bobby Vinton. Nancy Sinatra. Sissy Spacek. Dionne Warwick. Joe Walsh. Doc Watson. Esther Phillips. Joe Ely. Millie Jackson. Delbert McClinton. The Stray Cats. Olivia Newton-John. Connie Francis. Fats Domino. Frank Gorshin. Al Kooper. Michael Bloomfield. Vic Damone.

All this activity has occurred with little local fanfare. The business people of Music City are professional enough to keep these sessions with pop superstars quiet, and, in many cases, the Nashville music community is too busy tending to its own affairs to be interested in outside projects. Label executives are usually so buried in their own bailiwicks that they aren't even familiar with the rock and pop groups that do visit. (Gary Richrath of REO Speedwagon told me that when they came here to record their second LP in 1972 they dropped by the local office of their label to introduce themselves and talk shop. Nobody here knew who they were.)

Bob Dylan recorded four discs here—*Blonde on Blonde, John Wesley Harding, Self-Portrait,* and *Nashville Skyline*—but few Music City residents are aware of any Dylan recording done before the 1969 album that bears the town's name. (Later, when pressed about the Dylan sessions for *Blonde on Blonde,* one of the pickers who attended could provide few details beyond Albert Grossman's habit of throwing quarters into the ceiling to see if they would stick in

Joan Baez listens to a playback at Quadrafonic Studios in the early 1970s. (Photo: Marshall Fallwell, Jr.)

Neil Young checks to see if rust ever sleeps at the Steiner-Liff scrap-metals yard. Young has recorded in Nashville many times. (Photo: Marshall Fallwell, Jr.)

the acoustic tile, that Michael Bloomfield had walked into the studio from the rain carrying his guitar by the neck, and that Dylan hadn't said much but read a lot of movie star gossip magazines.)

In 1972 the Nitty Gritty Dirt Band, then a leading rock group, came to Music City to make a landmark three-LP set, *Will the Circle Be Unbroken,* a project that blended the five Dirt Band members with such leading country artists as Roy Acuff, the Carter Family, Merle Travis, and Earl Scruggs. The record stayed on the pop charts for thirty-two weeks and elicited raves from the rock press. However, the event was given scant attention by country journalists and the Nashville music writers failed to seize this opportunity to expound upon the coming country-rock fusion that was later labeled "progressive country."

Some years back I noticed Neil Young hanging out at the Exit/In, a former industry showcase club/watering hole. There he was, just sitting at a table like an ordinary person. He seemed a bit puzzled, though, at being completely ignored by the swarms of college coeds and industry hangers-on who were also in attendance. (Is too much anonymity better or worse than none at all?)

When Ray Charles came here to record in 1982 he stayed at Spence Manor, Music Row's only luxury hotel, and walked to the label offices two blocks away. No one bothered or even noticed the blind American music legend as he walked down the busiest street of Music Row.

This environment free from intrusion has proven attractive to stars weary of dodging fans, groupies, dope dealers, and sharpies at every turn. Word has reached both the East and West Coasts that Nashville is the place to come if you are serious about working without interruptions. The town's laissez-faire attitude also carries over to the reporting corps here, a mellow cadre far less aggressive in ferreting out muck and scandal than its counterparts in New York and Los Angeles. People here in the business knew long before it became common knowledge about Elvis Presley's drug habits; the maids who cleaned the rooms following his last attempt to record here (he never made it out of the hotel) reported huge piles of junk-food containers and used syringes left behind. This was never reported in the press, however. The habits of Elvis Costello's band and his manager, Jake Riviera, were also a source of considerable tongue-wagging, but no press ink, following their stay here to cut Costello's ill-advised *Almost Blue* disc.

Though this sort of wild and woolly behavior has been associated mostly with rock musicians, it should be remembered that country artists have been on the road quite a bit themselves, and they also have been known to seek pleasures during their off hours. Outrageous behavior is no stranger to Nashville, though for the most part it has diminished in the face of the conservative attitude brought by prosperity.

KAREN BROOKS
(Warner Bros.)

This lanky Texan, former sidekick to Jerry Jeff Walker and ex-wife of Austin songwriter Gary P. Nunn, could prove to be *the* country female singer of the 1980s. Her debut album, *Walk On* in 1982—brilliantly produced by Emmylou Harris's husband, producer Brian Ahern—showcased a versatile singer equally at home with Spanish-flavored acoustic ballads or full rock extravaganzas in the style of Roy Orbison. She scored her first No. 1 with "Faking Love," a duet with T. G. Sheppard, in 1983, and sang the theme for the TV miniseries "Thorn Birds." Although she writes infrequently, the songs she pens—which include "Tennessee Rose," "Couldn't Do Nothing Right," and "Walk On"—are exceptional. Her wry sense of humor and offbeat manner make her an interviewer's delight. She lives in a trailer on several hundred acres south of Nashville, and she spends her free time on horseback in barrel races or chasing down lost livestock.

In 1979 Local No. 257 of the American Federation of Musicians (AFM) reported that the number of noncountry recording sessions in Nashville surpassed country recording for the first time. This has been the case every year since. The AFM has also reported that Nashville, with production in excess of that reported for New York City or Los Angeles, is the singles capital of America. The rise in other forms of recording has not come at the expense of country music but is *in addition* to the thousands of country sessions booked annually by the studios of Music City.

In past years Nashville was thought to be merely an outpost for the recording of country music, but many acts now understand that recording in Nashville has much to offer them as well. In addition to a relaxed pace and freedom from intrusion, artists from outside the country music pantheon come here because of the lower cost of living and recording as compared to New York and Los Angeles. People have even come from as far away as Great Britain. A small cadre of writers and musicians from Britain made their way to Nashville during the 1970s, a migration led by Roger Cook, one of England's top pop writers at the time. Cook has since written hits for Don Williams and Crystal Gayle.

Studio time in Nashville costs less than in other recording centers partly because of the lower cost of living and partly because of the fierce competition among the town's forty-plus studios. In addition, Nashville lacks the traffic congestion common to New York or Los Angeles. The tidy Music Row arrangement also cuts down on expenses: musicians can stay in hotels within a ten-minute walk of the studio doors. The musicians and engineers throw themselves enthusiastically into whatever project comes along, creating a "family" atmosphere not found in other centers. Though double and triple the union scale rate is generally paid to the "best" players in other recording centers, only a few Nashville players can obtain double scale for their services.

All of this compactness has built a community of people who love music, whether they write, sing, engineer, produce, market, package, promote, or sell it. The people in the business get more personally involved in each of the steps of the process, a sort of Nashville intangible that

LINDA RONSTADT
(Asylum)

Although she wins the *Playboy* poll every year as "Best Female Country & Western Singer," Linda has recorded only one album, *Silk Purse from a Sow's Ear,* and the *Queenstown Trio* project, with Dolly Parton and Emmylou Harris, so far unreleased, in Nashville. Folks here would like to see her give Music City *studios* as much of a workout as Nashville songs. She's had country hits with "I Can't Help It if I'm Still in Love with You," "When Will I Be Loved," "Crazy," and "Blue Bayou." Expect her to "go country" later this decade when her pop/rock appeal fades even further.

Left: *Nashville's major rock promoter of the last 12 years, Joe Sullivan here combines business with pleasure. (Photo: Beth Gwinn)*
Right: *Loudon Wainwright and Kate McGarrigle's baby gets an early musical exposure during sessions for Loudon's* Attempted Moustache *LP. (Photo: Marshall Fallwell, Jr.)*

makes the creative part of the procedure run smoother. Nashville seems to have an uncanny ability to translate an artist's dreams into business profits with a minimum of difficulty.

Many visiting musicians have commented on the relaxed pace that represents full speed ahead in Nashville music circles. This pace, the use of the Nashville number system, and the overall ability of the participants here are the three factors that draw the most comment from outsiders.

This relaxed pace shouldn't be confused with that of a snail, however. Once in the studio, when the red light flicks on to signal a live "take," things move rapidly. A general spirit of camaraderie fills the air. The producer usually *solicits* suggestions from the assembled players, a far cry from the "you play this" attitude often found in other music centers. Discontent is suggested rather than shouted, and often cloaked with subtlety, as in: "That was pretty good. Why don't we try another take. Fred, is there something a little different you could play?"

The hands-off attitude of the Musicians Union has had a lot to do with the mellow atmosphere in the studios. The attitude of the union, led by the late George Cooper, for thirty-seven years the Nashville president, has been to allow the industry to police itself. Union officials don't pester the producers to collect the timecards or make sure no one runs into overtime without paying. The producer and engineers are expected to file the proper forms and pay the proper amount without close supervision. It's probably the best policy, since the intimacy of the local business prevents anyone from flouting the regulations for very long without being called on the carpet. Those who don't rectify matters find it very hard to do business here.

It should be noted that union officials do monitor sessions in other cities much more closely; they may sometimes interfere with legitimate recording activities in their efforts to prevent clandestine sessions.

For many years only one rate of payment existed for anyone who played on a recording, be it a master session contracted by a record company or a speculative, or "spec," session made in the hope that a later deal for the recording will surface. This encouraged many "scab" sessions (recording done without filing the proper forms with the union). The players and the engineer either donated their time or were paid in cash. To discourage this practice Cooper came up with a compromise in the 1960s: a "spec" rate set considerably lower than the rate paid for master sessions. This encouraged more experimentation, gained income the union would not otherwise have received, created an advantage over New York and Los Angeles sessions, and

Left: *Olivia Newton-John has never had a No. 1 country single, but that didn't stop her from winning a CMA Award as Best Female Vocalist in 1974. Bill Monroe, the father of bluegrass, gives her a Nashville welcome.*
Right: *Left to right, songwriter Will Jennings, Wilton Felder, Stix Hooper, Joe Cocker, and Joe Sample take a break during the Crusaders' (Felder, Hooper, and Sample) 1982 sessions in Nashville. (Photo: Melodie Gimple)*
Opposite: *Kevin Cronin and Gary Richrath of REO Speedwagon compare licks in this concert shot. The group's second album,* R.E.O./T.W.O., *was cut in Nashville. It remains one of their best. (Photo: Beth Gwinn)*

I KNOW ONE

Words & Music by:
Jack Clement

Notation by:
Art Sparer

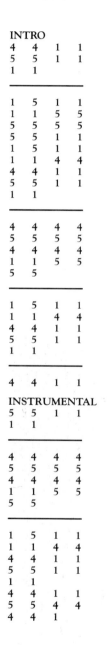

INTRO

4	4	1	1
5	5	1	1
1	1		

1	5	1	1
1	1	5	5
5	5	5	5
5	5	1	1
1	5	1	1
1	1	4	4
4	4	1	1
5	5	1	1
1	1		

4	4	4	4
5	5	5	5
4	4	4	4
1	1	5	5
5	5		

1	5	1	1
1	1	4	4
4	4	1	1
5	5	1	1
1	1		

4	4	1	1

INSTRUMENTAL

5	5	1	1
1	1		

4	4	4	4
5	5	5	5
4	4	4	4
1	1	5	5
5	5		

1	5	1	1
1	1	4	4
4	4	1	1
5	5	1	1
1	1		
4	4	1	1
5	5	4	4
4	4	1	

gave musicians the green light to participate in activities previously officially forbidden. If the recording gained eventual release as a major label record the players were then paid the normal master session rate to augment the lower "spec" rate already paid. This process has gradually moved outward from Nashville but is still not universally accepted.

The "Nashville Number System" has been in constant use here since it was developed by Neal Matthews of the Jordanaires, a vocal group that sang for hundreds of artists on thousands of sessions. The system is merely a quick way to map the chord changes in any piece of music. If the song is in the key of D then that key becomes a 1 for the remainder of the song. All other chords are then numbered accordingly: E=2, F=3, and so on. Other musical notation for sharps, flats, and naturals is used, so each song is reduced to a series of numbers, which the session leader takes down upon hearing the song for the first time. Copies are then distributed for all the participants to use. This leads to cryptic studio comments like this: "Gimme an 11-55, a 44-11, and another 11-55," chants that sound more like signals on a gridiron than instructions in a studio.

This system may sound simple but a musician must be very advanced to use it, particularly with the speed necessary to keep up when a sudden decision is made to change the key of the song: "Okay boys, let's try it in G instead of D." Bang! They're off— and if a musician doesn't know how to transpose this instantly in his head and modulate into the right key with the correct chords, then he won't be sought for studio work here very long.

The most amazing thing about this musical shorthand is that it isn't in widespread use elsewhere. Players in New York and Los Angeles generally work from prepared arrangements written out in charts or they record completely by "feel," that is, either in a structured or improvisational situation. The number system would seem to be the perfect middle ground, for it provides a framework that permits improvisation within limits.

This system, the musicians' ability, and their familiarity with each other's styles are three

Left: *Flat-picking guitar master Doc Watson has received 2 of his 3 Grammys for Nashville recordings. (Photo: Alan Mayor)*
Right: *Joe Tex was one of the hardest-working show business performers in addition to being one of the first major black artists to record in Nashville. (Photo: Charlyn Zlotnik)*

reasons why it wasn't at all rare in the 1950s and 1960s to find four, five, six, or more tracks recorded in one three-hour session. Brenda Lee recalls once recording the staggering total of ten songs in one session, at a pace that found her cutting a master track every eighteen minutes!

Recording doesn't roll quite as rapidly in modern times. The artists, engineers, and producers are even more skilled but the process has become much more complicated. Modern recording machinery resembles the equipment used in the 1960s about as much as the cockpit of a 747 resembles the one found in a 1930s biplane. While the sophisticated modern recording equipment has given artists the means to examine, modify, or even leave out any sound on every track of their disc, such scrutiny has slowed the completion of the process drastically. (Many artists spend several *hundred* hours in the studio to craft an album slightly less than thirty-five minutes long.)

Nevertheless, the speed of Nashville session players is always noticed by the many out-of-town guests the studios attract. It's always delightful to watch the reactions of visitors when a group of Nashville studio pickers hears a song once, jots down some numbers, and then renders a seamless track on the first try.

As a greenhouse maximizes the ability of plants to grow, so the Nashville atmosphere maximizes the chances for creative artistry to flourish.

Through the years Nashville has gradually attracted a growing number of talented musicians of every stripe. Though the city is still far from being the all-purpose recording nexus it will become, the change in the way Nashville is perceived by others in the business has changed dramatically. Ten years ago there were only two basic situations that would bring a major noncountry artist to town to record. In one case, the star or someone in an advisory capacity would decide that the time had come for the artist to make a country album. This

Burt Reynolds (left) has helped country music tremendously by using it in many of his films. Jerry Reed (right) co-starred with Reynolds in the Smokey and the Bandit *films before making his directing debut with* What Comes Around?, *filmed in Nashville in 1984. (Photo: Melodie Gimple)*

reasoning first brought Bobby "Blue" Bland, Ringo Starr, Millie Jackson, and many others to Music City.

Nashville has also been for years termed "the Mayo Clinic of the music business," a reference to another class of people who venture into the city's recording facilities. This class, always distinguished by lagging or nonexistent record sales, is usually made up of stars who earned their fame in pop music, films, sports, or TV. Over the years a weird and wonderful crew of such folk have arrived and departed, prime examples being Julie Andrews, Clint Eastwood, James Garner, Frank Gorshin, Dean Martin, Jack Palance, Twiggy, Nancy Sinatra, Connie Francis, George Burns, Carol Channing, Annette Funicello, and Terry Bradshaw.

Such appearances add luster to the town's image and make the nonmusic majority of citizens feel honored that their burg was touched by such royalty. Music Row takes it all in stride, however, for, if the truth were known, these visits produce significant recorded music about as often as country singers win Oscars or Emmys.

Over the years, the focus has shifted gradually from "a country album" to "a Nashville album." The musicians' ability has now overshadowed the end product—that is, *how* they play has finally eclipsed *what* they play.

As an early recording center Nashville played host to many artists simply because the city was one of the few to offer the necessary recording equipment. New York, Chicago, and Los Angeles also had facilities but Nashville was a heck of a lot closer for anyone living anywhere in the South, Texas, or some parts of the Midwest. During the 1950s it was a lot cheaper (and no doubt far less intimidating to the artist) to send artists to Nashville to record than to any of the other three capitals. When Elvis signed with RCA he was cut here at RCA's studio. Buddy Holly for Decca and Gene Vincent for Capitol also ventured to Nashville under those circum-

Carol Channing and Webb Pierce on the Grand Ole Opry, 1976.

Above: *English "New Wave" sensation Elvis Costello (right) meets his idol, George Jones. Costello's 1981 Nashville-recorded LP,* Almost Blue, *featured two songs written by Jones.*
Above, right: *"The Texas Troubadour" Ernest Tubb and "Easy Rider" Peter Fonda swap stories of the road in this mid-1970s meeting. (Photo: Alan Mayor)*
Below, right: *Johnny Lee and Cher discuss her purchase of a mechanical bull from Gilley's after Cher incorporated a bull ride into her Las Vegas show in 1981.*

stances. Nashville thus became the site of much important early rock recording simply by being in the right place at the right time with the proper equipment, a situation that also applied to Los Angeles's early years in the film business.

During the late 1960s and early 1970s, Nashville really began to hit its stride as a total recording center. After Bob Dylan began coming to Music City to make records, his stature as a mystical legend helped influence many others to try Nashville. (It should be noted that Dylan's popularity was at its zenith in the late 1960s and early 1970s. The rock press regarded him as a guru and had decided that he was the "heaviest" of the American musicians.) REO Speedwagon, Neil Young, Johnny Winter, Dan Fogelberg, Kansas, the Byrds, and many others found it easier and less expensive to make records in Music City than on the West or East Coast. And there was Nashville's special quaint charm, which Paul McCartney commented upon when he arrived to check things out in 1975, staying for several weeks in Curly Putman's house east of town. McCartney apparently spent very little time in the studio during his visit, for the only release to emerge was "Sally G," a selection that marked Paul's only appearance on the country charts. (It went to No. 51.)

Left: *Soul music star Millie Jackson, a frequent visitor to Music City studios, lays down a rap at a TV taping. Steel guitar legend Buddy Emmons is among the backing pickers.* (*Photo: Beth Gwinn*)
Below: *"New Wave" rocker John Hiatt lived in Nashville for several years in the mid-1970s before moving to California.* (*Photo: Jim McGuire*)

As the town's image as a center exclusively for country music began to recede, the technical minds in charge of operating the city's recording rooms began to upgrade the facilities to keep pace with the rapid innovation in the industry. By mid-1985 Nashville offered nearly as wide a range of options as was available anywhere in the world. By 1985 the city boasted 16-, 24-, and 48-track units for either analog or digital recording. Certain rooms specialized in capturing a "live" sound while others preferred a dampened or "dead" sound. The Nashville studios boasted a vast array of consoles that were made by all the leading manufacturers. By the mid-1970s Johnny Rosen's Fanta Sound was in place to specialize in on-site recording by bringing a fully equipped studio built into a truck to whatever remote spot was chosen by the producers.

Country music may have been a little slow to embrace the music video as ardently as did rock, but the city began preparing for the boom in the late 1970s. Film and video companies were established to provide the tools and knowledge to make the city as much of a film-video center as a music capital. The state film commission was established and funded with enough capital to accomplish the job of attracting major film companies to the area. Remote and stationary facilities for film and video recording were in place by 1983, once again giving Nashville a jump on its neighboring cities in terms of hardware. The planners of the new Grand Ole Opry House were well aware of this possibility in 1974—they equipped the facility to serve as a live venue as well as a TV/radio broadcast source and stocked it with the finest video and film equipment available.

By late 1984 some of the larger New York and Los Angeles video firms had offices here, ready for an expected boom in country video production. In August and September of 1984 Ted Turner's WTBS, MTV, and an independent group of California businessmen announced plans for "video channels" similar to MTV but much broader in musical scope, saying in so many words that country videos would now have the national exposure via this medium previously denied them by MTV's "rock videos only" play list.

As Nashville responded to the rock revolution with the Nashville Sound, so the city has reacted to video's new prominence by jumping into the field and establishing it from both within and without.

Left: *Paul McCartney's 1974 two-month visit to Music City resulted in "Sally G," a country charter for the ex-Beatle. His wife, Linda, stands beside him. (Photo: Alan Mayor)*
Right: *Ex-Beatle Ringo Starr recorded his* Beaucoups of Blues *LP in Music City in 1970. Producer Pete Drake (in sunglasses) waits while Ringo obliges the fans. (Photo: Marshall Fallwell, Jr.)*

Musical Nashville at Work

When you drive down the tree-lined streets of Music Row on a weekday morning, the area is so quiet and peaceful that it looks as if little is happening. There are few people in view, parking places are available on the streets, and there is no visible center of activity. At nine in the morning the Row is deserted. About the only thing being made is coffee, for the music business in Nashville is not an early riser.

The employees start drifting in around nine-thirty or ten, yawning and stretching while discussing the previous evening's activities. The casual observer might mistake them for graduate students or people on the dole, for standard industry apparel here revolves around blue jeans, slacks, open-collar shirts, or even T-shirts. It's hard to believe that these informally clad people are key cogs in an industry that sells over a half-billion dollars worth of recorded music in the United States alone every year. Additional income from music activities comes to Nashville from publishing, booking agencies, performance rights groups, live appearances, merchandise sales, management fees, and endorsements. The sum total has not been calculated, but it is a safe bet to say that the music business is worth several billion dollars annually to Nashville, not counting the additional tourist dollars the industry attracts.

By ten-thirty everyone is at work, in meetings or on the phone. Music Row business is conducted out of sight of those who walk or drive by on Music Square East (Sixteenth Avenue South) and Music Square West (Seventeenth Avenue South), the two major arteries of Music Row.

Despite the lack of street-side activity, there is intense work conducted behind closed doors. On a typical Monday morning, for example, all of the major label department heads meet to evaluate and discuss the projects they have on the market or in the stages that precede the release of a record. Policy decisions are made at these meetings to determine which of the label projects will receive concentrated effort, which of their records must be left to their own devices, which artists should be signed and which should be released from their contracts. Their staff of field promotion men reports in, letting the home office executives know where each of the releases stands in the area each covers. Marketing strategy sessions are held for each record. Advertising budgets for upcoming releases are set. New recordings are played and

MCA Nashville boss Jim Foglesong presents Barbara Mandrell a gold LP while aboard ship.

The late Tootsie Bess ruled Tootsie's Orchid Lounge with a sharp hatpin and a soft touch for almost 20 years. She treated the biggest stars and the smallest nobodies equally at her club, for years the major hangout of all who were or wanted to be somebody in country music. (Photo: Al Clayton)

BAR
IS
OPEN

discussed. Scheduling matters are determined so the company doesn't release its records too close together. Showcase performances are planned. The progress of the company's releases on the charts is evaluated. Calls are fielded from press, publishers, agents, and managers, all of whom want to know how particular artists are doing, how certain shows went over the weekend, and other vital data. Reports are printed and distributed among the staff. The various trade publications are devoured, always with an eye to uncovering something that will give a leg up on the competition.

Similar scenarios, but with different specific activities, are also in progress at booking agencies, management firms, publishers, performance rights groups, industry publications, and all the other elements in the music industry economy.

This activity goes on all day, a day that in Nashville can last until six-thirty, seven, or eight o'clock. Even then the work may not be completed. It is common for industry workers to attend evening functions: cocktail receptions in honor of artists whose records have been successful, showcase performances by label acts or new talent, visits to studios to monitor the progress of certain projects, late meetings with artists or managers who spend much of their time on the road and aren't always available during working hours.

Even then it isn't over. Many label executives listen to cassette tapes on the way to and from work. Evening hours at home quite often are partially occupied in listening to yet more recordings. With a work "day" like this, it's easy to understand why those in this business have a history of marital problems. (Some have a dossier of marriages longer than their list of gold records. Larry Butler, one of Nashville's top producers, has so far taken nine women to the altar, tying him with Jerry Seabolt for the industry lead.)

When you walk or drive down the streets of the Row you'll have a tough time even distinguishing which buildings are studios and which house publishing companies, booking agencies, management concerns, or other music-related endeavors. Many of the buildings aren't marked, and for good reason—the people in the industry know where they are, and those who aren't in the business aren't welcome to drop by and browse. Would you want strangers strolling through your work place while you toiled at your job?

This seems like a good place to pause briefly for an overview of the chain of events that occurs before a record becomes a hit. Perhaps if we back up and trace the process it will make all this a little easier to understand.

SONNY JAMES
(Dimension)

"The Southern Gentleman," born in Alabama, began professionally at the age of four. By the time he was seven, he had learned to play the violin. His 1957 smash, "Young Love," propelled him to "overnight" stardom in pop (No. 2) and country (No. 1). After this, he enjoyed little pop success, and he didn't get another No. 1 country hit until 1965. Then he exploded on the scene: his next twenty-four singles, over a seven-year period, all reached at least the Top 3; of these, twenty-three went to No. 2 and twenty-two to No. 1, including an unbroken record of *sixteen* consecutive chart-toppers! It seems odd that with *twenty-three* No. 1s, he has never won a CMA Award. His achievements merit selection into the Hall of Fame.

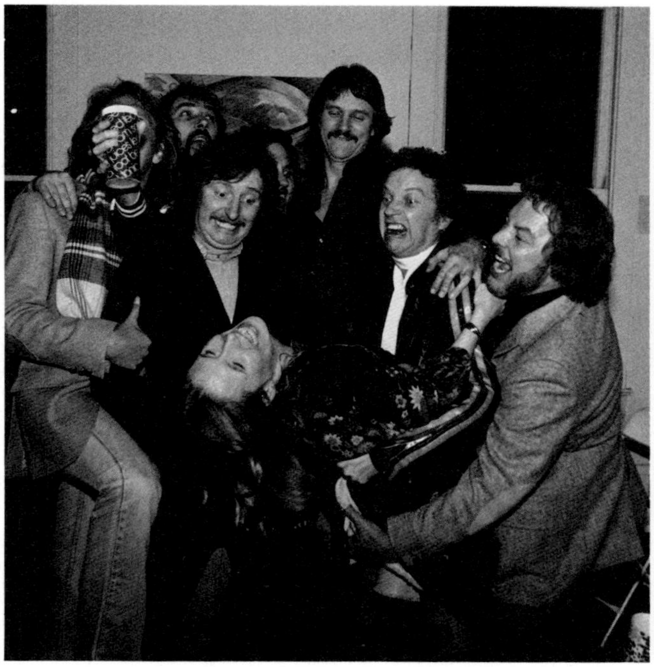

Left: *Picalic Inc. den mother Anita Hogin seems to be enjoying her ravishment at the hands of (left to right) Roger Cook, Frank Sheen, Craig Benson (partially hidden), Ralph Murphy, Tony Newman, and Charles Cochran. (Photo: Melodie Gimple)*
Right: *In this 1971 photo, Sonny James demonstrates what every major singer spends hours doing—looking for a hit. (Photo: Marshall Fallwell, Jr.)*

A Song's Journey From Idea to Hit

THE FIRST STEPS OF A SONG

Some years ago the Rolling Stones recorded a track with a key refrain that featured Mick Jagger singing, "It's the singer, not the song." No one in Nashville subscribes to this sentiment, however; the feeling in Music City is best summarized by the motto of the Nashville Songwriters Association, International: "It all begins with a song." It is a symbiotic relationship—a singer cannot function without a song to record and a song will languish forever without a singer to breathe life, meaning, and nuance into it.

How are those songs created and how do they get to the singers who so desperately need them?

Obviously, the songs are written by songwriters, but the methods and sources used by the writers are as different as the vocal shadings given the songs by their interpreters on vinyl. Some writers come to the office and write eight hours per day, putting in hours no different from those engaged in more conventional occupations. Bob McDill and the team of Rhonda "Kye" Fleming and Dennis W. Morgan put in their time between nine to five. Other writers do their work at home. Tom T. Hall likes to get up at 3:00 A.M. and write while most of Nashville sleeps. Some reach for inspiration as they fish, drive a car, sit in a bar, or play golf. Writer-performers have learned to scribble down the words to songs while traveling; many a song has begun with words hastily scribbled on napkins, menus, scraps torn from a paper sack, or the backs of business cards. Willie Nelson reports that he wrote "On the Road Again" while on a plane with film producer Sydney Pollack, taking five or ten minutes to get the words down. (However, the songs that Nelson wrote for his 1983 concept album *Tougher than Leather* took him over ten years to finish.)

Curly Putman (standing) and Bobby Braddock, authors of "He Stopped Loving Her Today," CMA Song of the Year in 1980 and 1981. Singly and together, they have won 45 BMI Awards for songwriting.

These last are writers who prefer a less regimented approach; they keep pad and pen handy and stand ready when inspiration strikes, feeling that songs that flow naturally are better than tunes that result from forced labor. Merle Haggard has told of writing several songs in one day while he drove his bus, with his then-wife Leona Williams frantically jotting down the words as he dictated them to her. Songwriters also keep paper and pen by the bed in case ideas come calling in their dreams. They waken long enough to scrawl a few words on the pad and return to sleep; in many cases, when morning comes they don't recall writing down the words.

Whatever the method of creation, once a song is written it must be recorded in order to make money for its writer and publisher. (The two generally share in the income generated on an equal basis.) Naturally, a singer who writes songs has a distinct advantage here over a writer who isn't also a recording artist. But there are pitfalls in this situation: singers who also write aren't always the best judges of their own efforts and often spurn better outside material in favor of mediocre selections they have written themselves.

Once a song is written it is put on a tape, or "demoed," as it is known in the business. (The exception to this procedure is the song written by a recording artist; why "demo" a song if you're going to record it yourself? In this case the finished track will function as the demo.) A songwriter obviously can't take the time to go around all day personally singing and playing the song to singers and producers. So a demo recording is made, usually at a studio considerably less elaborate than the type used for master sessions. The demo recording quite often consists of simply a vocal with guitar or piano, sung by the writer or by singers who have yet to land

Tom T. Hall, "The Storyteller," finishes one up in the studio. (Photo: Beth Gwinn)

TOM T. HALL *(PolyGram)*

"The Storyteller" came out of a town in Kentucky on few maps to become one of country music's all-time top songwriters: he has won twenty-seven BMI writing awards, five of them before "Harper Valley P.T.A." took him and Jeannie C. Riley to stardom. In 1971 he took to performing. Despite a mediocre voice, he posted seven No. 1 singles (all of his composition) by 1976 before cooling off. His best-known songs include "The Year Clayton Delaney Died," "Margie's at the Lincoln Park Inn," "Old Dogs and Children and Watermelon Wine," and "I'm Not Ready Yet." He has also written three books, including a novel. A Democrat who is very active in politics, he was once mentioned as a possible gubernatorial stalking-horse, and he still maintains relations with Billy Carter. He lives in Brentwood, Tennessee, with his wife, Dixie, and several hound dogs, where he rises early to work during the quiet hours. Possible Hall of Famer.

their own recording deals. (Janie Fricke, Karen Taylor-Good, and Kathy Mattea are three examples of singers who "graduated" from doing demo work to their own label pacts.) The idea here is not to turn in a virtuoso vocal performance, just to put the song on tape so that the words and melody can be plainly heard. If the writer has an adequate voice and can stay in time, on pitch, and in key, then that's sufficient for demo purposes. Writers who aren't good singers use a skilled vocalist. Or, if the song was written by a man for recording by a woman artist, or vice versa, the writer will need to use a singer of the opposite sex. If the song will be pitched as a male-female duet, then naturally the writer may want a singer of each gender.

In recent years a second school of thought has emerged in regard to demos. Some people in the business feel that a demo should be more elaborate and will go into the studio with a full rhythm section and written arrangements. While this approach does "dress up" the song, it costs more money and certainly does not guarantee that the song will be cut. When demos are made in this fashion it isn't unusual to find the same arrangement copied and slightly embellished on the finished track after the master session, overdubbing, and mixing are done.

When the demo is completed to everyone's satisfaction, the publisher then goes to work "pitching" the song to producers, artists, and record label representatives who evaluate material (known as A & R staffers). Prudent songwriters will also take part in this process of selling their song, some via the tape route and some by the more direct method of playing the song in person. The top writers will receive a steady stream of guests who are interested in hearing the new material the writer has completed.

Besides Miss Kimberly's method of putting a large sign next to a producer's car, songs have been pitched and recordings gained in many interesting ways. Kris Kristofferson, a licensed pilot, rented a helicopter and landed it in Johnny Cash's yard to pitch him "Sunday Morning Coming Down." Danny Tate and Blaise Tosti's song, "Affair of the Heart," reached Rick Springfield when Tosti followed Springfield into the men's room at the Hollywood Palace in Los Angeles, passing the singer a cassette while he passed water. The late Roger Bowling, writer of "Coward of the County," "Lucille," "Blanket on the Ground," and many other hits, got those songs cut in an even more unusual manner: he won four thousand dollars in a poker game with producer Larry Butler. Butler was about to be married (again) at the time and didn't have the money, so the two agreed Butler would pay Bowling off by recording some of his songs on a then washed-up pop singer by the name of Kenny Rogers, at the time trying a country comeback.

Naturally, the publisher tries to match a song to the style, range, and lyric content favored by a particular singer. (He will also know whether the producer, artist, manager, or other person responsible for screening material prefers to receive a tape on a reel-to-reel or cassette format.) No matter how well written the song is, there's no point in taking a cheating song to Don Williams or a song about a four-day drunk to Barbara Mandrell. Conway Twitty doesn't record any songs that put women in a bad light and it is doubtful that Alabama would sing about getting high on anything but love or nature. Songs pitched to the Oak Ridge Boys must have four-part harmonies involved, and Larry Gatlin tries to write all his own material. Hank Williams, Jr., isn't a likely candidate to cut "New York, New York" or any song placed north of the Mason-Dixon line.

Astute publishers also keep their ears to the ground to learn what particular type of song certain artists or their producers are seeking at any moment. If an artist is looking for a positive, uptempo love song, then there's little sense in bringing over a sad, slow ballad. This kind of information isn't printed in the trade papers or "tip sheets" that keep track of who is cutting and what they are seeking. It can only be gleaned from phone calls and personal relationships with those in a position to know what each artist currently seeks.

Once a song is pitched, the chances are the publisher won't hear anything if the artist or producer "passes" (turns down) the song. In theory, they should get the tape back with a note saying, "Thanks, but no thanks" or a phone call expressing these sentiments, but, in reality, since the top artists are swamped with hundreds of songs before they go in to record, such a courtesy is not often extended.

If there is interest in the song, the publisher will be contacted directly with a request to "hold" the song (discontinue pitching it to others). This usually means that the song is one of several that the artist feels strongly about and would like more time to consider. The length of time a publisher holds a song is entirely up for negotiation and must be balanced against the interest others have shown in it and the airplay expectations of the artists involved if more than one has expressed interest.

(It should be noted here that this situation is true only if the song has not been recorded. If the tune has appeared on vinyl before, anyone can record it without permission merely by filing a notice-of-use form with the publisher, a situation known as compulsory copyright. Thus, the only time a publisher or writer has any control over who records a song is at the beginning of the song's existence.)

LARRY GATLIN AND THE GATLIN BROTHERS *(Columbia)*

The west Texan Gatlins are led by the oldest brother, Larry, who writes the material, publishes it, and produces their records. Larry was discovered by Dottie West, who heard him singing gospel songs in Las Vegas. His superb voice generally deserves better songs than those he writes. The group's best years to date were 1977–80, when they made such hits as "Love Is Just a Game," "Night Time Magic," "Statues Without Hearts," "I Just Wish You Were Someone I Love," and "All the Gold in California." The Gatlins made a strong comeback in 1984 by incorporating Western swing touches; they tallied their biggest hits in five years with "Houston (Means I'm One Day Closer to You)" and "Denver," both produced by Rick Hall. Although they are good live performers, they'd be better if Larry wouldn't sit on a stool throughout. (Old bluesmen, Chet Atkins, and flamenco guitarists can sit down onstage, but a young, athletic country singer can't work a crowd properly from a seated position!)

Left: *Nashville emigré John Prine in the studio. (Photo: Marshall Fallwell, Jr.)* Right: *Songwriter/singer Mickey Newbury led a parade of Texas writers to Nashville during the 1970s, a list that includes Rodney Crowell, Guy Clark, and Townes Van Zandt. (Photo: Alan Mayor)*

Left: *There might have been rock 'n' roll without Sam Phillips—but it wouldn't have arrived in 1956. Phillips's Nashville studio employed Billy Sherrill when he first came here from northern Alabama. (Photo: Marshall Fallwell, Jr.)*
Right: *Dallas Frazier accepts Songwriter of the Year Award from the readers of* Music City News *in 1982. (Photo: Robert K. Oermann)*

Once a hold has been placed on a song the writer and publisher keep their fingers crossed, hoping that the artist will take the song into the studio and record it. Even then, they aren't out of the woods. It's common practice for artists to record more songs than they actually need for an album. Most of today's records are composed of ten songs. Artists and producers will commonly cut from twelve to fourteen "sides," then listen to all of them before deciding which ten tracks will make up the finished record. A song that has been recorded but not released is said to be "in the can," a location from which it may or may not escape. Waylon Jennings is notorious for the number of songs he has canned up, and the career of the late Jim Reeves has continued virtually unabated for twenty years since his death because of the amount of unreleased material he had amassed. Perhaps the most legendary material in the can is the "Million Dollar Quartet" recordings taped by Jack "Cowboy" Clement while Elvis Presley, Jerry Lee Lewis, Carl Perkins, and Charlie Rich were all under contract to Sam Phillips at Sun Records in the mid-1950s. These recordings of the four stars have not been officially released in the United States, although "bootleg" (illegally duplicated) copies do exist. A fictional magazine story from the psychedelic 1960s told the tale of an entire album of vintage Beatles material in the can; the writer went so far as to title this imaginary disc *Hot as Sun.*

Why are songs left in this special form of limbo? Artists may feel their vocals weren't up to snuff. Sometimes the producer will decide the instrumental tracks didn't "sparkle" with enough luster to merit release. Maybe that song just didn't fit well with the others on the album. Sometimes a really exceptional song is found just before recording is completed; adding the new entry when there are already ten songs on the record means that a song must be bumped. Sometimes the producer may not care for the overall "feel" of the song or maybe the project is over budget and he hasn't the funds left to add the string or horn parts he feels are necessary. Whatever the reason, having a song in the can leaves the writer and publisher with a bittersweet feeling.

When the song does make it onto the final disc, the writer and publisher wish, hope, drop down on their knees, pray, beg, and lobby for their song to be issued as a single release.

Why? Money and exposure. Songwriters and publishers gain income from two major sources: sales of the tunes on disc and exposure of the songs on broadcast sources, particularly radio. Country radio play lists are composed of current singles and golden oldies; while a single could easily log several hundred thousand performances in a few months, very few album cuts gain significant airplay.

A hit country song today will generate more money from airplay than sales, even though the amount paid to the publisher from sales of his songs on record was increased by the Copyright Act of 1976. The first Copyright Act was established in 1909. It required record labels to pay publishers 4¢ per song per record sold. That rate continued in effect for the next sixty-seven years, a circumstance that may give the reader a clue regarding the relative clout of record companies compared to that of publishers. (It's safe to say the labels raised the price of records a few times during this period.) The new copyright law raised this rate to 4¾¢, with provisions for gradual increases every two years until the entire situation would again be reviewed by the newly created Copyright Royalty Tribunal in 1987.

Since there are now over 2,200 full-time country radio stations, a hit record will accumulate an enormous amount of airplay income, funds that are collected by either Broadcast Music Incorporated (BMI) or the American Society of Composers and Publishers, the two major performance rights groups. (BMI is owned by broadcasters, ASCAP is owned by writers and publishers. A third group, SESAC, is privately owned and operates on a much smaller scale than BMI or ASCAP.) A song generates income, generally a few cents, each time it is played on the radio. The performance groups monitor radio stations on a sampling basis, then extrapolate to arrive at an approximation of the total airplay any song receives in any given period. The money to pay the writers and publishers these sums is paid to the performance rights society by each broadcast source according to a formula based on a percentage of its advertising revenues.

Broadcast sources pay annual fees to the performance rights groups for a "blanket license"—the right to use any songs in the repertoire of the group. Under this system, a modest country hit, say one that reaches the Top-15 level on the national charts, can earn the writer and the publisher $20,000. It would take sales of 800,000 copies to return that same $20,000 to the writer and publisher based on a payment of 5¢ per copy from the label to the publisher. There aren't many country singles that sell 800,000 copies. (In 1983 there were only forty-seven singles in all forms of music that sold a million copies, the number necessary for a 45 to earn certification as a "gold" single. John Anderson's "Swingin'" and the Kenny Rogers/Dolly Parton collaboration "Islands in the Stream" were the only gold country singles. Two million in sales of a single earns a disc a "platinum" certification, an honor accorded to only two records in 1983—Toni Basil's "Mickey" and the Rogers/Parton duet.)

The last few paragraphs presented a simplified explanation of how the system works when a song is released as a single. But, before the song gets to that stage, several steps must be taken. The next step in a song's journey from its birth to a place in the charts is another trip into the recording studio. This time, however, it won't be for demo purposes but at a master session. Why don't we proceed along and see what a Nashville recording session is like?

INSIDE THE STUDIO

There are five major components in a recording session: the song, the singer, the producer, the engineer, and the session musicians (or "players"). While it is technically possible with modern equipment for one person to write, sing, produce, engineer, and play all the instruments, as is the case with some of Paul McCartney's work, some of Todd Rundgren's discs, and recent records by Eddy Grant, John Fogerty, and Prince, I cannot recall any country recording done in this manner.

Many writers are also recording artists (Willie Nelson, Merle Haggard, Dolly Parton, Hank Williams, Jr., and Eddie Rabbitt, among others), and many singers are also involved in production. But, in most cases, singers will yield part of the control of their recording to an outside party.

Some of today's Nashville producers of the "old school" prefer to engineer the records they produce, but most will leave the minute dial settings to an engineer while they concern themselves with the overall sound or "feel" of the music.

MARTY ROBBINS
(Columbia)

Marty came out of Arizona in the early 1950s to become one of country's biggest stars. An entertainer deluxe, he wrote and sang hits drawn from all areas of America's pop music heritage. He was a regular for thirty years on the Opry until death claimed him late in 1982. One of the most popular country stars, Robbins was a Hall of Fame choice two months before he died. That was a fitting achievement, since he never won a CMA Award. "El Paso," which he wrote, was his most famous song, but Marty was also one of the premier balladeers of the music world, a talent evidenced in such immortal songs as "Among My Souvenirs," "You Gave Me a Mountain," "Don' Worry," and the tune that became his epitaph—"Some Memories Just Won't Die." The memory of Marty Robbins will also live, if not forever, then at least as long as country music does.

HANK WILLIAMS, JR.
(Warner Bros.)

The son of one of America's finest singer-songwriters, Hank seemed to have also inherited his father's inner turmoil. Wrecked cars, broken marriages, whiskey, pills, and a suicide attempt almost claimed him before he suffered a near-fatal fall down the side of Ajax Mountain in Montana. Since then, he has settled down to become a great songwriter, gifted singer, ferocious guitarist, compelling entertainer, and one of the top concert attractions in music. Hank sings his father's songs, his own, and those of everyone else from Robert Johnson and John Lee Hooker to the Allman Brothers and ZZ Top. On the cutting edges between country, rock, and blues, Hank draws a crowd so young that few are old enough to remember the Beatles, much less his father. At thirty-six, he has had twenty-three years of live performance experience. Within a decade, he should be in the Hall of Fame.

Gene Watson and Chubby Wise, one of country music's best fiddlers, listen to a playback in this 1970 photo.
Opposite: *Jimmy Bowen wears a hat indoors. You could too if you've produced Frank Sinatra, Crystal Gayle, Conway Twitty, Dean Martin, Hank Williams, Jr., George Strait, and the West Coast Pop Art Experimental Band. Bowen also heads MCA Records's Nashville office. (Photo: Beth Gwinn)*

JIM GLASER *(Noble Vision)*

Quiet, firm, soft-spoken, highly professional, and technically gifted are terms that apply to the youngest member of the award-winning Glaser Brothers. The group became famous in the late 1960s, but Jim was overshadowed by the more flamboyant Tompall and the more methodical Chuck, the most business-minded of the trio.

Though the Glasers enjoyed considerable success on the charts from 1967–73, Jim began trying to establish a solo career as early as 1968. He labored in vain for years to post a hit as a vocalist despite such songwriting successes as "Woman, Woman," a 1967 pop hit for Gary Puckett and the Union Gap.

In 1983 Jim made another try as a soloist, this time on a tiny independent label called Noble Vision, brainchild of former A & M Records promotion man Don Tolle. To the astonishment of everyone, he posted six Top-20 records from his first album, including "You're Gettin' to Me Again," a No. 1 smash in the fall of 1984. Now established as an airplay artist, Glaser has yet to flex the album-sales muscle that distinguishes the superstars from the near-greats.

A smooth balladeer, Glaser is widely regarded in Nashville as the most musically talented of the Glaser clan.

Though the common perception of recording sessions places them in the dead of night, most Nashville studio work is conducted from ten in the morning to nine at night. Sessions commonly run for three hours and are scheduled at ten, two, or six o'clock. The very best players can be booked to work for the same artist on each session or they may perform on different projects.

The normal country session will feature bass, drums, rhythm guitar, a keyboard instrument, an acoustic guitar, and possibly a steel guitar (though the use of a "steel" is not as prevalent as it was in previous years). The fancy lead guitar parts and other hot licks on fiddle, banjo, dobro, additional guitars, or other instruments are usually added later in "overdub" sessions, as are horns, strings, and backing vocals, according to the wishes of the producer.

To the uninitiated, a Nashville recording session looks so easy it's hard to believe that the participants are actually working. About a half-dozen people are in the studio, most dressed in duds like those you'd wear to go into the yard to pull weeds. They are standing around a tape recorder, listening to a demo of the song they will soon record. One of the group is scribbling numbers on a scrap of paper, using the Nashville number system (see example on page 168). At the finish of the demo, all the players nod, jot down the numerical notation from the session leader, then amble back to their instruments.

Though the informal dress and jocular attitude of the players may lead one to believe that they aren't taking the work seriously, their attitude becomes all business once the red light that indicates "live" recording flashes on. Within ten minutes, and often on the first "take" (attempt), this core group has "laid down" (recorded) the basic track for the record. While the take is in progress any of the assembled crew of "pickers" will signal if he or she catches a mistake. Quite often, the producer or engineer will hear a wrong note or an out-of-tune instrument and they will halt the machinery. The tape will spin back to the beginning and the process will start again.

Modern recording machinery exists that can simultaneously record on twenty-four, thirty-six, forty-eight, or more separate tracks, but most Nashville recording is accomplished on twenty-four track machines. When the basics are done, the engineer or producer takes a strip of tape and sticks it to the bottom of the recording console. This tape is then marked according to which instruments are on which tracks in the following manner:

1	2	3	4	5	6	7	8	9	10	11	12	13	14	15	16
	Drums		Rhythm Guitar	Rhythm Guitar	Bass Guitar	Piano		Lead Guitar	Lead Vocal	Harm. Vocals	Steel Guitar	Dobro	Strings	Sax	

It's customary to leave the first and last tracks blank since they are on the edges of the two-inch-wide tape and are thus more likely to be damaged than those nearer the middle.

This information is eventually transferred to a sheet of paper—all studios use preprinted forms for this purpose—which is then stored in the box with the master tape for reference during the later overdubbing and mixing stages. Woe to the engineer who loses this "map" of the recording of a song!

The singer, if he or she is present, may sing a "scratch" or reference vocal, but in many cases the star won't even come in during this stage, preferring instead to sing to the completed rhythm track at a later date. (There are, however, some artists who, feeling they will be more inspired by the presence of the backing musicians, try to go for a finished vocal during the session. Ricky Skaggs, Willie Nelson, the Kendalls, and Don Williams are among those who prefer this approach. If they don't get a satisfactory vocal on this attempt then they are still free to return and do it later.)

TELETRONIX
1
2
3
4
5
6
2

Faron Young, "The Singing Sheriff," stretches for a note in the studio. Some of Young's offstage shenanigans would embarrass George Jones. (Photo: Marshall Fallwell, Jr.)

Similarly, many duets are recorded by singers at different times and often at different studios. Even though two people are credited as partners, one should not assume that they were there to harmonize together in the studio. It's far more common for one to add his or her vocal half before or after the partner has done his or her portion. This is not due to any personal preference but because scheduling difficulties may arise when two major stars come together on a project.

In many cases the producer or engineer may feel that the take is almost there or that the crew can do just a *little* better, so, although the music may sound just fine, the process will be repeated. The first take is stored and the repeat will follow it on the master tape. It's not at all unusual for a crew of Nashville players to "hook it" (get a perfect take) on the first try. When this occurs most producers will punch the "talk-back" button (an intercom that connects them to the participants in the studio) and say, "Hey, that sounded real good. Why don't we do another just to be on the safe side?"

Once the producer and engineer are satisfied, one of them will punch the button and tell the players, "Sounds great, why don't we listen to a playback?" All ears then fasten onto the track as each player listens intently to make sure that everything is in order. If all is not right, then the miscreant who bungled is publicly embarrassed and the troupe does the track over until it's just right. If all is well, there will be congratulations all around; someone may sneak in a quick joke or tell a tale of someone else's rowdy behavior or compliment someone on his or her playing. Then it's back to the trenches for the next selection.

This method can yield two to five finished rhythm tracks for each three-hour session. It looks awfully simple, but the truth of the matter is that recording this way requires extraordinary musical ability, patience, and experience. This core group must play with the precision of a chamber music group to achieve a good take, and the pressure of recording the same song over and over in a room with no windows is very hard on the nerves.

Once this process is completed to the producer's satisfaction it's time to move on to an even more difficult stage—overdubbing and mixing.

Passing the torch—Willie Nelson records with Billy Joe Shaver's son Eddy, age 12.

OVERDUBBING AND MIXING

A novice to the recording process will have a hard time shaking the eerie feeling that will come over him during an overdubbing session. From the control room it sounds as if the entire crew of session musicians is out in the studio, playing furiously away. But, as he peers through the control-room glass, he may see only one person out there, painstakingly adding a part to the basic tracks. This process is called overdubbing—placing additional instrumentation or voices onto the basic tracks. Overdubbing is utilized because it's impractical to have everyone who makes a musical contribution to a record do so simultaneously. Besides the logistics involved in coordinating such a crowd, trying to record the rhythm track, background vocalists, string section, horn parts, singer, and other elements at one time would complicate matters tremendously. The various additional sounds are therefore placed on the record after the rhythm tracks have been made.

During this stage the singer may put down a finished vocal or maybe just "punch in" a few notes here and there.

Modern recording equipment has made this possible. Up until the late 1950s all recording machinery consisted of but one track, so all the sounds captured on tape had to be recorded simultaneously. When two-track recording was invented, recording artists could then record the instruments and the vocals on two separate tracks. The tape could then be played back and one of the tracks could be redone without erasing the other. (Many home machines offered for sale today have this feature, which is a boon to anyone who needs to record vocal and instrumental tracks separately.)

Once the recording technology was created for two-track machines, it didn't take long for the two-track to yield to three-, four-, and then eight-track machines. Today's recording equipment is so sophisticated that forty-eight, sixty-four, or even more tracks can be recorded separately, a process unnecessary for most popular music but of considerable value in the recording of music using a full orchestra or for movie soundtrack purposes.

DONNA FARGO
(Columbia)

The teaching profession's loss became country music's gain in the early 1970s when Donna's two hits, "Happiest Girl in the Whole U.S.A." and "Funny Face"—both composed by her—blanketed pop, country, and a-c radio. Born in North Carolina and raised in southern California, Donna has posted six No. 1 country singles, won a CMA Award, a Grammy, and eleven BMI citations. Her husband, Stan Silver, acts as her producer and manager. In 1978, she learned that she had multiple sclerosis, an affliction that forced an end to her heavy appearance schedule. Since her illness was diagnosed, she has continued to tour on a limited basis and has posted chart discs every year. She also works tirelessly to help others with the same affliction. Her courage in the face of disaster deserves a higher award than the CMA or the National Association of Recording Arts and Sciences (NARAS) can give. A velvet butterfly with a will of steel.

When all the overdubbing is complete, the most tedious part of the recording process begins: mixing. Basically, this aspect involves balancing the sounds on all the tracks with one another to create the most pleasing overall sound. Mixing also involves deciding which sounds to subtract from the finished tape—as opposed to overdubbing, in which sounds are being added to the tape. The mixing process usually involves only the producer and engineer, although in some cases artists prefer to be included. Those who are on hand to mix the tape must be rather patient individuals; the basic tape will be replayed dozens, even hundreds of times before everyone is satisfied that the finished work sounds as good as is humanly possible. With today's advanced recording equipment there are literally thousands of variations possible for any sound on any one track. When you have sixteen, twenty, or twenty-four tracks involved, each with thousands of possible variations, the combinations soar well into the millions. It is common for this mixing phase to require more time than the initial recording and overdubbing phases put together.

(One of the catch phrases in Nashville studios is, "Oh well, we'll fix it in the mix." While some things can be masked or enhanced during this process, it should be remembered that the mixing phase involves no added instrumentation. You've got to work with what's already there. If a song gets to this stage and it is discovered that the drum or bass track does not mesh with the rest of the sound, the producer is stuck—he can't go back and overdub the instruments that comprise the basic rhythm track since all that has followed was keyed to them. When this situation arises, it's a sure sign of inexperience or ineptitude on the part of the producer and the engineer; one or the other should have caught such a basic mistake long before the mixing stage.)

When that final mix has been accomplished, then it is time to transfer the sixteen or twenty-four tracks to a two-track copy, a process called the "mix-down." During this phase, all the sounds on the two-inch recording tape are switched to a two-track tape that measures one-quarter inch in width. This step is necessary for the next procedure in the recording process—mastering.

MASTERING AND PRESSING

Mastering is the last step a tape goes through before it is taken to the pressing plant to be miraculously transformed into a flat disc for shipment to wholesalers and retailers. The art of mastering a record requires such unique technical knowledge and skill that there are many who specialize in this phase of the recording process exclusively. They are known as mastering engineers, and the best ones are in great demand, for this stage represents the last opportunity to catch any mistakes or make any changes before the tape becomes vinyl. The producer, engineer, and sometimes the artist will be present during a mastering session. All will listen as intently as possible, desperately straining to mentally step back so they can listen to the tape with a fresh perspective.

The end result is a reference disc, also known in the trade as a lacquer. It's the size of a twelve-inch disc and looks like one except for the plain white label from the mastering lab that identifies the artist, title, label, and record number. All the participants take copies of this lacquer home and listen to it there as well as in the studio, in their office, or in whatever location they most prefer. "Vinyl is final" in this business—once the order is given to press a record there's no turning back!

When everyone is satisfied that the final mastered copy sounds as good as it possibly can, the lacquer is taken to the pressing plant to be made into records for shipment to wholesalers, retailers, and radio. The mechanical steps involved in this process are every bit as technical and highly specialized as those in the recording, mixing, and mastering stages. The complex process involved in this area has engendered a technical jargon unique to this phase of the industry. That lingo encompasses such words as "mother"—the disc from which the records are stamped out as they are pressed—and many other arcane terms best left to the specialists.

The fruit of their labors is a completed record, all labeled and boxed, ready to be shipped to sellers, radio stations, and those in the business whose chore it is to listen to and review new products of the recording arts. The chain of events that began with the scribbling of a few words on paper has now culminated in a finished record.

Now a new series of events begins to unfold—discovering if radio will like the record enough to play it and if the public will cherish it enough to purchase it.

RADIO

Now that the record has been written, demoed, pitched, held, recorded, overdubbed, mixed, mastered, pressed, and shipped, the radio stations that play country music have the task of deciding whether or not to give it public exposure. Today that job is infinitely more complicated than it was thirty years ago when there were far fewer country stations and far fewer records released in any given week. The latest figures compiled by the Country Music Association show that there are 2,265 radio stations that play country records full-time. Most of the major companies will ship at least one copy of the record to each of those stations, a process that costs nearly two thousand dollars in postage alone for every single issued.

Instead of the two-sided record that is made available to retailers and jukebox buyers, the stations receive one-sided records. Actually, these do have two sides—but both contain the same song. The labels do this to prevent stations from splitting the airplay on any given release; it won't do a great deal of good if 1,500 stations play the "A" side while the other 765 are play-

T. G. SHEPPARD
(Warner Bros.)

Born Bill Browder in Texas, Sheppard moved to Memphis at age sixteen. He later launched his show business career there as Brian Stacy, but pop audiences weren't impressed. He became Bill Browder again and began a new career as a men's clothing salesman before landing a job as a promo man for RCA.

He found a song by Bobby David ("Devil in the Bottle") but couldn't attract any major label interest. He signed on with Melodyland Records, a newly formed country division of Motown Records, a company known for black artists such as the Supremes, Stevie Wonder, Marvin Gaye, and the Jacksons.

Bill became T. G. Sheppard at that point. He scored a No. 1 with "Devil in the Bottle" and followed it with additional hits. T. G. moved over to Warner Bros. in 1974 and tallied his first No. 1 there in 1979. He has enjoyed eleven chart-toppers there through the end of 1984, though his success with singles has far surpassed his album-sales figures. Smart, hard-working, and personable, Sheppard has made the most of his somewhat limited talent and is also known as a very alert businessman.

Susan Anton, T. G. Sheppard, and two unidentified dancers work on their disco steps during an appearance on "The Mike Douglas Show."

ing the "B," or flip, side. This will result in confusion and less concentrated airplay. And, in today's highly competitive world of radio airplay, concentrated turntable spins lead the way to hit status.

When a record arrives at a radio station, it is placed in a stack with the other new releases that have arrived during the week. The number of new releases varies from week to week and can range up to one hundred. The music director and the program director (MD and PD, respectively) of each station have the unenviable chore of deciding which of the new records will be played, which will be ignored, and which will be held over for consideration the following week. After the selection process is done, most stations end up adding from two to six records. As of mid-1985, the average play list of a station included only forty songs.

Of the 2,265 country stations, about 400 are monitored weekly to determine which records are the most popular in the United States. These outlets, known as "reporting stations," notify one or more of the four trade publications that monitor the music industry of their selections weekly. The four publications are *Billboard, Radio 'n' Records, The Gavin Report,* and *Cashbox,* listed in order of importance. Each publication depends on one to two hundred stations for reports. There is some overlap among reporting stations; the biggest and most influential radio outlets report to all four publications, some report to three, some to two, and the remainder to one of the four magazines.

Billboard and *Radio 'n' Records* are by far the most important of the four publications today. The two magazines compile their charts in a different manner: *Billboard*'s lists are compiled with consideration of airplay and sales while *Radio 'n' Records*'s chart is assembled with airplay as the sole criterion, as does *The Gavin Report. Cashbox* compiles its charts using methods akin to *Billboard*'s. *Billboard* and *Cashbox* list one hundred records in their charts while *Radio 'n' Records* carries fifty and *The Gavin Report* uses thirty. Not surprisingly, the competition to get a record played on the reporting stations is fierce.

If this were a perfect world, the MD and PD would listen to each record in its entirety, then make the decision to play or not to play a record based only on the intrinsic merit of the disc. In reality, the first step taken is to weed out records on small labels, discs by artists far past their glory years, and platters by artists whose names aren't known. These are given or thrown away, a process that reduces the size of the pile under consideration dramatically.

The remaining records are then divided into two stacks: the first consists of discs by the top stars. These are usually put into the station's "rotation," or play list, quickly. The rest are left in a stack of records that will receive further consideration.

The job of getting records in the "further consideration" pile played is the responsibility of the promotion department of each record label. These hard-working men and women call each reporting station weekly and do their best to have these records added to the list of discs that the station plays. Many companies also engage independent promotion people when they feel a record will need extra assistance. These "indies" simultaneously work several different records from different labels. Often, the publishing company that publishes the song, the artist, or the act's management will engage independents, in the hope that their relationships and credibility with the MDs and PDs will prove to be vital. They are paid two to three thousand dollars (for the "life" of the record) or are engaged by the week ($250). In many cases their efforts mean the difference between success and failure.

The conversation that transpires between a label or independent promo person and a radio station functionary may well seem ridiculous to an outsider, but it is a very serious matter to all who are involved with the record under consideration. A typical dialogue sounds something like this:

Promo: Hi Joe, how's it going today?
MD/PD: Oh, okay, how're you doing?
Promo: Pretty good. I was wondering how you're feeling this week about "Dogfight," our new single on Kitty Katt?

MD/PD: I dunno, it's on my desk right now. What's it do in the charts next week?
Promo: Goes into *Billboard* at 83 with a bullet.
MD/PD: I'm not sure that it's right for my market. Is Joe Doe playing it at WACK?
Promo: He says he'll go on it if Dan Tan plays it at WUKE. Dan told me last week he's strongly considering it.
MD/PD: Is Bob Cobb on it at WOMB?
Promo: Added it as an extra yesterday.
MD/PD: Then I'll listen to it again. Call me back in a few days. I make my picks on Wednesday. Lemme know if Joe or Dan puts it on the air before then.

Sharp-eyed readers may have noted that the quality of the record doesn't seem to be an important consideration. Acceptance at key radio stations and chart ranking are much more important factors today than artistic merit.

The average promotion person will make 90 to 120 such calls every week, and in most cases he or she will be working on two to ten different records. When the record does reach one or more of the charts of the four trade papers, his/her job becomes easier in some respects but more difficult in others. Some stations wait for "chart action" before they add a disc, so it becomes easier to get a record played once it is anointed by national chart recognition. Other stations, however, require a record to attain a greater degree of chart success than this. They may not add the record until it hits the Top 60, 50, 40, 30, or even Top 20. In rare instances a station may not *ever* play certain releases, even if they go to the top of the charts. The MD, PD, or both may simply dislike the record, they may feel that it isn't the right record for their listeners, or they may have a personal feud going with the artist or his/her label. Records by artists perceived as being too "hard country" (traditional) may be excluded by stations in urban areas, a situation that has prevented Ricky Skaggs and George Jones records from receiving unanimous airplay.

Conversely, radio in more rural areas may feel that particular records aren't country *enough,* a fate that befell Ronnie Milsap's "Stranger in My House" and T. G. Sheppard's "Without You" in 1983, in spite of the fact that each artist had posted nine consecutive country No. 1s over the three preceding years.

Obviously, a new record would never get charted if all the reporting stations waited for chart action. Fortunately, there are a few dozen stations that will add a new record, even one by a new artist, as soon as it is released. These stations are known as "starter stations"; by accumulating enough points with them a record can gain entry to the charts and rise to a point when it will be considered by the majority of the reporting outlets.

That word "charts" keeps cropping up. Let's head on to a brief look at what these charts are, how they work, and how they influence what you hear on the radio every day.

THE CHARTS

As the ultimate umpires of a record's progress or lack of movement, the charts published weekly in the four music trade magazines are alternately cursed and praised, depending on how the records released by any particular company fare in a given week. Each of the four trade publications has its own method of compiling a chart, and it would be far too exhausting a project to explain the methods of all. Our time would be better served if we focus on one chart and examine it in some detail. For this purpose, let's look at the country singles chart published by *Billboard,* the oldest and most widely read trade paper in the record business.

Billboard began publication in 1905. Its first chart listing country records was published in 1948 under the title of "Best Selling Folk and Country & Western Records." It has continued to publish such a weekly list in the thirty-seven years since. That first chart listed only fifteen records; today one hundred appear each week under the title of "Hot Country Singles."

DON WILLIAMS *(MCA)*

Known as "The Gentle Giant," Don grew up in south Texas, near Floydada. In the late 1960s, he was lead singer for Pozo Seco Singers, a group that had several minor pop hits. When the group disbanded, Don moved to Nashville to work for Jack "Cowboy" Clement and Allen Reynolds, founders of JMI Records. After making two albums for JMI, he departed for ABC (now MCA) and, in 1974, began posting No. 1s. Quiet and religious, Don has been happily married for over twenty years. His idea of a high time is taking his two sons fishing or hunting. As smooth as Jim Reeves and as straight as a West Texas highway, Don is parsimonious with words and has been called country music's Gary Cooper. He has won two CMA Awards and is a superstar in England, where Eric Clapton and Pete Townshend are among his admirers. Possible Hall of Famer.

JOHNNY LEE *(Full Moon/Asylum)*

The second-most-famous star from Gilley's nightclub, Johnny was raised on a dairy farm in Alta Loma, Texas, just south of Houston. He was involved in rock in the early 1960s. Later in the decade, he served in the navy, spending some time in Vietnam. He finagled Gilley into letting him sit in with him and eventually was hired to play trumpet in the combo. Minor hits on ABC/Dot and GRT preceded his "Lookin' for Love" smash from the film *Urban Cowboy* in 1980. Until early 1983 he toured with Gilley but now headlines on his own. He was married to television actress Charlene Tilton ("Dallas").

JANIE FRICKE *(Columbia)*

Countless back-up vocal sessions and commercial jingles preceded Janie's apparent "overnight" rise in 1982, when she was chosen CMA's Best Female Vocalist, a feat she repeated in 1983. A Hoosier by birth, she earned a degree from Indiana University before setting her sights on a music career in 1972. She arrived in Music City in 1975 by way of Dallas, Los Angeles, and Memphis. Her first big hit was a duet with Charlie Rich, "On My Knees," in 1978. In 1982, she broke through as a solo with the chart-toppers "Don't Worry 'bout Me Baby" and "It Ain't Easy Bein' Easy." Extensive touring with Alabama during this period aided her career considerably. She lives near Dallas with her husband-manager Randy Jackson, overseeing a menagerie that includes four buffaloes, three horses, two goats, and an albino donkey.

GLEN CAMPBELL
(Atlantic)

The road from Delight, Arkansas, to Hollywood doesn't stop in Nashville. Campbell's hits were recorded in California, a fact that did not prevent him from conquering the country charts many times, most memorably with "Gentle on My Mind," a John Hartford masterpiece. Glen's 1968 *Wichita Lineman* LP topped the *Billboard* pop charts—only the third country disc to do so. A formidable guitar picker, Campbell is a master of the a-c/country sound once referred to as "countrypolitan," now called "contemporary country." Campbell's well-publicized on-again, off-again romance with Tanya Tucker briefly threatened George Jones's position atop the gossip charts in 1981 and 1982. In 1984, Campbell began to inch his way back to country prominence through recordings made in Nashville with Harold Shedd, Alabama's producer.

Each record listed is identified by artist, label, and the record number each label gives to its releases. In addition, data about the songwriter(s), publisher(s), producer(s), and appropriate performance rights organization(s) is carried after the song, title, and artist identification. If you look at this chart, you will notice that some of the records have the number circled in black ink. This mark, known in the business as a "bullet," indicates the records that are, to quote *Billboard,* "demonstrating the greatest airplay and sales gains this week (Prime Movers)." Some fifty-five to sixty records receive this coveted designation in any given week. Once a record gains a place on the chart its progress becomes easy to monitor. If it has a bullet it will invariably advance in next week's chart—unless it's No. 1, in which case it has nowhere to go but down. If the disc does not have a bullet it will begin to plummet from the chart, an occurrence label personnel describe thusly: "It was 93 with a parachute."

That's clear enough, but how does a record gain entry on that select list of one hundred in the first place? Records gain entry to the *Billboard* chart by accumulating points from the approximately 130 radio stations that have been designated *Billboard* reporting stations by the magazine. The magazine also gives each station a "weight" of either six, four, three, two points, or one point according to its judgment of the station's relative importance. If the record is added at a station playing sixty-five or fewer records it will receive the weight of the station (six, four, three, two, or one points). If a station plays more than sixty-five records, the record must rank from No. 1 to 65 on its local chart in order to earn any points. In February of 1985 there were ten six-pointers, thirty-six were tagged as four-point outlets, two were worth three points, twenty-three were rated at two points, and the remaining fifty-nine stations carried the weight of but one lonely point.

Each of the 130 stations publishes its own local chart weekly. They transmit this chart to *Billboard,* the results are fed into a computer, and a point readout is made for every record each week. How many points does it take to gain entry into this elite circle of the nation's top one hundred records? Well, that depends on how many records are in competition during a week and how their points stack up with each of the other releases. As a practical matter it usually takes forty-five to sixty points for a record to be added to *Billboard*'s chart. Six to ten records are added in each week in the order of their point totals.

Records can also accumulate points once they reach the level of forty or better on the local charts. Bonus points are given for each five notches a record advances up these local charts, so a record that advances from any number above forty to a number from thirty-five to forty will receive one bonus point. If the record moves from any number above forty to numbers thirty through thirty-five it will receive an additional bonus point. An extra bonus point is given for a No. 1 record. The maximum number of bonus points possible then would be nine, one for each five-point hop and one for being the top record on the local chart that week.

Once a record makes the charts it will advance, decline, or hold its position according to this same internal point schedule. The higher up the chart a record advances, the more points it takes to continue the climb.

When a record ascends into the Top 30 an additional factor is introduced: sales. *Billboard* monitors local retail and wholesale outlets to see which records are actually being sold and which are simply "airplay hits," records that gain plenty of radio exposure but don't sell. Retail sales also gain points for the record, and these are added to the total resulting from the airplay movement.

It doesn't take a genius to figure out that these 130 stations and the people who report retail sales to *Billboard* are in a position of influence in the business. Though no one in the industry will admit to the practice, it's not unusual to find these individuals on the receiving end of free trips, merchandise, and other hard-to-trace favors best left to the imagination.

This intense effort to gain airplay and sales for singles seems strange, because the record business makes far more money from LP and cassette sales. Those configurations retail for six to ten times the shelf price of a single, and they far outpace 45s in terms of unit sales. In 1982, 425 million units of LPs and cassettes were sold, compared to 137 million singles.

Gary Stewart's talent deserves more attention than the rambunctious singer gives it. (Photo: Gary Gershoff)

JERRY REED

Known as "The Alabama Wildman," Jerry is actually a native of Atlanta. His accomplishments as a singer, actor, and guitarist have overshadowed his songwriting, which has earned him eighteen BMI Awards. Jerry was discovered by Bill Lowery and first recorded in 1955. Sixteen years of misses preceded Reed's first No. 1 in 1971, titled, ironically, "When You're Hot, You're Hot." His record career since then is dotted with far more misses than hits, although he struck pay dirt again in 1973, 1977, and 1982. During dry spells, he forged an acting career as Burt Reynolds's sidekick in the *Smoky and the Bandit* movies. Twice CMA Instrumentalist of the Year, Reed is more inclined to pick guitar—or fish—than most *anything* else. In 1984, he moved into film and video production with his own multimillion-dollar company, adding another important cog to Nashville's burgeoning visual arts industry.

In terms of gross dollars alone, singles represent a very small percentage of the total dollar income. But a hit single is a wonderful two- to four-minute advertisement for the album from which it springs—and it is a free ad that will be repeated thousands of times daily if the single is a smash hit nationally. Since country radio rarely plays album cuts anymore, a hit single is the major exposure that an album is likely to receive.

In bygone times, country albums were quite often composed of one or two hits and eleven or ten pieces of "filler," material far too weak to ever obtain release as a 45. Now that LP and cassette sales have become the dominant factor in the profit picture, labels and artists have upgraded their album song selection. Today, artists strive to go for a single every time a track is recorded. This is certainly a more cost-effective approach for the labels: each album can yield three, four, or even five singles (Anne Murray released five from her *Where Do You Go When You Dream* album). An LP will thus remain active on retail shelves for longer periods than in years previous, when an artist would issue a new disc every few months. Albums are too expensive now to release that often unless the artist routinely sells two hundred thousand copies each time, a total few acts in any popular field attain regularly. (The record company must pay the shipping costs to send records to retailers and wholesalers. It also pays the cost when the unsold discs are returned by the stores, a practice known in the business as "eating." "Yeah, we shipped one hundred thousand, sold twenty thousand, and wound up eating the other eighty thousand.")

Who buys country singles? Label sales personnel estimate that 50 to 75 percent of their singles sales are to jukebox operators. The remaining 25 to 50 percent are bought mainly in the South and Midwest. Thirty-five- to forty-nine-year-old women buy more country singles than any other group, demographic facts that the top country songwriters never forget.

Singles also represent a cheaper way to bring a new artist to the market. Today many artists can obtain only a "singles" deal from a major label. Quite often the release of a subsequent album by the artist is tied to chart performance of the single. ("We'll do an album when you get a single into the Top 20.") In 1982 RCA's country division began to experiment with the shortened LP concept, putting fewer tracks on an album and offering it for sale at a reduced price. This is a variation on the "EP" that first appeared in the 1950s. (The EP, or extended play disc, is the size of a 45 but it plays at 33 RPM speed and offers four songs instead of the two found on a single. Elvis issued many EPs and the Beatles were the last major act to issue them until the late 1970s.) Since singles sell for about $1.98 and albums cost the customer $7.00 and up, there's quite a bit of room for price maneuvering within this range by offering the consumer more music than a single but less than an album.

RCA's first efforts in this area were discs by Louise Mandrell, Leon Everette, and the duet team of Gary Stewart and Dean Dillon. The company dubbed the discs "mini LPs" and set a price that would permit retail sale at about five dollars for the six songs included. These packages were the same size and featured the graphics of a ten-cut album. They also contained liner notes, a glossy cover, and full recording information. As of the end of 1984, no other country labels had followed suit, although some diskeries were offering one or two dollars off list price for releases by their "developing artists."

As the reader may quickly surmise, the current chart system has many flaws in addition to the unfortunate concentration of power in a very small percentage of radio stations (less than 6 percent). As a result, the 2,135 nonreporting stations tend to ignore any local research and simply add records that make the *Billboard* chart, which prevents many fine records from having a chance to gain public exposure. The suggestion has been made that, given the computerization of modern times, this sample could be enlarged dramatically. Indeed, it's technically feasible to make each of those 2,265 country stations reporters by having each transmit its own chart to *Billboard*'s computer each week. Aside from the huge additional cost to *Billboard,* such an approach has not gained favor among the six biggest recording corporations that dominate country music. As things stand, they control about 97 percent of the Top 40 and thus are hardly interested in a method that would give the smaller labels a better chance to erode their dominance. Unless *Billboard* voluntarily decides to change the system, it appears that the current approach will be the one that determines which records you hear and which ones you don't for the immediate future.

HOW MUCH DOES A SUCCESSFUL RECORD EARN?

Now let's assume that a record does become a hit, that a song that started out as a few verses on a writer's pad is able to make it onto the radio, charges onto the trade lists, and finishes at or near the top of the country music charts. How much will that single make for the singer?

For the purposes of this exercise let's pretend that the hypothetical single "Dogfight" by Kitty Katt does become a big hit. Katt's contract calls for a royalty rate of 8 percent. The record sells 500,000 copies and the retail price is \$1.99. A math expert will then figure that Katt earned \$79,600 from the sales of "Dogfight" ($500 \times 1.99 \times 8\%$). Unfortunately this is true only in the dreams of would-be singing stars. In reality Katt would earn much less.

First of all, almost every recording contract stipulates that the record company be allowed a 10 percent "packaging deduction." This reduces our basic figure of \$1.99 per disc sold to \$1.79. The record companies also claim a 25 percent allowance for "free goods," records shipped free to radio, press, and television. This is also standard in most recording contracts, and it reduces the number of records that Katt is paid on from 500,000 to 375,000 copies.

A record company shouldn't have to pay Katt for records that were shipped but not sold, now should they? An unsold record shipped to retail but later sent back is known as a "return," and most recording contracts allow the label to deduct a "reasonable reserve" for returns. Katt's label deducts another 25 percent for a reserve, thus subtracting another 125,000 records from the amount Katt will be paid for selling. (If only 80,000 records are returned then Katt's account is credited later and adjustments are made.)

Now we are ready to begin figuring. Under the revised figures Katt's totals look like this: records sold (250,000) times the royalty rate (8%) times the base price (\$1.79). This figures up to a total of \$35,750 for Katt. Will this be the amount she receives from the label? No, because the label doesn't pay outright for the cost of making the record—it advances Katt the recording costs. In effect it makes Katt a loan to pay for the recording. The costs of making the record along with any other advances given to Katt must be deducted before Katt receives any money. Thus Katt will make what is left after recording costs, and any outstanding advances are deducted from the \$35,750.

Now let's further assume that "Dogfight" is included on Katt's album, *The Soulful Meows of Kitty Katt,* and that the record sells another 500,000 copies at a royalty rate of 9 percent. How much does Katt earn from the sales of this disc if the retail price is \$8.98? First, the packaging deduction (10%) reduces the base price from \$8.98 to \$8.08. The label's "free goods" policy is somewhat tighter, so only 20 percent is deducted for freebies, giving Katt a net sales figure of 400,000 copies. The "reasonable reserve" clause nicks off 25 percent of that 500,000 copies, which reduces Katt's net figure of sales to 275,000 copies. Katt thus earns $275{,}000 \times \$8.08 \times 9\%$, or \$200,750, before the label's further recoupment of recording costs and any outstanding advances.

Now this may sound like a lot of money, but remember that there were 275,000 copies of the album sold at retail for \$8.98. Thus the record that earned Katt \$200,000 less recording costs and advances generated 275,000 times \$8.98—or \$2,469,500—at the retail counter.

Anyone who studies the examples above can easily see why the artists spend a lot of their time out on the road playing for customers in a live situation at fees ranging from \$3,000 up to \$100,000 per night in addition to the income they can generate from the sales of merchandise at the shows, such as T-shirts, photo books, hats, sweaters, tapes, and other paraphernalia.

SHELLY WEST
(Warner Bros.)

In her mid-twenties, Dottie's only daughter made her own solo move in 1983 with "Jose Cuervo," an uproarious morning-after testimonial to tequila. In glamour and vocal ability, she can stand up to any of the new women singers. In 1982, she presented Dottie with her first grandchild, and she travels with her new daughter, Tess, in a "nursery on wheels." Her youth belies her seven years of onstage experience.

B. J. THOMAS
(Cleveland International)

In the course of his up-and-down career, this Texan singer has put forty songs on the pop charts and has scored No. 1 singles in country (three), pop (two), and a-c (four), the best known being "Raindrops Keep Fallin' on My Head," "Hooked on a Feeling," and "(Hey, Won't You Play) Another Somebody Done Somebody Wrong Song." Heavily into cocaine at one point, he turned his life around through a loving wife and religion. He sang only gospel in the late 1970s and won Grammys in that field annually from 1977–80. In 1983, he returned to secular music with "Whatever Happened to Old-Fashioned Love," which became a No. 1 smash. He has co-written two biographies of his life.

You can also see how tempting it is for an artist to try to record his or her own songs, since the income from the songs will supplement the recording figure. The biggest stars in music make the bulk of their income from live appearances rather than from recording unless they consistently sell lots of records, which will then entitle them to higher royalty rates and other contract concessions when a new recording pact is negotiated.

THE FUTURE OF COUNTRY MUSIC AND NASHVILLE

The Future of Country Music and Nashville

Since 1968 country music has expanded its territory so that it now includes styles or "flavors" to suit the taste of almost any listener. A large percentage of today's top country acts, among them Alabama, Eddie Rabbitt, the Oak Ridge Boys, Barbara Mandrell, Hank Williams, Jr., Crystal Gayle, Razzy Bailey, Rosanne Cash, Anne Murray, Lee Greenwood, T. G. Sheppard, Charly McClain, Kenny Rogers, and Ronnie Milsap, would have had most of their recent releases excluded from country radio play lists during all of the 1960s and most of the 1970s. Even though these artists sing country songs, the arrangements and modern production touches that make them appealing to a wide variety of fans today would have doomed the same records to airplay oblivion in previous years. The program directors (PDs), music directors (MDs), and consultants who, in place of the disc jockeys of yesterday, now make the programming decisions would have simply passed judgment upon them with a curt "too rock," "too pop," or "too adult-contemporary," evaluations that were damning indictments in the past.

Many veteran country writers, singers, and producers have remarked that the country music of today would have been considered rock in the 1950s and early 1960s. Could you imagine "9 to 5," "Drivin' My Life Away," or "Nobody" even making Top 20 on the country charts in 1959 or 1969 or even 1973? Yet all three were No. 1 country singles that also attained peaks of No. 1, No. 5, and No. 15 respectively on the pop charts in 1981 and 1982. How would Alabama have fared with "The Closer You Get" on the country lists way back in 1969?

Today it is nearly impossible for a well-known country singer to put out a "pop" record that will be rejected by country radio. And record producers and artists deliberately target their records to appeal to as many different kinds of audiences as is possible, a practice that has been termed "horizontal programming." It is now felt that a record must be a hit in at least three radio formats to really make the cash registers jingle. This "neither fish nor fowl" approach often results in records that sacrifice their country elements for enough pop touches to gain airplay on the "Hot 100" or adult-contemporary lists; in the process, these "slicked up" records usually lose the grit and soul that lie at the heart of country music. More production means more distractions in the way of hearing the feeling the singer puts into the song. Since country music is built around conveying emotion the extra production usually detracts from rather than enhances the song.

However, these production touches can also mean the difference between a record that sells 200,000 copies to an audience made up entirely of country listeners and one that crosses over to sell over a million copies to listeners in several formats. In view of such a payoff it's not surprising that many artists opt for an approach that attempts to "have its cake and eat it too" by combining country songs with pop production.

As more and more radio stations employ country formats it becomes even harder to determine what is and what isn't country music. The same rule that applies to committees is at work—the more members a committee has, the harder it is to reach a consensus. Now that there are over two thousand stations that program country music full-time, this "country music committee" has swollen to a size that makes a consensus impossible without the use of the almighty "Hot Country Singles" chart published by *Billboard* magazine.

Many of the MDs and PDs at these stations either are newcomers to radio or have recently moved over from pop and rock stations to country outlets. Naturally, those who were brought up on pop or rock 'n' roll will have wider definitions of country music than will long-time

CHARLY McCLAIN *(Epic)*

The most glamorous of the new female singers, Charly is a native of Memphis. Her frothy vocals draw from the more modern side of country. Though usually heard singing lushly produced ballads, Charly had her biggest hit with "Who's Cheatin' Who," a driving rocker. She has made more dramatic television appearances than any of country's young stars, with "Hart to Hart," "CHiPs," and "Fantasy Island" already to her credit. (Her husband is Wayne Massey, a star of daytime soaps.) In 1983, she and Mickey Gilley hit it big with "Paradise Tonight," and they continue to join forces as a duet team.

RAZZY BAILEY *(MCA)*

Alabaman Razzy Bailey was a honky-tonk and club veteran in the South for thirteen years before landing an RCA deal in 1979. Before this, the numerous discs he had made on smaller labels had gone nowhere, but with RCA he hit immediately, kicking off a string of twelve Top 10s by mid-1983, including consecutive No. 1s in 1980–82, highlighted by "Loving Up a Storm" and "She Left Love All over Me." Unfortunately, his success in radio was not followed by significant album sales. He wrote Dickey Lee's hit "9,999,999 Tears." Friendly and diligent, Razzy lives in Nashville with his wife, Sandra, and their children.

country programmers. The hard truth of the matter is that many of these radio workers don't really care a whit about what is and what is not country music. Their main concern is ratings, so they are content to "play the hits," whether it's Ronnie Milsap bemoaning the "Stranger in My House," Mickey Gilley and Charly McClain harmonizing on "Paradise Tonight," or Sylvia doing her best to deliver pop-slanted numbers. The higher a station's rating, or "numbers," in the periodic measurement by Arbitron, the largest such service, the more listeners that station theoretically has. A rise in this listening audience translates into a raise for the station's advertising rates.

If this sounds like the same game played by TV networks with their Nielsen ratings, it is. A radio station also has a finite amount of time to sell to advertisers, so the amount it can charge for this time determines its profit. It's a sad fact of our modern age that radio, like television, panders to the lowest common denominator. Today's country radio stations are more afraid of losing listeners by playing something different than they are interested in gaining listeners by daring to be unusual.

This muddled situation has gotten so confusing that Ikie Sweat, a fine country singer from Houston, was rebuffed when he made his last trip to Nashville to seek a record deal. He was told he was "too country." "If I'm 'too country' for Nashville," he lamented, "where do I go?" Where indeed!

Country purists don't need to swap acoustic guitars for synthesizers quite yet, however. The last few years have seen a resurgence in the popularity of traditional country stylists, such as Ricky Skaggs, George Strait, David Frizzell, Reba McEntire, Gene Watson, John Anderson, the Whites, John Conlee, and Earl Thomas Conley, who stepped into the traditional-country vacuum created by the pursuit of crossover hits by others. In addition, such grizzled warhorses as George Jones, Merle Haggard, Conway Twitty, and Johnny Rodriguez have been enjoying career resurgences. It's too early to tell whether this is a boom or just a boomlet, but it does offer some hope that country won't lose all touch with its basic elements in the years ahead.

Ironically, some of the artists who have had the most crossover success have found themselves on the pop charts without mounting a calculated campaign to get there. Way back in 1975 Waylon Jennings remarked, "I couldn't go pop with a mouthful of firecrackers," but the fact remains that he has had quite a bit of success on the "Hot 100" chart ever since. So far ten of his singles have made this elite list and two, "Good-Hearted Women" (the duet with Willie that helped launch the "outlaw" era) and "Luckenbach, Texas (Back to the Basics of Love)," have climbed to No. 25. What happened was not that Waylon "turned pop" but that the enormous influx of younger fans attracted to his outlaw image and the huge growth in country-formatted radio stations gave him the necessary airplay and sales to make headway on the pop charts.

Country music's future is uncertain—as is the future of life on this orb. If the cycles of boom and bust continue as they have in the past, country could well be riding for a fall. All types of popular music go through cycles of popularity; the public is a fickle master that tires very easily upon overexposure to any one type of music. So there would seem to be a down side in country's future, particularly since the music has been blanketing radio so thoroughly since 1980.

So the question then becomes: How far down? It would be easier to answer if country had remained a separate and distinct form of music rather than an amalgamation of many influences. Today if a record does well on the country charts then it is considered country regardless of how it sounds. My guess is that country music will lose some of its appeal but will bottom out at a level of popularity far above what it had attained before the English invasion of 1964.

The advancing age of the American population (our final "bumper crop" of babies came in 1964, the last year in which over four million were born) and country's increasing overseas appeal should combine to cushion any fall that may come from overexposure. It should also be remembered that country music today has a following among the under twenty-five set that it

GENE WATSON *(MCA)*

Silken-voiced Gene—one of the finest "pure" country singers around—was a mechanic and body man at a repair shop before "Love in the Hot Afternoon" brought him his first hit in 1974. Watson's career has suffered from lack of publicity—*Playboy* magazine called him a secret in 1982 when he had already posted twelve Top-10 hits. Onstage, he's shy on patter or artifice but long on diamond rings and honky-tonk ballads. The man just stands there and sings, sans guitar, with a voice as smooth as warm honey. He lives quietly in Houston with his wife, Mattie; his front yard is full of cars he's repairing.

MICKEY GILLEY *(Epic)*

His cousin Jerry Lee Lewis had been a star for seventeen years when Mickey scored his first No. 1 in 1974, on the George Morgan hit "Room Full of Roses" from 1949. Prior to that, Gilley had spent "nearly twenty years grinding out other people's hits in a succession of busthead skull orchards," as my colleague Bob Claypool so delicately puts it. By early 1985 Mickey had posted eighteen No. 1s (more than Loretta Lynn had) and was coproprietor of Gilley's multimillion-dollar club-recording studio-rodeo arena complex. Mickey is one of the finest live performers in music. He enjoys dusting off pop classics like "True Love Ways," "Stand by Me," "Talk to Me," and "You Don't Know Me." He is also a standout honky-tonk piano-pounder in his own right. He should continue enjoying hits throughout the decade.

MERLE HAGGARD *(Epic)*

The finest American singer-songwriter of the post–Hank Williams era, Merle is a certain future Hall of Famer. Others may call themselves outlaws or publicly use pot, but Haggard was actually in San Quentin Federal Prison. In his songs, he chronicles the plight of the workingman, social problems, and inner distress, and he does it as well as any American since Woody Guthrie. He heads one of the finest, most versatile bands extant, and will in time be classed as one of America's finest living musicians. When he turned twenty-one, he was in prison; later, he entertained at the White House. He now lives in northern California, touring when his mood is good and the fishing isn't.

has never before enjoyed. Some of those listeners may leave the bandwagon in favor of whatever style label advertising convinces them is the "hippest" of the moment, but such attrition is to be expected. Country will patiently be waiting for these youngsters when they mature and tire of the sound of disco or English synth-pop acts like Duran Duran, the Human League, or Depeche Mode.

There are two main groups of acts that should be able to weather this downturn without seeing their careers capsize. The traditionalists will do nicely, for they represent the basic elements of country music that have proven appealing to fans since the 1920s. Though they have reached back in time to more basic forms of country, the modern production touches that these artists have applied make their records sound fresh to the millions of new listeners country music has attracted in the previous five years.

These traditionalists will have to be very skilled musicians—the ears of the American public become harder to fool as time waltzes on. Artists who can take a little Hank Williams, a smidgen of Roy Acuff, a dash of Bob Wills, and a pinch of Lefty Frizzell (sounds like a recipe for a Merle Haggard) and blend these elements with their own style will fare much better than acts that merely imitate the sound or feel of any one artist.

Those who draw their influences from many different branches of popular music—call them modernists—should also thrive, provided that they too can weld these influences together into a unique style. Singers who can straddle the pop-country fence will be able to attract significant audiences from each pasture.

Regardless of the kind of music played, the successful artists of tomorrow will be visually appealing. The video revolution, which has changed many of the rules in popular music, is altering the marketing approach in country as well. The days are long gone when an artist could attain massive success from radio airplay alone. (A classic example of this was Razzy Bailey. He knocked out five No. 1s in a row between 1980 and 1982. However, his recordings didn't sell enough and RCA let him go in 1983.) The dimension of sight has been added to recorded music. Physically unattractive acts with awkward stage movements and little presence on the boards will be taking back seats (if they are allowed on the bus at all) to artists who look good, move with grace, and exude charisma. The days of the homely star—long a unique characteristic in country music—may be gone for good.

Long before MTV, this same visual revolution rewrote the rules of national politics. How would FDR or Harry Truman have fared against more glamorous opponents had they been subjected to the sort of televised scrutiny that today's political candidates receive? We'll never know if they could have passed that test, but nowadays elections seem to be won by whoever looks and sounds the most "presidential."

And so it will be in show business tomorrow, the substance ignored in favor of a glistening shadow. This will open the door to a new breed of artist who can sing passably enough, given the benefits of a few million dollars worth of equipment, studio musicians, and a skilled producer, but who looks and moves the way the public feels that a star should.

The same technology that can make a mediocre singer sound almost great is also preparing new methods for the manufacture and delivery of recordings. Face it, we've been making and playing our records in the same fashion since flat discs replaced glass and porcelain cylinders almost seventy years ago. The change to cassette tapes as the most desired recorded format is only the first step; the 1980s and 1990s will see today's LPs and singles consigned to the same boneyard that houses cylinders, "mono" discs, and 78 RPM platters.

Tapes and new laser-encoded records will be the formats of recorded music during the rest of this century. That music will be recorded using digital equipment rather than by the analog methods in use since recording began. The compact disc (CD), brought onto the market earlier in the 1980s, is even more indestructible than records made from Dynaflex, the thinner vinyl introduced in the early 1970s. CDs are about the size of a single with a picture sleeve, so you'll be able to pack them around almost as easily as cassette tapes. The discs do require a different type of player, but this system utilizes existing speakers and amplifiers. The player,

A Gibson guitar is fine-tuned at the factory in Nashville. (Photo: Greg Kinney)

LEE GREENWOOD
(MCA)

Raised in northern California, Lee was a promising high school athlete before casting his lot with show biz. In the 1960s, he began recording for Paramount Records and then went to Las Vegas, where he learned all aspects of the performance spectrum. He writes, plays guitar, piano, and saxophone, arranges music, and sings with commanding authority and compelling conviction. Greenwood is one of the most talented artists to hit country music in the last twenty years. He is best at lush, fully produced ballads, and will be a superstar if he doesn't fall victim to accident or egotism. A tremendously hard-working, intelligent artist, he could well become the next Kenny Rogers. He surprised many by capturing the CMA's Male Vocalist honor in 1983, a feat he repeated in 1984.

Opposite, above: *Intense Lee Greenwood moved from a support role in Vegas showrooms to country stardom in the early 1980s. (Photo: John Carnes)*
Below: *Ronnie Milsap tickling the ivories. (Photo: Robin Hood)*
Left: *Earl Thomas Conley in action at Fan Fair. (Photo: John Carnes)*
Overleaf: *A close-up of the Fan Fair audience. (Photo: Robin Hood)*

ELEVENTH ANNUAL
FAN FAIR
FAN FAIR
FAN FAIR

I GOT THE FEELING IN NASHVILLE
FAN FAIR

REBA McENTIRE *(MCA)*

Long regarded as a bright prospect, Reba matched her billing in 1983 with her first two No. 1s. Traces of Patsy Cline sparkle in her powerful vocal delivery. Both born and married into professional rodeo families, she lives on a ranch in Chockie Mountain, Oklahoma—near her girlhood home—where she tends cattle belonging to her and her husband, Charlie Battles. Reba, who can claim the best freckles in country music, has the potential to become the leading country female singer of the 1980s, a prediction underlined by her selection in 1984 as CMA's Female Vocalist of the Year. She has it all: talent, looks, personality, dedication, and stage presence.

Above, left: *The view west from outside the Country Music Hall of Fame and Museum. Note the tour buses in front of the Country Corner U. S. A. building (now the Nashville headquarters for Mickey Gilley and Johnny Lee souvenirs). (Photo: John Carnes)*
Above, right: *Oklahoma's Reba McEntire at Fan Fair. (Photo: John Carnes)*
Below, left: *R. C. Bannon and Louise Mandrell show off the latest in natty threads. (Photo: John Carnes)*
Below, right: *The Country Music Hall of Fame and Museum, seen from across Music Square East (formerly 16th Avenue South). (Photo: John Carnes)*
Opposite: *Roy Acuff—"The King of Country Music"—fiddles on the Opry. (Photo: Bob Schatz)*

which "reads" the sound on the record by a laser beam, is only slightly larger than the disc itself, so the unit will be able to fit into car dashboards. You'll find that six to ten CD discs will fit easily into the glove compartment.

It seems reasonable to assume that the new methods of presenting music, added to the existing ones, will create records with an even shorter shelf life than at present. The principle of diminishing returns applies to hearing music just as it does to eating chocolate éclairs. I enjoyed hearing Men at Work sing "Down Under" the first one hundred times, but after six weeks of it nonstop that joy was significantly diminished. Had I been *seeing* them sing it as well all that time I suspect that I would have become saturated even sooner.

This will also have an impact on career longevity. Acts will "burn out" their public welcome much faster with this increased exposure. Artists in the pop fields will become megastars for a short time, then vanish from the Top 40 quicker than you can say "Blondie, the Knack, or Cheap Trick."

The payoff at the top will be even more monumental than it is today, because companies will try to maximize their returns by crossing hits in one country over to the charts of others. With the satellite capabilities we now have, we could create a worldwide music program with a planetary hit parade. Such a network, as well as providing entertainment, could be a vital step toward building understanding among all of the world's citizens.

Nashville itself should do just fine in the next twenty years. The city already boasts the audio, film, and video hardware necessary to create the entertainment programs, films, and records that will be desired by consumers in the years ahead—years that should see ever-increasing demands for leisure-time entertainment, provided, that is, that we don't bomb ourselves into the Stone Age. The people to make the "software"—the music, words, and images—are already here or are on the way. With its small-town charm, Nashville should attract even more artistically inclined immigrants who weary of big-city life—provided, of course, that Nashville manages to retain some of this charm in the face of the rapid growth the city is now undergoing.

They will be lively years, for the city is now seeing the leadership and power of the music business shift to another generation. The men and women who have made Nashville the music capital it has become are now for the most part dead or retired. The heroes of the past, those who hacked out a place for Nashville in the 1940s, 1950s, and 1960s, will be venerated for their achievements, but the new breed of leaders here have their own methods of doing business and creating music.

As of 1985 this new breed of leaders had assumed control of the fate of the four most important labels in country music: CBS, RCA, MCA, and Warner Bros. Their Nashville operations were headed by men forty-five years old or younger—and all these men came to Nashville after gaining their music business experience on the West and East Coasts. These four men—Rick Blackburn at CBS, Joe Galante at RCA, Jimmy Bowen (who moved from Warner Bros. to MCA in 1984), and Jim Ed Norman, Bowen's successor at Warner Bros.—are aggressive, competitive individuals, so the battle for country supremacy during the rest of the 1980s should be a spirited one.

These men will need new methods in the years ahead because the business of popular music has changed significantly in just a few years. Marketing, for instance, is stressed much more today than it was in the past decades. The advent of video as a promotion and sales tool has given label executives a new method to employ in the battle for increased sales. (The early country videos have ranged from the sublime mystery of Willie Nelson and Merle Haggard's portrayals of Mexican bandits in "Pancho and Lefty" to the mundane—Hank Williams, Jr., as a plantation owner in his "Queen of My Heart"—to ridiculous exercises in tedium like Mark Gray's eight-and-a-half-minute "mini-movie," which depicted him as a hitchhiker before, during, and after the some three minutes of "Left Side of the Bed" was performed.)

Album production and talent costs have risen dramatically in the past two decades, requiring greater sales to recoup the label's investment. The vast increase in the number of

EXILE *(Epic)*

The history of Exile begins with J. P. Pennington, cousin of legendary country singer Lily Mae Ledford, way back in the early 1960s. The group endured numerous personnel changes and years of obscurity before blasting to the top of the pop charts with "Kiss You All Over" in 1978. Subsequent releases fell far short of this success, but the group remained together, stabilizing its present roster—Pennington, Sonny LeMaire, Les Taylor, Marlon Hargis, and Steve Goetzmann—in the early 1980s.

Their Kentucky backgrounds and the country songwriting success of Pennington and former member Mark Gary encouraged the quintet to try for a country music career in 1982. The group formed an alliance with top Nashville publisher-producer Buddy Killen, who helped them gain a deal with Epic Records. The band's first country discs were issued in 1983. They quickly became a huge success story in 1984, closing out the year with their second album, *Kentucky Hearts*, at the top of the country album charts.

Although its members are older than those of Alabama—thus with less appeal to the 18–25 age group—Exile is a far more accomplished group.

Hank Williams, Jr., in performance. Hank plays for over two hours at every show and makes the most varied and interesting albums of any of today's country superstars. (Photo: John Carnes)

country stations, coupled with postal rate hikes, have sent mailing costs skyrocketing through the roof. The tightening of radio play lists in the 1980s has made it harder for the labels to establish new artists, a situation that spells long-term problems for any type of music.

Indeed, as of mid-1985, Alabama was the only new country act of the decade to consistently attain multi-platinum sales levels. The sales of country music fell dramatically during 1984, as measured by the number of gold and platinum certifications. The industry discovered that the tried-and-true formula revolving around singles airplay no longer guaranteed album sales success. The public accepted the new artists on the radio—a free source of music—but balked at spending eight dollars to buy their albums. Country label executives openly talked of finding a "savior" to lead them out of the sales doldrums—but as of mid-1985 none had materialized.

Nashville has what it takes to become the most important center for popular music in America, but the people in the industry here will have to shed their self-image of the city as the country music capital of the U.S.A.—a goal met long ago—and aim considerably higher. As successful as it has become, I don't have the sense that Nashville has yet truly "dared to be great." The immediate goals of cutting a record that will go to No. 1 on the country charts, cross over to pop, and pave the way for a platinum album have taken hold to such a degree that the creators of music in Nashville are content to play it very safe. They don't seem to be willing to work hard enough or take the risk necessary to create music bold enough to chart a course of its own. It is my perception that Nashville music makers let radio dictate to them what sort of music to fashion. Thus informed, the "Music City U.S.A." craftsmen repair to the studio and crank it out.

However, the most successful creators of music have been those leaders who made music so compelling, so new, and so intense that radio and the public were entranced. Writers, musicians, and producers should stop worrying so much about radio and strive to make their music so good that people *demand* it. Radio will eventually hear the clamor and will play what the people want to hear, just as they eventually had to play Elvis Presley in the 1950s, the Beatles and Bob Dylan in the 1960s, disco and country music in the 1970s, and European synth-pop in the 1980s.

Nashville will never attain the greatness that is within its grasp as a source of popular music until the music creators of the city realize that it's their job to *lead* radio rather than to pander to it.

To do this Nashville will have to open its ears to the music of other forms and from other parts of the world, as Moe Bandy and Joe Stampley did in their Culture Club-influenced 1984 release, "Where's the Dress?" The city will have to be more inventive, less calculating, and less conservative in the music that it produces. No one can accurately predict what type of music will become the next big thing, but every major musical trend that has emerged in the past thirty years has at one time been scorned by the establishment. Nashville must be willing to endure these slings and arrows of scorn in order to create the kind of music that will be as vital to this city as were the pop hits it produced in the "Golden Age" of 1957 to 1964.

Creators are not followers, they are leaders.

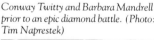

Conway Twitty and Barbara Mandrell prior to an epic diamond battle. (Photo: Tim Naprestek)

Bibliography

A partial listing of sources that were helpful in the writing of this book.

PERIODICALS

Billboard, Cash Box, Country Music, Country News, Country Rhythms, Country Song Roundup, Country Style, The Gavin Report, Journal of Country Music, Music City News, Music Row, The Nashville Gazette, Radio 'n' Records, Record World, Variety.

NEWSPAPERS

Atlanta Journal-Constitution, Austin American-Statesman, Chicago Tribune, Houston Post, Los Angeles Times, Nashville Banner, New York Times, The Tennessean, Washington Post, Washington Star.

BOOKS

ADAMS, GEORGE ROLLIE, AND CHRISTIAN, RALPH. *Nashville: A Pictorial History.* Virginia Beach, Va., 1981.

ALLEN, BOB. *George Jones: The Saga of an American Singer.* Garden City, N.Y., 1984.

———. *Waylon Jennings and Willie Nelson.* New York, 1979.

ATKINS, CHET, WITH BILL NEELY. *Country Gentleman.* Chicago, 1974.

BALE-COX, PATSI. *Rocky Mountain Country.* Denver, Colo., n.d.

BANE, MICHAEL. *The Outlaws.* New York, 1978.

BART, TEDDY. *Inside Music City.* Nashville, 1970.

BREWER-GIORGIO, GAIL. *Orion.* Atlanta, Ga., 1979.

CARESS, JAY. *Hank Williams: Country's Tragic King.* New York, 1979.

CARR, PATRICK. *Illustrated History of Country Music.* Garden City, N.Y., 1979.

CASH, JOHNNY. *Man in Black.* New York, 1975.

CHARLES, RAY, AND RITZ, DAVID. *Brother Ray.* New York, 1978.

CLAYPOOL, BOB. *Saturday Night at Gilley's.* New York, 1980.

COE, DAVID ALLAN. *Just for the Record.* N.p., 1978.

CORBIN, EVERETT. *Storm over Nashville.* Nashville, 1980.

CORNFELD, ROBERT, AND FALLWELL, JR., MARSHALL. *Just Country.* New York, 1976.

DELLAR, FRED, AND THOMPSON, ROY. *Illustrated Encyclopedia of Country Music.* New York, 1977.

DELLAR, FRED, AND WOOTTON, RICHARD. *Best of Country Music.* New York, 1980.

DENISOFF, R. SERGE. *Waylon: A Biography.* Knoxville, Tenn., 1983.

FABER, CHARLES. *Country Music Almanac.* Vols. I and II. Lexington, Ky., 1978.

FLIPPO, CHET. *Your Cheatin' Heart.* New York, 1981.

FOWLER, LANA NELSON. *Willie Nelson Family Album.* Amarillo, Tex., 1980.

GAILLARD, FRYE. *Watermelon Wine.* New York, 1978.

GENTRY, LINNELL. *A History and Encyclopedia of Folk, Country and Western and Gospel Music.* Nashville, 1961.

GREEN, DOUG. *Country Roots.* New York, 1976.

GRIFFIN, SID. *Grievous Angel.* Unpublished.

GURALNICK, PETER. *Feel Like Going Home.* New York, 1971.

———. *Lost Highway.* Boston, 1979.

HAGGARD, MERLE, WITH PEGGY RUSSELL. *Sing Me Back Home.* New York, 1981.

HALL, TOM T. *How I Write Songs: Why You Can.* New York, 1976.

———. *The Storyteller's Nashville.* New York, 1979.

HEMPHILL, PAUL. *The Nashville Sound.* New York, 1970.

HOPKINS, JERRY. *Elvis.* New York, 1971.

HORSTMAN, DOROTHY. *Sing Your Heart Out, Country Boy.* New York, 1975.

HUME, MARTHA. *Kenny Rogers: Gambler, Dreamer, Lover.* New York, 1980.

HURST, JACK. *The Grand Ole Opry.* New York, 1975.

KOSSER, MICHAEL. *How to Become a Successful Nashville Songwriter.* Nashville, 1981.

KRIAILOVSKY, WILLIAM, AND SHEMEL, SIDNEY. *This Business of Music.* Rev., enl. ed. New York, 1971, 1973–74.

LEVINE, ARTHUR D. *The Nashville Number System.* Nashville, 1981.

LOMAX, ALAN. *Folk Songs of North America.* New York, 1960.

LOMAX, JOHN A. AND ALAN. *Folk Song U.S.A.* New York, 1947.

LYNN, LORETTA, WITH GEORGE VECSEY. *Coal Miner's Daughter.* New York, 1976.

MALONE, BILL C. *Country Music U.S.A.* Austin, Tex., 1968.

———. *Southern Music, American Music.* Lexington, Ky., 1979.

MILLER, JIM. *Rolling Stone Illustrated History of Rock and Roll.* New York, 1976.

MORRIS, EDWARD. *Alabama.* Chicago, 1985.

MORTHLAND, JOHN. *Best of Country Music.* Garden City, N.Y., 1984.

MURRELLS, JOSEPH. *Book of Golden Discs.* London, 1978.

NASH, ALANNA. *Dolly.* New York, 1978.

NASSOUR, ELLIS. *Patsy Cline.* New York, 1981.

NICKERSON, MARINA, AND FARAH, CYNTHIA. *Country Music: A Look at the Men Who Made It.* El Paso, Tex., 1981.

OERMANN, ROBERT K., WITH DOUGLAS B. GREEN. *Listeners Guide to Country Music.* New York, 1983.

PORTERFIELD, NOLAN. *Jimmie Rodgers.* Urbana, Ill., 1979.

READER'S DIGEST. *Reader's Digest Country and Western Songbook.* Pleasantville, N.Y., 1983.

REID, JAN. *The Improbable Rise of Redneck Rock.* Austin, Tex., 1974.

RILEY, JEANNIE C., WITH JAMIE BUCKINGHAM. *Jeannie C. Riley.* Lincoln, Va., 1981.

ROONEY, JIM. *Bossmen: Bill Monroe and Muddy Waters.* New York, 1971.

ROXON, LILLIAN. *Rock Encyclopedia.* New York, 1969.

SCOBEY, LOLA. *Dolly Parton.* New York, 1977.

———. *Willie Nelson, Country Outlaw.* New York, 1982.

SHELTON, ROBERT, AND GOLDBLATT, BURT. *The Country Music Story.* Indianapolis, Ind., 1966.

STAMBLER, IRWIN. *Encyclopedia of Pop, Rock and Soul.* New York, 1974.

STAMBLER, IRWIN, AND LANDON, GRELUN. *Encyclopedia of Folk, Country and Western Music.* 1st and rev. eds. New York, 1969, 1983.

THOMAS, B. J., WITH JERRY B. JENKINS. *Home Where I Belong.* Waco, Tex., 1978.

TOSCHES, NICK. *Country: The Biggest Music in America.* New York, 1977.

———. *Hellfire.* New York, 1982.

TOWNSEND, CHARLES. *San Antonio Rose: The Life and Times of Bob Wills.* Urbana, Ill., 1976.

VON SCHMIDT, ERIC, AND ROONEY, JIM. *Baby, Let Me Follow You Down.* Garden City, N.Y., 1979.

WHITBURN, JOEL. *Joel Whitburn's Record Research Reports.* Menomonee Falls, Wis., 1973–83.

———. *Music Yearbook 1983.* Menomonee Falls, Wis., 1984.

———. *Top Pop 1940–1955.* Menomonee Falls, Wis., 1973.

———. *Top Pop 1955–1982.* Menomonee Falls, Wis., 1983.

WILLIAMS, ROGER. *Sing a Sad Song.* Urbana, Ill., 1970.

WILLIAMS, JR., HANK, WITH MICHAEL BANE. *Living Proof.* New York, 1979.

WOOTTON, RICHARD. *Honky-Tonkin'.* Charlotte, N.C., 1980.

———. *Illustrated Country Almanac.* New York, 1982.

The World Almanac. New York, 1982–84.

WREN, CHRISTOPHER. *Winners Got Scars, Too.* New York, 1971.

WSM INC. *Grand Ole Opry WSM Picture-History Book.* Ed. Jerry Strobel. Nashville, 1976.

WYNETTE, TAMMY, AND DEW, JOAN. *Stand by Your Man.* New York, 1979.

CHRONOLOGY OF DATES RELATING TO NASHVILLE'S MUSIC INDUSTRY

1877

Invention of the microphone
Invention of the phonograph

1887

Emile Berliner patents the first flat disc

1889

Formation of Columbia Records
First commercial record players on market in Germany

1891

First "jukeboxes" offer opera singers on rotating cylinders for 5¢

1894

Billboard, the first music industry trade paper, founded

1895

Variety magazine begins chronicling the world of entertainment

1896

American Federation of Musicians (AFM) founded

1901

Formation of Victor Talking Machine Co.

1902

AFM Local No. 257 founded in Nashville

1903

First royalty system established for recording artists

1904

First double-sided records issued

1906

Victor markets first Victrola

1907

Invention of 3-vacuum tube by Lee DeForest

1909

Passage of first musical Copyright Act
First orchestra recordings released

1914

Formation of American Society of Composers, Authors and Publishers (ASCAP)

1917

First jazz recordings issued

1919

Formation of RCA Corp.

1920

First commercial radio station, KDKA, established by Westinghouse in Pittsburgh; election returns carried over it
Clara Smith makes first blues records on Columbia

1922

Fiddlin' John Carson and Clayton McMichen broadcast live over WSB, Atlanta
Eck Robertson and Henry Gilliland make first country records in New York City for Victor Talking Machine Co.

1923

Fiddlin' John Carson recorded by Ralph Peer in Atlanta
Henry Whittier records "Wreck of the Old Southern '97"
WBAP in Fort Worth, Texas, starts first "Barn Dance" program

1924

Vernon Dalhart's "Wreck of the Old '97"/ "The Prisoner's Song" becomes the first country record to sell one million copies
WLS "National Barn Dance" established in Chicago

1925

George D. Hay moves to Nashville from WLS in Chicago
WSM begins broadcasting
WSM starts its own "Barn Dance" show
Victor and Columbia issue first commercial electrical records

1926

DeFord Bailey becomes first black to play the WSM "Barn Dance"
Uncle Dave Macon joins "Barn Dance," becomes its first big star
Peer-Southern music publishing company founded

1927

WSM "Barn Dance" becomes "Grand Ole Opry"
Ralph Peer first records Jimmie Rodgers and the Carter Family
NBC and CBS radio networks founded (1927–28)

1928

Victor Recording Machine Co. makes first Nashville recordings, waxing Opry string bands
Bradley Kincaid publishes first country star songbook

1929

RCA acquires Victor Talking Machine Co.
Warner Bros. buys Brunswick Radio Co.
Jimmie Rodgers makes *The Singing Brakeman*, a 15-minute film
Gene Autry makes his first recordings

1930

"Border" radio (radio stations based in Mexico, thus immune to FCC restrictions on transmission power) begins at XER, outside Del Rio, Texas, in Ciudad Acuña, Mexico
Ken Maynard becomes first singing cowboy

1931

Delmore Bros. make first recordings
RCA demonstrates first 33⅓ RPM disc

1932

WSM gets clear-channel status, ups power tenfold to 50,000 watts
WSM begins booking Opry acts for personal appearances
The Delmore Brothers join the Opry

1933

Jimmie Rodgers dies in New York City
WLS gets a one-hour radio spot on NBC—the first national country music show
WWVA "Jamboree" begins in Wheeling, West Virginia
Fred Rose visits Nashville; lands "Song Shop" program on WSM
Bob Wills and Tommy Duncan form Bob Wills and the Texas Playboys

1934

Decca Records launched in United States as a budget line
RCA markets cheap combination radio–record-player

1935

Wills and Texas Playboys make first records
Patsy Montana records "I Want to Be a Cowboy's Sweetheart," believed to be the first million-seller by a female country artist

1936

Kitty Wells makes radio debut at WSIX in Nashville
Roy Acuff cuts "Wabash Cannonball" and "Great Speckled Bird"
Ernest Tubb makes his first records
Duets begin in earnest: Monroe Bros., Blue Sky Boys, Dixon Bros.
Hank Snow makes his first records

1937

Pee Wee King joins "Grand Ole Opry"
Leonard Slye leaves the Sons of the Pioneers, eventually becomes Roy Rogers

1938

J. L. Frank, later an important talent promoter, moves to Nashville
Roy Acuff moves to Nashville; joins Opry
Country musicians first invited to perform at the White House
Carter Family joins border radio station XER
CBS reactivates Columbia label

1939

WSM gains network feed status from NBC; Opry carried over NBC radio net for first time in half-hour segments
Bill Monroe joins the Opry
Red River Dave becomes one of the first televised performers, at the New York World's Fair
Formation of Broadcast Music Incorporated (BMI)

1940

First recording industry charts published in *Billboard*
Germany produces first magnetic tape recorder
Minnie Pearl joins "Grand Ole Opry"

1941

WSM launches first commercial FM radio station
ASCAP and BMI join battle, and ASCAP pulls its songs from most radio play lists
Billboard publishes list of top hillbilly hits
Bing Crosby has big pop hits with "New San Antonio Rose" and "You Are My Sunshine"

1942

AFM strike under leadership of Joseph Petrillo results in recording ban
Acuff-Rose music publishing company founded, and affiliates with BMI
Formation of Capitol Records
"Hi-fi" technology bows in England
Elton Britt gets first official country gold recording for "There's a Star-Spangled Banner Waving Somewhere"
Eddy Arnold joins "Grand Ole Opry"

1943

"Grand Ole Opry" moves to Ryman Auditorium
Al Dexter's "Pistol-Packing Mama" hits No. 1 on pop charts
Ernest Tubb joins the "Grand Ole Opry"

1944

Formation of Ernest Tubb Fan Club by Norma Barthel (still in existence)
Jimmie Davis elected governor of Louisiana
Billboard introduces "Most Played Juke Box Folk Records" charts
Eddy Arnold of RCA records in WSM's studios; beginning of commercial recording in Nashville
Jimmie Davis stars in MGM film *Louisiana*, first cinematic biography of country music star

1945

Wesley Rose moves to Nashville
Paul Cohen directs first Decca sessions in Nashville at WSM with Red Foley, Kitty Wells, and Ernest Tubb
Mercury Records established in Chicago
Hill & Range publishers established; soon active in Nashville
Lester Flatt and Earl Scruggs in place in Bill Monroe's band; founding of bluegrass music follows

1946

Acuff-Rose signs Hank Williams
Chet Atkins moves to Nashville
Grady Martin debuts on the "Grand Ole Opry"
Castle Recording Company, first commercial recording studio in Nashville, opens

1947

Owen Bradley begins producing for Decca
MGM Records is established
First full-time country station, WARL in Arlington, Va., begins
Magnetic tape introduced in U.S.
Francis Craig's "Near You" hits No. 1 pop, remains there for 12 weeks; first No. 1 pop single cut in Nashville
Ernest Tubb highlights country show at Carnegie Hall in New York City, first country package show to play there

1948

Chet Atkins cuts his first records as a featured artist
Columbia markets 33 RPM records
"Tennessee Waltz" first recorded
Eddy Arnold becomes superstar, has Top-5 pop album
Francis Craig and his Orchestra hits No. 4 on pop singles chart with "Beg Your Pardon"
NBC carries live country music concert from Washington, D.C., first national TV exposure for form
Mercury issues its first C & W discs
Country charts renamed "Best Selling Retail Folk Records" by *Billboard*
Dinning Sisters get No. 7 pop hit with Nashville-recorded "Buttons and Bows"
Bullet Records opens city's first record-pressing facility to keep up with demand for "Near You"

1949

Billboard begins calling charts "Best-Selling Folk and Country & Western Recordings"
RCA introduces 45 RPM disc
3-speed record players come onto market
Jimmie Rodgers's memorial LP goes to No. 4 pop 16 years after he died
Eddy Arnold's *To Mother* LP goes to No. 2 pop
Gordon Stoker joins Jordanaires; modern quartet established in 1958
Country Song Roundup (the longest-lived country music magazine) begins publication

1950

WSM establishes Nashville's first TV station
Capitol becomes the first label to locate an office here, which it labels its "country division"
"Tennessee Waltz" becomes huge pop hit, goes to No. 1 for Patti Page
"Chattanoogie Shoe Shine Boy" hits No. 1 pop
Eddy Arnold Sings hits No. 5 in pop LP chart
Boudleaux and Felice Bryant move to Nashville
Carl Smith joins the "Grand Ole Opry"
Hank Snow moves here, joins the Opry
Johnnie Lee Wills's "Rag Mop" on Nashville-based Bullet Records hits No. 10 pop, spawns many cover versions

1951

Hubert Long moves to Nashville, later becomes successful talent agent
"Slow Poke" goes to No. 3 on pop charts for Pee Wee King
"Cold, Cold Heart" hits No. 1 for Tony Bennett, signaling the discovery of Hank Williams's songs by popular audiences
Del Wood's instrumental "Down Yonder" hits No. 6 pop; only million-selling instrumental ever achieved by a woman

1952

Kitty Wells becomes first woman to gain a No. 1 country single when she answers Hank Thompson's "The Wild Side of Life" with "It Wasn't God Who Made Honky Tonk Angels"
Owen Bradley establishes his first studio, dubbed the "Quonset Hut"
First DJ Festival held in Nashville
Mercury opens Nashville office
Recording Industry Association of America (RIAA) formed
Ray Price joins the Opry
"Jambalaya" (No. 3 for Jo Stafford) and "Half as Much" (No. 2 for Rosemary Clooney), both songs first exposed by Hank Williams, are huge pop hits
Hank Williams asked to leave the Opry due to his drinking problem
Eddy Arnold replaces Perry Como on NBC-TV series

1953

Hubert Long forms first Nashville talent agency
Marty Robbins joins the Opry
Jimmy Dean goes on CBS network TV with a country show
Hank Williams dies on New Year's Day
Joni James takes Williams's hit "Your Cheatin' Heart" to No. 7 on pop singles list

1954

Jim Denny leaves WSM, forms own agency and publishing company
Country Music Disc Jockey Association formed
Boots Randolph moves here, gains fame as a saxophonist
Faron Young moves here, joins the Opry
Fred Rose dies

First Elvis Presley recordings
Bill Haley records "Rock Around the Clock"
First use of pedal steel guitar on a recording: Webb Pierce's "Slowly"
Owen Bradley moves his Quonset Hut to 804 Sixteenth Avenue South, first music enterprise in what is now called "Music Row" area

1955

Opry first telecast nationally on ABC
Floyd Cramer moves to Nashville
George Jones posts first chart hit
Rosemary Clooney records here

1956

Bobby Helms and Gene Vincent claim Top-10 pop hits on Nashville side
Johnny Ray and Guy Mitchell attain Top-10 pop successes with songs by Nashville writers
Elvis signs with RCA, records "Heartbreak Hotel" and other sides in Nashville, hits No. 1 in pop
Stereo tape now available
Buddy Holly records here
Elvis LPs cut in Nashville go to No. 1 pop
Stonewall Jackson moves here
Brenda Lee begins recording in Nashville
Roger Miller moves here
Billboard now calls chart "Country and Western" (C & W)

1957

Country music makes its first visit to Broadway: Roy Acuff, Kitty Wells, Johnnie & Jack headline at Palace Theater
Everly Brothers join the Opry
Ferlin Husky rises to No. 4 pop with Ken Nelson-produced "Gone"
Everly Bros. hits: "Wake Up Little Susie" (No. 1 pop) and "Bye, Bye Love" (No. 2), both written by Boudleaux and Felice Bryant
Marty Robbins scores a No. 2 pop hit with "A White Sport Coat (and a Pink Carnation)"
Sonny James goes to No. 2 pop with "Young Love"
Roy Orbison moves here from Memphis
Porter Wagoner joins the Opry

1958

Owen Bradley signs with Decca for Artists & Repertoire (A & R) post
Chet Atkins produces Don Gibson's "Oh Lonesome Me" (No. 7 pop), which kicks off the Nashville Sound, an attempt to upgrade country music production
Country Music Association (CMA) founded
BMI opens Nashville office
Stereo LPs introduced
Sheb Wooley records "Purple People Eater" in Nashville; it tops the pop chart
First Grammy Awards presented; "Tom Dooley" wins best "C & W recording" for Kingston Trio
Gary Burton records here with Chet Atkins
Everly Bros. rack up 2 No. 1 pop singles for "All I Have to Do Is Dream" and "Bird Dog"
Dallas Frazier moves here
The Glaser Brothers move here
Conway Twitty scores No. 1 pop hit with "It's Only Make Believe"

1959

Starday Records moves to town
Marty Robbins's *Gunfighter Ballads* makes No. 6 on pop LP lists
Johnny Horton scores huge pop hit with "The Battle of New Orleans"
The Browns hit No. 1 pop with "The Three Bells"
Stonewall Jackson and the Everlys rack up No. 4 pop singles
Hank Cochran and Dottie West move to Nashville
Mark Dinning records No. 1 "Teen Angel" in Nashville; Guy Mitchell hits No. 1 with "Heartaches by the Number"
Billy Grammer's No. 4 "Gotta Travel On" paves way for Monument's move to Nashville in 1960

1960

Brenda Lee scores two pop No. 1s and becomes an international star
Marty Robbins's "El Paso" hits No. 1 pop
Roy Orbison, Jim Reeves, and Johnny Horton all post No. 2 pop hits
Brenda nabs 2 Top-5 pop LPs
Everly Bros. net 2 Top-10 pop LPs
Brenda has a third Top-5 pop single
"Cathy's Clown" goes to No. 1 for Everly Bros.
"The Battle of New Orleans" becomes first Nashville recording to win a Grammy
Willie Nelson moves here from Texas, Harlan Howard from California
Chet Atkins invited to Newport Jazz Festival
Nashville recordings ride No. 1 on *Billboard*'s "Hot 100" for 28 of year's 51 weeks
Conway Twitty scores with Top 10s
Jimmie Davis again elected governor of Louisiana
Porter Wagoner begins syndicated TV show
Hank Locklin and Bob Luman gain Top-10 pop singles
Monument Records moves to Music City from Baltimore
Burl Ives records here
Johnny Horton killed in automobile accident
Robert Shelton and Burt Goldblatt publish *Country Music Story*

1961

Country Music Hall of Fame created: Jimmie Rodgers, Fred Rose, Hank Williams first to be inducted
FM stereo gets FCC approval
Billy Sherrill moves here to work in Sam Phillips's studio
Joe Dowell, Elvis, and Jimmy Dean hit No. 1 on Nashville recordings
Roy Orbison hits No. 1 pop with "Running Scared"; "Cryin'" hits No. 2
Leroy Van Dyke nabs only pop hit with "Walk on By"
Chet Atkins Workshop LP hits No. 7 on pop charts
Johnny Horton's Greatest Hits peaks at No. 8 on pop charts
Floyd Cramer, Marty Robbins, Brenda Lee, Sue Thompson, and Patsy Cline post Top-10 pop singles
Ray Stevens moves here
First country music reference tool published: Linnell Gentry's *A History and Encyclopedia of Country, Western and Gospel Music*

1962

Columbia buys Quonset Hut studio from Owen Bradley
Ray Charles's *Modern Sounds in Country & Western Music* hits No. 1 on pop LP list
Tommy Roe, Johnny Tillotson record smash pop hits here
Claude King and Sue Thompson rack up Top-10 pop singles
Jerry Reed moves here
Roy Acuff inducted into Country Music Hall of Fame
Lester Flatt and Earl Scruggs record the theme for TV series "Beverly Hillbillies"
Jim Reeves tours South Africa, makes film, *Kimberly Jim*, there
Burl Ives cuts two Top-10 hits in Music City

1963

Brook Benton, Dixiebelles become first black acts to cut pop hits here
Bobby Bare hits with "500 Miles"; ignites folk cover boom by country acts
Skeeter Davis hits No. 2 pop with "The End of the World"
St. Louis Cardinals begin holding "country music night" at baseball park
Ray Charles's *Modern Sounds in C & W Music, Vol. II* hits No. 2 on pop LP charts
Bill Anderson posts Top-10 pop single
Patsy Cline, Hawkshaw Hawkins, and Cowboy Copas killed in plane crash
Music City News begins publication

1964

RCA spends $1 million renovating studios for Nashville office
National Academy of Recording Arts & Sciences opens Nashville branch
George Hamilton stars in *Your Cheatin' Heart* film bio of Hank Williams
Roy Orbison hits No. 1 pop with "Oh, Pretty Woman" single
The Best of Jim Reeves hits No. 9 on pop LP lists
Roger Miller and Skeeter Davis post Top-10 singles on pop lists
Buck Wilkin forms Ronny & the Daytonas; "G.T.O." hits No. 4 pop
Sesac, performance rights organization, opens Nashville office
Academy of Country Music founded
Jim Reeves dies in plane crash
Dolly Parton, Tom T. Hall, Connie Smith, and Sonny Throckmorton move here
Bobby Goldsboro hits No. 9 pop with "See the Funny Little Clown"
Tex Ritter inducted into Hall of Fame
Johnny Cash records Bob Dylan's "It Ain't Me, Babe"
Acuff-Rose invents the Newbeats; group has pop hit with "Bread & Butter"

1965

First Academy of Country Music Awards presented
Kris Kristofferson moves to Nashville
Owen Bradley opens Bradley's Barn, the first suburban Nashville studio
Gene Pitney and Joe Tex record here
Eddy Arnold's *My World* LP goes to No. 7 pop
Roger Miller posts 3 Top-10 pop singles and 2 Top-6 pop LPs
Eddy Arnold scores No. 6 pop single with "Make the World Go Away"
Roger Miller wins five Grammy Awards
Tammy Wynette moves here
Ernest Tubb chosen for Country Music Hall of Fame
Tex Ritter joins the Opry

1966

Roger Miller gets NBC-TV network show
Tape cartridges introduced
Vikki Carr records in Nashville
Cincinnati Redlegs inaugurate "country music night" at baseball park
Waylon Jennings moves to Nashville
Roger Miller wins six Grammies
Statler Brothers snag No. 4 pop single for "Flowers on the Wall"
Eddy Arnold, Jim Denny, George D. Hay, and Uncle Dave Macon chosen for Country Music Hall of Fame
S. Sgt. Barry Sadler cuts "Ballad of the Green Berets" here at RCA
Robert Shelton and Burt Goldblatt's *A Picture History of C & W Music* published
Dylan first records here; *Blonde on Blonde* goes to No. 9 on LP lists; "Rainy Day Women #12 and 35" hits No. 2 pop on singles list

1967

Country Music Hall of Fame opens museum
First CMA Awards presented
Woodland Studios opens
Bob Dylan records *John Wesley Harding* here, LP goes to No. 2 in 1968
Kenny Rogers hits No. 5 with Mickey Newbury's "Just Dropped In"
The prices of monophonic records rise to equal those of stereo records, the first step in the phase-out of mono
Nashville studios top 5,000 sessions for the first time
CMA membership tops 2,000
Buffy Sainte Marie records in Nashville
Glen Campbell's *Gentle on My Mind* hits No. 5 on pop LP charts
David Allen Coe moves here
Overall record and tape sales top $1 billion for the first time
Red Foley, Jim Reeves, Steve Sholes, J. L. Frank picked for Hall of Fame

1968

"Harper Valley P.T.A." and "Honey" hit No. 1 on pop singles chart
CMA Awards shown for first time on network TV (32 share)
Doc Watson, Albert Collins, the Byrds, Dinah Shore, and the Beau Brummels all cut records in Nashville
American Guild of Authors and Composers establishes Nashville office
Jerry Foster and Bill Rice, Lynn Anderson, Barbara Mandrell, and Jimmy Buffett all move here
Liquor by the drink passes in "dry" Nashville—becomes law in 1970 (it helps the growth of tourist trade, restaurants, live music)
April-Blackwood publishing opens Nashville office
Porter Wagoner and Dolly Parton appear on "The Tonight Show"
Al Gallico opens publishing office here
Billy Sherrill assumes A & R control of CBS and Epic Records
Glen Campbell posts No. 1 pop LP with *Wichita Lineman*
Bill Malone's *Country Music U.S.A.*, first book-length, scholarly look at country music, published
Chet Atkins named RCA vice-president
Bob Wills chosen for Hall of Fame

1969

Glen Campbell and Johnny Cash both star in network variety shows
ABC debuts "Hee Haw" program
Ann-Margret, Jerry Jeff Walker, Leapy Lee, and Jack Elliott record here
Bob Dylan records *Nashville Skyline*, which features Johnny Cash as a guest artist
Hubert Long opens Hollywood branch office
Country invades England via first Wembley Festival
Johnny Cash hits No. 2 on pop singles list with "A Boy Named Sue"
Country music franchise food boom, in which stars lend their names to fast food chains (none survive the 1970s)
Sessions here top the 7,000 mark
Johnny Cash at San Quentin hits No. 1 on pop LP charts
Glen Campbell posts No. 2 pop LP with *Galveston*
"Little Green Apples," written by sometime Nashville resident Bobby Russell, wins overall Song of the Year honors at the Grammy Awards
Gene Autry chosen for Hall of Fame
Irwin Stambler and Grelun Landon write *The Encyclopedia of Folk, Country and Western Music*, the first such reference tool in the field

1970

Hello, I'm Johnny Cash hits No. 6 on pop LP lists
"Everything Is Beautiful" hits No. 1 on pop singles chart for Ray Stevens
"Amos Moses" goes to Top-10 on pop lists for Jerry Reed
Tracy Nelson and Even Stevens move here
Tex Ritter runs for U.S. Senate
Bill Monroe selected for Hall of Fame
The Carter Family selected for Hall of Fame
Ground-breaking for Opryland
Jack Clement Recording Studios open
Everly Brothers replace Johnny Cash for summer TV series
Ringo Starr, Clint Eastwood, Jack Palance, Georgia Gibbs, Linda Ronstadt, Arthur Prysock, Steve Miller, Country Joe McDonald, James Brown, Leontyne Price, and Frank Gorshin record in Nashville
Mike Douglas schedules a complete week featuring country programs
First in-depth radio documentary on country music produced by WEXL (Detroit)
Joe Allen moves here
Recording sessions top 8,500
Roger Miller opens a hotel called the King of the Road
Johnny Cash is invited to the White House
Nashville Songwriter's Association formed
Dylan records his last Nashville-cut LP, *Self-Portrait*, which hits No. 4 pop

1971

Sonny James, Loretta Lynn, Conway Twitty, Porter Wagoner, Dolly Parton, Del Reeves, Faron Young, and Jim Ed Brown sell out Madison Square Garden
Goldie Hawn, Joan Baez, Manhattan Transfer, Gordon Lightfoot, and Sandy Posey record in Music City
Nitty Gritty Dirt Band records 3-LP set in Nashville with all-star country cast
MUZAK holds first Nashville sessions
First international conference on video recording held
Nashville sessions top 13,000
CMA counts 525 full-time country music radio stations
Country Music Hall of Fame Library and Media Center opens
Donna Fargo, Jimmy Bowen, Guy and Susannah Clark move here; Willie Nelson goes back to Texas; John Conlee moves here
Sammi Smith, Lynn Anderson, and Jerry Reed post Top-10 pop singles
Billy Joe Shaver gets first recordings
Art Satherley chosen for Hall of Fame
Kris Kristofferson has big pop hits on covers by Smith, Janis Joplin

1972

Opryland musical theme park opens for business
Fan Fair is spun off of DJ Week to provide event for fans
George Gobel, Neil Young, and REO Speedwagon record in Nashville
Tanya Tucker and Don Williams move to Nashville
"Funny Face" becomes a Top-5 pop single for Donna Fargo
Jimmie Davis is inducted into the Hall of Fame
Neil Young records *Harvest LP* partly in Nashville

1973

Dan Fogelberg, Leon Russell, Johnny Winter, John Stewart, and Paul Kelly cut in Music City
Larry Gatlin, Johnny Rodriguez, and Ronnie Milsap move here
Jack Clement makes the first country music video ("Come Early Mornin'" by Don Williams)
Charlie Daniels posts a No. 9 pop single with "Uneasy Rider"
Behind Closed Doors by Charlie Rich hits No. 8 pop LP
Loretta Lynn featured on cover of *Newsweek*
Chet Atkins and Patsy Cline chosen for Hall of Fame

1974

Grand Ole Opry House opens with President Nixon in attendance
Carol Channing, Paul McCartney record in Nashville
Vinyl shortage grips industry
Nashville recordings hit No. 1 on pop singles charts three times: "The Streak" by Ray Stevens, "I Can Help" by Billy Swan, and "The Most Beautiful Girl" by Charlie Rich
George Hamilton IV becomes the first country artist invited to tour Russia
Robert Altman comes to town to film *Nashville*
Merle Haggard makes the cover of *Time*
Pee Wee King and Owen Bradley selected for Hall of Fame

1975

Kenny Rogers, Joe Simon, and Delbert McClinton record in Nashville
$4.98 becomes LP list price
Freddy Fender, with "Before the Next Teardrop Falls," and B. J. Thomas, with "(Hey, Won't You Play) Another Somebody Done Somebody Wrong Song," snag No. 1 pop singles
"I'm Not Lisa" hits No. 4 on pop singles lists for Jessi Colter
Janie Fricke moves here, becomes top session singer
Minnie Pearl chosen for Hall of Fame
W. W. and the Dixie Dance Kings filmed here; Don Williams and Jerry Reed make their film debuts

1976

Disco begins to take off
LP list price goes to $5.98
Ozark Mountain Daredevils record here
Kitty Wells and Paul Cohen chosen for Hall of Fame
RCA issues *Wanted—The Outlaws*, a compilation LP featuring Willie Nelson, Waylon Jennings, Jessie Colter, and Tompall Glaser; it becomes the first country LP to be certified platinum

1977

Opryland Hotel opens in Opryland
New copyright law passes—the first revision since 1909
LP list price goes to $6.98
Frank Sinatra, Jr., Joe Ely, and Kansas record in Nashville
Crystal Gayle takes "Don't It Make My Brown Eyes Blue" to No. 2 on pop singles chart
"Lucille" goes to No. 5 on pop singles chart for Kenny Rogers
Merle Travis received into Country Music Hall of Fame

1978

PBS carries the Opry live annually (to 1981)
$7.98 now LP list price
Sales of records and tapes in U.S. tops $4 billion
Digital recording starts to become a viable recording option
Disco peaks
Gail Davies moves here
Grandpa Jones admitted into Hall of Fame
Kansas's Nashville-recorded "Dust in the Wind" single hits No. 6 pop

1979

Steve Forbert records here
Kenny Rogers scores three Top-10 pop singles, No. 5 pop LP
Charlie Daniels Band hits Top-5 on pop singles list with "The Devil Went Down to Georgia," scores Top-5 pop album with *Million Mile Reflections*
Hubert Long and Hank Snow selected for Hall of Fame
Pro baseball returns to Nashville; Conway Twitty, Jerry Reed, Cal Smith, and Richard Sterban are among its bankrollers

1980

The film *Urban Cowboy* spreads country fever and makes famous Gilley's club in Pasadena, Texas
MCA debuts first video disc system
Elvis Costello, Linda Ronstadt, the Allman Brothers, and Sissy Spacek all cut discs in Nashville
Kenny Rogers's *Greatest Hits* goes to No. 1 on pop LP lists
The soundtrack for *Urban Cowboy* hits No. 3 pop
Alabama signed to RCA, racks up first No. 2 hits
Dolly Parton's "9 to 5" hits No. 1 in pop, country, and a-c charts
Eddie Rabbitt hits No. 1 on pop singles chart with "I Love a Rainy Night" and hits No. 5 with "Drivin' My Life Away"
Johnny Lee scores a No. 5 pop single with "Lookin' for Love"
Sissy Spacek stars in film of Loretta Lynn story, *Coal Miner's Daughter*
Larry Butler named Producer of the Year at Grammys — the first Nashville producer so honored
Johnny Cash, Connie B. Gay, Sons of the Pioneers make the Hall of Fame
Dan Fogelberg begins string of Nashville-waxed pop hits

1981

MTV debuts
B. B. King, George Burns, John Denver, Don McLean, and Dave Brubeck record in Nashville
Ronnie Milsap, Eddie Rabbitt, and the Oak Ridge Boys all post Top-5 pop singles
Leon Russell, John Prine, Rosanne Cash, and Rodney Crowell move here
Country Rhythms magazine begins publication
Vernon Dalhart, Grant Turner chosen for Hall of Fame
Kenny Rogers and Kim Carnes hit No. 4 pop for their Nashville-cut duet

1982

WSM and Associated Press launch Music Country Network via satellite
Marty Robbins passes away following heart surgery
The Crusaders, Joe Cocker, Tom Jones, Ray Charles, Dean Martin, Dionne Warwick, Engelbert Humperdinck, and the Marshall Tucker Band record in Nashville
Nashville-based writers win majority of BMI pop awards for first time
"Always on My Mind" hits No. 5 pop for Willie Nelson as a single
Marty Robbins, Lefty Frizzell, and Roy Horton to Hall of Fame
Fan Fair outgrows Ryman Auditorium; moves to state fairgrounds
Twitty City opens

1983

WSM and Group W satellite Communications debut the Nashville Network to 7 million cable-TV homes
Joe Cocker, Neil Young, and Engelbert Humperdinck return here to record
"Always on My Mind" wins overall Song of the Year honors at Grammy Awards
Eddie Rabbitt and Crystal Gayle post No. 7 pop hit with "You and I"
Nashville writers win bigger share of BMI pop awards
Mutual Radio first simulcasts CMA Awards Show to worldwide audience
Publication of revised and expanded edition of Stambler and Landon's *Encyclopedia of Folk, Country & Western Music*
Bob Seger takes Rodney Crowell's "Shame on the Moon" to No. 2 pop
Dolly Parton lures Sylvester Stallone to Nashville for some of the filming of *Rhinestone*, her third movie
Complete Opryland complex bought by Gaylord Communications for a sum reported to be in excess of $250 million
"Little" Jimmy Dickens inducted into Hall of Fame

1984

Floyd Tillman and Ralph Peer inducted into Hall of Fame
Patsy Cline film bio, *Sweet Dreams*, filmed in Nashville
Huge increase seen in country music video clip production
Nashville's film activity increases dramatically: portions of *Starman*, *Songwriter*, *Marie*, and *The Bear* filmed here
TV crews from England, Japan, France, and Norway film specials here
The Nashville Network claims penetration into over 20 million homes
Jim Owens Entertainment program, *This Week in Country Music*, is now seen in over 60 million homes
Charlie Daniels's "Volunteer Jam" gains worldwide audience through association with Voice of America
Hank Williams, Jr., and Ronnie Milsap videos aired on MTV
The Judds come from out of nowhere to post two No. 1s and gain CMAs Horizon Award for developing artists
Lionel Richie makes surprise appearance at CMA Awards
Fan Fair attendance tops 19,000 registrants
Emmylou Harris and noted West Coast sidemen like Jim Horn, Barry Tashian, and Willie Weeks move here. Famed producer-sidemen Steve Cropper and Barry Beckett move here, highlighting large influx of out-of-town talent to Music City
Sharp decrease in country record sales becomes apparent
Huge construction and renovation boom in Music Row area
Barbara Mandrell Country highlights country star-theme museum craze
Expansion continues at Twitty City
Tender Mercies wins Oscar; uses country music for soundtrack
First all-digital album recorded in Nashville by Deborah Allen
Gary Morris becomes first country music star to star in a Broadway opera, playing opposite Linda Ronstadt in *La Bohème*
Gibson Guitars moves entire manufacturing operation to Nashville
Ricky Skaggs hit of Bill Monroe's song "Uncle Pen" becomes first bluegrass song to make No. 1 on country charts
Alabama becomes first act to win three Entertainer of the Year awards from the CMA
Roy Acuff honored at Kennedy Center in Washington, D.C.
Big-time booking agencies like ICM and ATI establish Nashville offices; William Morris beefs up local operation
MTM Enterprises, a large TV production company, establishes MTM Music Group, which comprises a label, publishing company, and other enterprises in Nashville
Ernest Tubb passes away

MULTIPLE NO. 1 SINGLES 1968–84

This chart shows the country singers who posted more than one No. 1 single on the country charts in any given year. Note that discs stayed at No. 1 longer at the beginning of the chart than at the end, thus more artists were able to post multiple No. 1s toward the end of the list than at the beginning.

The number preceding the names tells how many No. 1 singles each artist tallied.

1968

3 Merle Haggard, Sonny James, Tammy Wynette
2 David Houston

1969

3 Sonny James, Buck Owens
2 Glen Campbell, Johnny Cash, Jack Greene, Merle Haggard, Conway Twitty

1970

4 Sonny James, Charley Pride
2 Merle Haggard

1971

3 Lynn Anderson, Sonny James, Loretta Lynn, Charley Pride, Conway Twitty

1972

3 Merle Haggard, Freddie Hart, Conway Twitty
2 Donna Fargo, Sonny James, Jerry Lee Lewis, Charley Pride, Tammy Wynette

1973

3 Charley Pride, Conway Twitty
2 Donna Fargo, Merle Haggard, Freddie Hart, Loretta Lynn, Ray Price, Charlie Rich, Johnny Rodriguez, Tanya Tucker, Tammy Wynette

1974

5 Charlie Rich
4 Dolly Parton
3 Merle Haggard
2 Mickey Gilley, Tom T. Hall, Waylon Jennings, Loretta Lynn, Ronnie Milsap, Conway Twitty, Tammy Wynette

1975

4 Merle Haggard
3 Freddy Fender, Johnny Rodriguez
2 John Denver, Mickey Gilley, Ronnie Milsap, Charley Pride, T. G. Sheppard, Tanya Tucker, Conway Twitty, Don Williams

1976

3 Conway Twitty, Tammy Wynette
2 Mickey Gilley, Ronnie Milsap, Willie Nelson, Marty Robbins, Don Williams

1977

3 Charley Pride, Conway Twitty
2 Crystal Gayle, Waylon Jennings, Ronnie Milsap, Elvis Presley, Kenny Rogers, Don Williams

1978

3 Ronnie Milsap, Willie Nelson, Dolly Parton, Kenny Rogers
2 Crystal Gayle, Waylon Jennings, Eddie Rabbitt, Margo Smith

1979

3 Anne Murray, Kenny Rogers
2 Moe (Bandy) & Joe (Stampley), the Bellamy Brothers, John Conlee, Waylon Jennings, Charley Pride, Don Williams

1980

4 Ronnie Milsap
3 Mickey Gilley
2 Alabama, Crystal Gayle, Waylon Jennings, Willie Nelson, the Oak Ridge Boys, Dolly Parton, Charley Pride, Eddie Rabbitt, T. G. Sheppard, Conway Twitty, Don Williams

1981

3 Alabama, Razzy Bailey, T. G. Sheppard, Hank Williams, Jr.
2 Rosanne Cash, Crystal Gayle, Merle Haggard, Johnny Lee, Ronnie Milsap, the Oak Ridge Boys, Dolly Parton, Eddie Rabbitt, Conway Twitty

1982

3 Alabama, Ronnie Milsap, T. G. Sheppard, Ricky Skaggs, Conway Twitty
2 The Bellamy Brothers, Janie Fricke, Mickey Gilley, Merle Haggard, Willie Nelson, Charley Pride, Eddie Rabbitt

1983

3 Alabama, Mickey Gilley
2 John Anderson, John Conlee, Earl Thomas Conley, Janie Fricke, Crystal Gayle, Merle Haggard, Reba McEntire, Ronnie Milsap, the Oak Ridge Boys, Charley Pride, Kenny Rogers, Ricky Skaggs, B. J. Thomas, Don Williams

1984

3 Alabama, Earl Thomas Conley, Exile, Merle Haggard, Ricky Skaggs, George Strait
2 John Conlee, Crystal Gayle, the Judds, Johnny Lee, Ronnie Milsap, Willie Nelson, the Oak Ridge Boys, Conway Twitty, Don Williams

Sources: Joel Whitburn's Record Research Reports. Billboard magazine.

COUNTRY HITMAKERS 1948–84

TOP-10 RECORDS	ARTIST	NO. 1 RECORDS
65	George Jones	13
63	Merle Haggard	35
63	Eddy Arnold	15
61	Conway Twitty	37
51	Charley Pride	29
51	Loretta Lynn	16
46	Buck Owens	20
46	Johnny Cash	11
46	Jim Reeves	9
45	Webb Pierce	9
44	Dolly Parton	18
43	Marty Robbins	14
43	Waylon Jennings	14
41	Ray Price	7
39	Sonny James	23
38	Tammy Wynette	20
38	Mel Tillis	6
37	Bill Anderson	7
36	Faron Young	3
35	Hank Snow	6
33	Willie Nelson	15
32	Ronnie Milsap	25
31	Red Foley	4
30	Mickey Gilley	17
29	Don Williams	16
28	Hank Williams, Jr.	6
28	Porter Wagoner	2
27	Crystal Gayle	15
27	Kenny Rogers	14
27	Hank Williams	7
27	Jerry Lee Lewis	6
26	Carl Smith	4
26	The Statler Brothers	2
25	Kitty Wells	2
24	Elvis Presley	8
24	David Houston	7
23	Eddie Rabbitt	12
22	Hank Thompson	1
21	T. G. Sheppard	13
21	The Oak Ridge Boys	10
21	Tom T. Hall	7
21	Barbara Mandrell	6
21	Glen Campbell	5
20	Anne Murray	9
20	Don Gibson	6
20	Johnny Rodriguez	6
20	Emmylou Harris	5
20	Connie Smith	1
19	Billy "Crash" Craddock	3
18	Lynn Anderson	5
18	Moe Bandy	2
18	Gene Watson	1
17	Charlie Rich	9
17	Tanya Tucker	6
17	Joe Stampley	4
16	Donna Fargo	6
16	John Conlee	6

Sources: Joel Whitburn's Record Research Reports. Billboard magazine.

COUNTRY ACTS ON POP CHARTS 1940–84

TOP-20 RECORDS	ARTIST	TOP-10 RECORDS	NO. 1 RECORDS
68	Elvis Presley	42	15
22	Everly Brothers	15	4
22	Roy Orbison	9	2
20	Kenny Rogers	11	2
19	Brenda Lee	12	2
9	John Denver	7	1
8	Anne Murray	4	1
8	B. J. Thomas	5	2
7	Glen Campbell	4	1
7	Marty Robbins	3	1
6	Johnny Cash	1	—
5	Roger Miller	5	—
5	Bobby Goldsboro	2	1
5	Eddie Rabbitt	3	1
5	Charlie Rich	1	1
4	Patsy Cline	1	—
4	Mac Davis	1	1
4	Dolly Parton	3	2
4	Ray Stevens	4	2
3	Tennessee Ernie Ford	3	1
3	Bobby Bare[1]	2	—
3	Floyd Cramer	3	—
3	Charlie Daniels	2	—
3	George Hamilton	2	—
3	Johnny Horton	3	1
3	Dickey Lee	1	—
3	Jerry Lee Lewis	3	—
3	Ronnie Milsap	1	—
3	Willie Nelson	2	—
3	Juice Newton	3	—
3	Conway Twitty	3	1

[1]Bare's first hit, "All American Boy," was erroneously credited to Bill Parsons on the label copy.

Sources: Joel Whitburn's Record Research Reports. Billboard magazine.

THE GROWTH OF COUNTRY RADIO 1961–84

YEAR	TOTAL RADIO STATIONS	FULL-TIME COUNTRY STATIONS	% COUNTRY STATIONS
1961	4,653	81	1.74%
1963	5,083	97	1.91
1965	5,495	208	3.79
1967	5,909	?	—
1969	6,745	606	8.98
1971	7,148	525	7.84
1972	7,331	633	8.63
1973	7,500	764	10.19
1974	7,807	856	10.96
1975	8,034	1,116	13.89
1976	8,240	?	—
1977	8,408	1,140	13.56
1978	8,608	1,150	13.36
1979	8,748	1,434	16.39
1980	8,933	1,534	17.17
1981	9,092	1,785	19.63
1982	9,160	2,114	23.08
1983	9,320	2,266	24.31
1984	?	2,265	?

Note: Although the CMA refers to its radio survey as an "annual" event, it was unable to provide the number of full-time country radio outlets for the following years: 1962, 1964, 1966, 1967, 1968, 1970, 1976.

Figures for the number of radio stations in 1984 were not available at the time of publication. Judging from previous years, a slight increase would be expected, resulting in a slight decrease in the percentage of full-time country stations.

Sources include the annual published by *Broadcast* magazine for the total number of radio stations and the Country Music Association "annual" survey for the number of full-time country outlets.

COUNTRY MUSIC MARKET SHARE 1973–83

YEAR	TOTAL RECORDED MUSIC SALES	GROSS COUNTRY SALES	PERCENT COUNTRY SALES
1973	$1,436,000,000	$150,180,000	10.5
1974	2,200,300,000	255,234,000	11.6
1975	2,360,000,000	276,120,000	11.7
1976	2,737,100,000	331,189,000	12.1
1977	3,500,000,000	451,603,200	12.4
1978	4,100,000,000	426,544,000	10.2
1979	3,680,000,000	437,456,000	11.9
1980	3,670,000,000	526,526,000	14.3
1981	3,625,000,000	529,250,000	14.6
1982	3,592,000,000	538,800,000	15.0
1983	3,815,000,000	495,950,000	13.0

Note: Figures for 1984 sales were not available at the time of publication, but gross sales figures for 1984 reflect a healthy increase through November of that year. Estimates for country music's market share in 1984 range from 9 to 12 percent.

Sources: Annual surveys published by the National Association of Record Merchandisers (NARM) and the Recording Industry Association of America (RIAA). Ed Morris. *Billboard* magazine: *International Talent Buyer's Guide* (annual).

COUNTRY SINGERS' GREATEST YEARS

This list ranks the artists by the maximum number of weeks they have had singles charted in *Billboard* in any given year. Because songs stayed on the charts longer in the 1940s and 1950s and there were fewer artists, the majority of entries are from the pre-1970s.

YEAR	ARTIST	NO. WEEKS	NO. OF SINGLES	LABEL(S)
1954	Webb Pierce	132	5	Decca
1951	Lefty Frizzell	112	6	Columbia
1959	Johnny Cash	110	10	Sun, Columbia
1983	Merle Haggard	107	7[1, 2]	Epic, MCA, Mercury
1955	Eddy Arnold	106	6	RCA
1949	Eddy Arnold	105	8	RCA
1959	Ray Price	104	4	Columbia
1959	Faron Young	104	7	Capitol
1949	Hank Williams	103	6	MGM
1955	Webb Pierce	103	4	Decca
1964	George Jones	101	6[3]	UA, Mercury
1965	Buck Owens	99	6	Capitol
1983	Willie Nelson	98	7[2, 4, 5]	Columbia, Epic, Monument
1958	Johnny Cash	97	5	Sun, Columbia
1951	Eddy Arnold	96	7	RCA
1980	Willie Nelson	96	8[4, 6]	Columbia, RCA, Songbird
1970	Hank Williams, Jr.	95	7[7, 8]	MGM
1956	Elvis Presley	94	4	RCA
1971	Conway Twitty	94	7[9]	MGM, Decca
1978	Willie Nelson	94	8	Columbia, RCA, UA, Lone Star
1956	Johnny Cash	93	3	Sun
1961	Webb Pierce	93	5	Decca
1951	Hank Williams	90	7	MGM
1962	George Jones	89	7[10]	Mercury, UA
1964	Buck Owens	89	4	Capitol
1950	Red Foley	87	10[11]	Decca
1976	Joe Stampley	86	7	ABC-Dot, Epic
1955	Kitty Wells	85	5[12]	Decca
1964	Kitty Wells	84	5[13]	Decca
1972	George Jones	83	7[14]	Epic
1963	George Jones	81	6[10]	UA
1980	George Jones	81	6[14, 15]	Epic
1971	Porter Wagoner	81	6[16]	RCA
1975	Tanya Tucker	81	6	Columbia, MCA
1972	Tammy Wynette	81	6[14]	Epic
1950	Eddy Arnold	80	7	RCA
1964	Johnny Cash	80	5	Columbia
1956	Kitty Wells	80	4[12]	Decca
1975	Joe Stampley	80	7	ABC-Dot, Epic

[1]Merle Haggard and Leona Williams; [2]Merle Haggard and Willie Nelson; [3]George Jones and Melba Montgomery; [4]Willie Nelson and Waylon Jennings; [5]Willie Nelson and Brenda Lee; [6]Willie Nelson and Ray Price; [7]Hank Williams, Jr., and Lois Johnson; [8]Hank Williams, Jr., as Hank the Drifter, Jr.; [9]Conway Twitty and Loretta Lynn; [10]George Jones and Margie Singleton; [11]Red Foley and Ernest Tubb; [12]Red Foley and Kitty Wells; [13]Kitty Wells and Webb Pierce; [14]George Jones and Tammy Wynette; [15]George Jones and Johnny Paycheck; [16]Porter Wagoner and Dolly Parton

Sources: Joel Whitburn's Record Research Reports. Billboard magazine.

TOP-10 AND No. 1 RECORDS (1968–84)

TOP-10	NO. 1
61 Conway Twitty	**37** Conway Twitty
56 Merle Haggard	**32** Merle Haggard
48 Charley Pride	**29** Charley Pride
43 Dolly Parton	**25** Ronnie Milsap
42 George Jones	**18** Tammy Wynette
41 Waylon Jennings	**18** Dolly Parton
40 Loretta Lynn	**17** Mickey Gilley
38 Mel Tillis	**16** Sonny James
35 Tammy Wynette	**16** Don Williams
32 Ronnie Milsap	**15** Crystal Gayle
31 Willie Nelson	**15** Loretta Lynn
30 Mickey Gilley	**15** Willie Nelson
29 Don Williams	**14** Alabama
27 Kenny Rogers	**14** Waylon Jennings
27 Crystal Gayle	**14** Kenny Rogers
26 Sonny James	**13** T. G. Sheppard
26 Hank Williams, Jr.	**10** Oak Ridge Boys
23 Bill Anderson	**9** George Jones
23 Eddie Rabbitt	**9** Anne Murray
23 Statler Brothers	**9** Charlie Rich
21 Tom T. Hall	**7** Bellamy Brothers
21 Marty Robbins	**7** Tom T. Hall
21 T. G. Sheppard	**6** Johnny Cash
20 Glen Campbell	**6** John Conlee
20 Jerry Lee Lewis	**6** Donna Fargo
20 Johnny Rodriguez	**6** Freddie Hart
20 Emmylou Harris	**6** Barbara Mandrell
19 Buck Owens	**6** Johnny Rodriguez
19 Billy "Crash" Craddock	**6** Mel Tillis
18 Moe Bandy	**6** Tanya Tucker
17 Johnny Cash	**6** Hank Williams, Jr.
17 David Houston	**5** Lynn Anderson
	5 Razzy Bailey
	5 Glen Campbell
	5 Emmylou Harris

Sources: Joel Whitburn's Record Research Reports. Billboard magazine.

NASHVILLE GRAMMY WINNERS

Alabama *(2)*
Lynn Anderson *(1)*
Asleep at the Wheel *(1)*
Chet Atkins *(7)*

Bobby Bare *(1)*
Blackwood Brothers *(7)*
Jimmy Bowen *(1)*
Larry Butler *(2)*

June Carter *(2)*
Johnny Cash *(6)*
Johnny Christopher *(2)*
Cortelia Clark *(1)*
Roy Clark *(1)*
Cynthia Clawson *(1)*

Charlie Daniels Band *(1)*
Danny Davis *(1)*
Jimmie Dean *(1)*
Al De Lory *(2)*

Donna Fargo *(1)*
Lester Flatt &
Earl Scruggs *(1)*
Tennessee Ernie Ford *(1)*

Larry Gatlin *(1)*
Crystal Gayle *(3)*
Amy Grant *(2)*
Lee Greenwood *(1)*

Tom T. Hall *(1)*
John Hartford *(3)*
Johnny Horton *(1)*
David Houston *(2)*

Mark James *(2)*
Waylon Jennings *(2)*
Bobby Jones *(1)*
George Jones *(1)*

The Kendalls *(1)*
Anita Kerr Singers *(3)*
Kris Kristofferson *(3)*

Johnny Lee *(1)*
Richard Leigh *(1)*
Les Leverette *(1)*
John D. Loudermilk *(1)*
Loretta Lynn *(1)*

Charlie McCoy *(1)*
James Malloy *(1)*
Barbara Mandrell *(2)*
Jody Miller *(1)*
Roger Miller *(11)*
Ronnie Milsap *(3)*
Chips Moman *(1)*
Bob Morrison *(1)*

Willie Nelson *(6)*

Oak Ridge Boys *(5)*
Kenny O'Dell *(1)*
Roy Orbison *(1)*

Dolly Parton *(3)*
Gary S. Paxton *(1)*
Ben Peters *(1)*
Elvis Presley *(3)*
Ray Price *(1)*
Charley Pride *(3)*

Jerry Reed *(2)*
Mike Reid *(1)*
Charlie Rich *(1)*
Jeannie C. Riley *(1)*
Hargus "Pig" Robbins *(1)*
Marty Robbins *(2)*
Kenny Rogers *(2)*
Bobby Russell *(2)*

Don Schlitz *(1)*
Jeannie Seely *(1)*
Billy Sherrill *(2)*
Shel Silverstein *(1)*
Joe Simon *(1)*
Sammi Smith *(1)*
Joe South *(2)*
Statler Brothers *(3)*
Ray Stevens *(2)*
Glenn Sutton *(1)*

B. J. Thomas *(4)*
Wayne Carson Thompson *(2)*
Merle Travis *(1)*
Conway Twitty *(1)*

Porter Wagoner *(3)*
Doc Watson *(2)*
Merle Watson *(1)*
Dottie West *(1)*
Tammy Wynette *(2)*

Source: National Academy of Recording Arts and Sciences (NARAS)

CORPORATE CHART SHARES 1980–84

LABEL	(SINGLES) 1980	1981	1982	1983	1984	SUB-TOTAL	(ALBUMS) 1980	1981	1982	1983	1984	SUB-TOTAL	TOTAL
Columbia	59	51	49	48	43	250	33	32	21	25	28	139	389
Epic	50	41	38	48	43	220	20	21	19	28	29	117	337
													726
Warner Bros.	39	32	34	41	46	192	12	12	10	12	23	69	261
Elektra	41	39	43	13	—	136	13	10	14	9	—	46	182
Associated labels	26	54	49	32	24	185	8	6	32	29	7	82	267
													710
RCA	77	69	73	78	86	383	38	31	33	38	40	180	563
MCA	57	67	58	66	62	310	36	31	31	26	31	155	465
Capitol, United Artists, and associated labels	56	37	52	37	34	216	31	13	18	17	12	91	307
Mercury	26	27	19	17	33	122	8	?	7	6	11	32	154

Notes: Associated labels for Warner Bros. and Elektra include Viva, Curb, and Asylum. Associated labels for Capitol and United Artists include Liberty and EMI. Cleveland International was figured into Epic's totals. Monument was figured into Columbia's totals.

Sources: Billboard's World of Country Music: 1980, 1981, 1982, 1983, 1984. Pocket calculator

COUNTRY MUSIC HALL OF FAME MEMBERS

1961

Jimmie Rodgers
Fred Rose
Hank Williams

1962

Roy Acuff

1964

Tex Ritter

1965

Ernest Tubb

1966

Eddy Arnold
Jim Denny
George D. Hay
Uncle Dave Macon

1967

Red Foley
Joe Frank
Jim Reeves
Steve Sholes

1968

Bob Wills

1969

Gene Autry

1970

A. P. Carter
"Mother Maybelle" Carter
Sara Carter
Bill Monroe

1971

Art Satherly

1972

Jimmie Davis

1973

Chet Atkins
Patsy Cline

1974

Owen Bradley
Pee Wee King

1975

Minnie Pearl

1976

Paul Cohen
Kitty Wells

1977

Merle Travis

1978

Grandpa Jones

1979

Hubert Long
Hank Snow

1980

Johnny Cash
Connie B. Gay
Sons of the Pioneers
- Roy Rogers
- Bob Nolan
- Tim Spencer
- Lloyd Perryman
- Karl Farr
- Hugh Farr

1981

Vernon Dalhart
Grant Turner

1982

Lefty Frizzell
Roy Horton
Marty Robbins

1983

Little Jimmy Dickens

1984

Ralph Peer
Floyd Tillman

TOP CMA AWARD WINNERS 1967–84

9	Alabama, the Statler Brothers
8	Loretta Lynn, Willie Nelson
7	Chet Atkins, Roy Clark, Ronnie Milsap
6	Johnny Cash, Danny Davis & the Nashville Brass, Merle Haggard, Dolly Parton
5	Charlie Rich, Kenny Rogers
4	Charlie Daniels, Waylon Jennings, Barbara Mandrell, Ricky Skaggs, Conway Twitty
3	George Jones, Jack Greene, Charley Pride, Porter Wagoner, Tammy Wynette
2	John Anderson, Bobby Braddock, Buckaroos, Glen Campbell, Wayne Carson-Thompson, Johnny Christopher, Charlie Daniels Band, John Denver, Janie Fricke, David Frizzell, Crystal Gayle, Tompall Glaser, Lee Greenwood, Freddie Hart, Mark James, Charlie McCoy, Anne Murray, the Oak Ridge Boys, Buck Owens, Curly Putnam, Jerry Reed, Ricky Skaggs Band, Buck Trent, Dottie West, Shelly West, Don Williams

TOP ACADEMY OF COUNTRY MUSIC AWARD WINNERS 1965–84

19	Merle Haggard
12	Billy Armstrong
11	Loretta Lynn
10	Al Bruno, Archie Francis
9	Alabama, J. D. Manness
8	Roy Clark
7	Floyd Cramer, Buddy Emmons, Mickey Gilley, Johnny Gimble, Hargus "Pig" Robbins, Kenny Rogers, the Strangers, Jerry Wiggins
6	Charlie McCoy, Conway Twitty
5	Moe Bandy, Glen Campbell, Donna Fargo, Billy Graham, Freddie Hart, Billy Mize
4	Tony Booth, Larry Booth Garner, Crystal Gayle, Barbara Mandrell, Buck Owens, Red Rhodes

Source: Academy of Country Music

NASHVILLE SONGWRITERS ASSOCIATION, INTERNATIONAL, HALL OF FAME

1970

Gene Autry
Johnny Bond
Albert Brumley
A. P. Carter
Ted Daffan
Vernon Dalhart
Rex Griffin
Stuart Hamblen
Pee Wee King
Vic McAlpin
Bob Miller
Leon Payne
Jimmie Rodgers
Fred Rose
Redd Stewart
Floyd Tillman
Merle Travis
Ernest Tubb
Cindy Walker
Hank Williams
Bob Willis

1971

Smiley Burnette
Jenny Lou Carson
Wilf Carter
Zeke Clements
Jimmie Davis
Alton Delmore
Rabon Delmore
Al Dexter
Vaughn Horton
Bradley Kinkaid
Bill Monroe
Bob Nolan
Tex Owens
Tex Ritter
Carson J. Robison
Tim Spencer
Gene Sullivan
Jimmy Wakely
Wiley Walker
Scotty Wiseman

1972

Boudleaux Bryant
Felice Bryant
Lefty Frizzell
Jack Rhodes
Don Robertson

1973

Jack Clement
Don Gibson
Harlan Howard
Roger Miller
Ed Nelson, Jr.
Steve Nelson
Willie Nelson

1974

Hank Cockran

1975

Bill Anderson
Danny Dill
Eddie Miller
Marty Robbins
Wayne Walker
Marijohn Wilkin

1976

Carl Belew
Dallas Frazier
John D. Loudermilk
Moon Mullican
Curly Putman
Mel Tillis
Special Award: Stephen Foster

1977

Johnny Cash
Woodie Guthrie
Merle Haggard
Kris Kristofferson

1978

Joe Allison
Tom T. Hall
Hank Snow
Don Wayne

1979

Reverend Thomas A. Dorsey
The Louvin Brothers,
Charlie and Ira
Elsie McWilliams
Joe South

1980

Huddie "Leadbelly" Ledbetter
Mickey Newbury
Ben Peters
Ray Stevens

1981

Bobby Braddock
Ray Whitley

1982

Chuck Berry
William J. "Billy" Hill

1983

W. C. Handy
Loretta Lynn
Beasley Smith

1984

Hal David
Billy Sherrill

THE ULTIMATE COUNTRY CHART

"The Ultimate Country Chart" presents more factual data about past, present, and future country stars than any previous source. You want facts? This chart contains over 2,400! Before you feast your eyes on this fabulous banquet of information kindly stay tuned long enough to learn how it was compiled and what information it conveys.

Everyone on the U.C.C. has had at least one No. 1 single on *Billboard's* country charts (except Clint Eastwood and Jay Huguely—a.k.a. Cledus Maggard—neither of whom could be considered country music singers).

The U.C.C. is arranged chronologically with each artist entered for the year when he or she first appeared on any position on the *BB* lists. The year of the first No. 1 is next, followed by the grand totals of Top 10s and No. 1 singles garnered as of December 31, 1984.

A check in the next column indicates membership in the Country Music Hall of Fame, the ultimate honor in the field. The next two columns detail the number of awards won from the Country Music Association and the Academy of Country Music. The next figure tells you how many Grammy Awards the act has received from the National Academy of Recording Arts and Sciences.

Selection to the Hall of Fame of the Nashville Songwriter's Association, International, is indicated by a check mark in the next column, followed by the number of singles the artist has placed in *BB's* "Hot 100" list of the national pop hits. The next number indicates the highest position gained on those same pop singles charts.

The next two columns show the artist's success in the Middle of the Road (MOR) and adult-contemporary (a-c) lists. The number of Top-20 singles and the top marks achieved in those fields are indicated in that order.

The next column lists the number of BMI Awards won by the act for songwriting. Present (✓) or former (X) membership with the Grand Ole Opry follows. The next-to-last row of figures shows how many *Music City News* Awards the star has won. (The *MCN* Awards are fan-voted; CMA, ACM, and Grammy Awards are awarded by industry professionals.)

A check mark in the last column indicates whether that artist is represented among the 242 folk, country, and gospel recordings included in the official White House Library. Two checks indicate the artist's work was chosen in 1973 and in 1978, the only two occasions when 1600 Pennsylvania Avenue has gone to the record shop.

Sources for the data include *Billboard* magazine, *Joel Whitburn's Record Research Reports*, BMI, CMA, ACM, NARAS, NSAI, the Grand Ole Opry, *Music City News*, and the White House. All data were compiled and cross-checked by the author.

	Artist	1st No. 1	Top-10 Singles	Total No. 1s	Hall of Fame	CMA Awards	ACM Awards	Grammy Awards (NARAS)	NSAI Hall of Fame	Songs on Pop Charts	Best Pop	Top 20 MOR/a-c	Best MOR/a-c	BMI Awards	Grand Ole Opry	*Music City News* Awards	White House Library
1948	Red Foley	1950	31	4	✓					3	1				X		✓
1949	Hank Snow	1950	35	6	✓				✓	2	68			5	✓		✓
	Ernest Tubb	1950	17	1	✓		1		✓					6	X	1	✓
	Pee Wee King	1951	3	1	✓				✓	1	3			5	X	1	✓
	Hank Williams	1949	27	7	✓		1		✓	1	23			26	X		✓
	Tennessee Ernie Ford	1950	11	2			1	1		16	1			1			✓
	Eddy Arnold	1949	63	15	✓	1				23	6	14	1	12	X		✓
	Hank Thompson	1952	22	1						1	99			3			✓
	George Morgan	1949	8	1										2	X		✓
	Hank Locklin	1960	8	1						3	8			1	✓		✓
1950	Lefty Frizzell	1951	13	3	✓				✓	1	85			12	X		✓
1951	Carl Smith	1951	26	4						3	43			1	X		✓
1952	Ray Price	1956	41	7		1	3	1		11	11	2	4	5	X		✓
	Kitty Wells	1952	25	2	✓					1	78		1	1	X		✓
	Webb Pierce	1952	45	9						6	24			21	X		✓
1953	Jimmie Dean	1961	8	2				1		12	1	9	1	2			✓
	Jim Reeves	1953	46	9	✓					23	2	6	10	7	X		✓
	Marty Robbins	1956	43	14	✓		1	2	✓	24	1	6	4	19	X	6	✓
	Skeeter Davis	1953	12	1						8	2	5	1		✓		✓
	Faron Young	1959	36	3						6	12	1	13	10	X	1	✓
	Jean Shepherd	1953	8	1						1	16				✓		
1954	Billy Walker	1962	11	1										2	✓		✓
1955	George Jones	1959	65	13		3	3	1		5	73			11	X	2	✓✓
	Johnny Cash	1958	46	11	✓	5	2		✓	48	2	8	1	23	X		✓
	Porter Wagoner	1962	28	2		3		3		1	92			1	✓	3	✓
	Ferlin Husky	1957	8	3						4	4			2	X		✓
	Elvis Presley	1955	24	8				3		149	1	37	1	5		1	✓
1956	Sonny James	1956	39	23						18	1	1	22	7	X		✓
	Jim Ed Brown	1959	16	2		1	1			3	1	1	16	1	✓	3	✓
	Johnny Horton	1959	7	2				1		8	1			4			✓
	Everly Brothers	1957	6	4						38	1	4	4	3	X		✓
1957	Jerry Lee Lewis	1957	27	6			1			18	2	1	23	1			✓✓
	Patsy Cline	1961	8	2	✓					13	9	4	2		X		✓
	Bobby Helms	1957	3	2						6	6						
1958	Mel Tillis	1972	38	6		1			✓				44	23	X	6	✓
	Don Gibson	1958	20	6					✓	14	7	1	15	27	✓		✓
	Stonewall Jackson	1959	11	2						4	4			1	✓		✓
1959	Buck Owens	1963	46	20		2	4			9	25	2	18	28		6	✓
	Bill Anderson	1962	37	7					✓	5	8	2	3	48	✓	1	✓
	Freddie Hart	1971	14	6		2	5			1	17		28	10			
	Wynn Stewart	1967	5	1										2			
1960	George Hamilton IV	1963	9	1						11	6	1	4		✓		
	Loretta Lynn	1966	51	16		8	11	1	✓	4	52			9	✓	24	✓✓
	Roy Drusky	1965	13	1						1	35			5	✓		✓
	Roger Miller	1964	11	3			2	11	✓	15	4	11	1	22			✓
	Del Reeves	1965	8	1						1	96			1	✓		✓
1961	Dave Dudley	1970	10	1						2	32	1	13	2			✓
1962	Willie Nelson	1975	33	15		7	1	4	✓	8	5	8	2	16			✓✓
	Bobby Bare	1974	14	1				1		8	2	5	4	2	X		✓

	Artist	1st No. 1	Top-10 Singles	Total No. 1s	Hall of Fame	CMA Awards	ACM Awards	Grammy Awards (NARAS)	NSAI Hall of Fame	Songs on Pop Charts	Best Pop	Top 20 MOR/a-c	Best MOR/a-c	BMI Awards	Grand Ole Opry	*Music City News* Awards	White House Library
	Glen Campbell	1968	21	5		2	5	5		37	1	30	1			1	✓
	Sheb Wooley	1962	2	1		1				9	1						
	Claude King	1962	6	1						4	6	2	3	2			
1963	Merle Haggard	1966	63	35		6	17		✓	7	28	1	16	42		7	✓✓
	Dottie West	1979	13	4		2		1		4	14	1	7	4	✓	1	✓
	David Houston	1966	24	7				2		4	24	1	18		✓		✓
	Melba Montgomery	1974	1	1						1	39			1			✓
	Roy Clark	1973	8	1		7	8			6	19	4	6			11	✓
1964	Hank Williams, Jr.	1970	28	6						8	67			11		1	✓
	Red Sovine	1965	4	3						2	40			5	X		
	Connie Smith	1964	20	1										1	✓	1	✓
	Johnnie Wright	1965	1	1										2	X		
1965	Waylon Jennings	1974	43	14		4		2		11	21	2	16	13		1	✓✓
	Statler Brothers	1978	26	2		9	2	3		3	4	1	18	26		22	
	Jack Greene	1967	9	5		3				1	65				✓		✓
	Johnny Paycheck	1977	10	1			1			1	92			3			✓
	Jerry Wallace	1972	4	1						13	8	2	2				
1966	Conway Twitty	1968	61	37		4	6	1		20	1		37	16		17	✓✓
	Tammy Wynette	1967	38	20		3	1	2		11	19	2	11	13	X	2	✓✓
	Charley Pride	1969	51	29		3		3		10	21	1	7			5	✓✓
	Lynn Anderson	1970	18	5		1	2	1		6	3	3	5				✓✓
1967	Ed Bruce	1982	4	1										8			
	Dolly Parton	1970	44	18		6	2	3		15	1	11	1	25	✓	4	✓✓
	Tom T. Hall	1969	21	7				1	✓	5	12	1	2	22	✓	1	
	Jerry Reed	1971	6	3		2		2		9	8	1	6	18			✓
	Johnny Duncan	1971	8	3													
	Henson Cargill	1968	2	1						1	25						
	Cal Smith	1972	4	2		1	2			1	64					1	
	Vern Gosdin	1984	10	1													
1968	Jeannie C. Riley	1968	6	1		1		1		5	1	1	4				✓
	Mickey Gilley	1974	30	17			7	1		4	20	2	3			1	
	Sammi Smith	1970	3	1		1	1	1		2	8	1	3				
	Bobby Goldsboro	1968	2	1						26	1	20	1	10			
	Billy Jo Spears	1975	5	1			1			2	78						
	Charlie Rich	1973	17	9		5		1		13	1	10	1				✓✓
	Jim Glaser	1984	4	1		1				1	92			3			
1969	Barbara Fairchild	1972	3	1						3	32	1	9				
	Barbara Mandrell	1978	21	6		4	4	1		3	31	1	6		✓	9	✓
	Kenny Rogers	1977	27	14		5	5	2		35	1	26	1			4	✓
1970	Crystal Gayle	1976	27	15		2	4	3		11	2	14	2			1	
	David Frizzell	1981	7	2		2	2									2	
	Anne Murray	1974	20	9		2	1	3		26	1	26	1				
	The Kendalls	1977	11	3		1		1		1	69					1	
	Billy "Crash" Craddock	1974	19	3						4	16	1	15				
1971	Dickey Lee	1975	4	1						6	6	1	2	6			
	Jeanne Pruett	1973	5	1						1	73				✓		
	Joe Stampley	1972	17	4		1	2			1	37	1	17	3			
	Nitty Gritty Dirt Band	1984	3	1						11	9	3	10				
1972	Tanya Tucker	1973	15	6			1			8	37	1	7	2		1	
	Don Williams	1974	29	16		2	1			1	24	1	8	3	✓	1	
	Kris Kristofferson	1973	1	1		1	1	3	✓	7	16	4	2	33		6	✓
	Donna Fargo	1972	15	6		1	5	1		8	5	3	5	11		1	
	Johnny Rodriguez	1973	20	6			1			3	13			2		2	
1973	Marie Osmond	1973	1	1						3	5	3	1				
	Ronnie Milsap	1974	32	25		7		3		14	5	11	1		✓	1	✓
	Larry Gatlin	1977	14	3			3	1		1	84		36	14	✓	6	
	Charlie Daniels	1979	1	1		4	2	1		9	3		30	5		1	✓
	John Denver	1974	5	3		2	2			25	1	23	1				✓
	Gary Stewart	1975	3	1										2			
1974	Linda Ronstadt	1975	6	1			1	2		32	1	12	2				
	T. G. Sheppard	1974	20	12						4	37	3	3			1	
	Eddy Raven	1984	3	1													
	Eddie Rabbitt	1976	23	12			1			14	1	10	1	19		3	✓
	Moe Bandy	1979	18	2		1	4										
	C. W. McCall	1975	2	1						4	1	1	19				✓
	Billy Swan	1974	1	1						4	1	1	6	4			
1975	Emmylou Harris	1976	20	4		1		3		4	37	3	10				
	Gene Watson	1982	17	1													
	Jessi Colter	1975	4	1		1				3	4	1	16	3			

	Artist	1st No. 1	Top-10 Singles	Total No. 1s	Hall of Fame	CMA Awards	ACM Awards	NARAS	NSAI Hall of Fame	Songs on Pop Charts	Best Pop	Top 20 MOR/a-c	Best MOR/a-c	BMI Awards	Grand Ole Opry	Music City News Awards	White House Library
	Freddy Fender	1975	8	4		1	1			7	1	3	9	1			
	Johnny Lee	1980	9	5			1	1		2	5	1	10				
	Margo Smith	1977	8	2									37	1			
	B. J. Thomas	1975	5	3				4		25	1	14	1		✓		
	Dave & Sugar	1976	11	2									32				
1976	Reba McEntire	1982	9	2		1											
	Oak Ridge Boys	1978	21	9		3	3	5		4	5	3	8			2	✓
	Juice Newton	1981	2	1			1			9	2	8	1				
	Earl Thomas Conley	1981	10	7													
	Charly McClain	1980	10	2												1	
	Bellamy Brothers	1979	12	6						4	1	1	2				
	Razzy Bailey	1980	13	6									41	1			
	Michael Murphey	1982	3	1						6	3	5	1	3			
1977	Janie Fricke	1978	11	6		2										3	
	Alabama	1980	14	14		9		2		6	15	6	5	5		6	
	Cristy Lane	1980	7	1												1	
	John Anderson	1982	10	3		1				1	43			3			
	Debby Boone	1980	2	1			1	2		3	1	3	1			1	
	Ronnie McDowell	1981	10	2						2	13		42	1			
1978	John Conlee	1978	13	6			1							2	✓		
	Steve Wariner	1981	5	1													
1979	Sylvia	1981	7	2						1	15	1	5				
	Rosanne Cash	1981	5	3						1	22	1	6	2			
1980	Ricky Skaggs	1982	9	7		4									✓	4	
1981	George Strait	1981	11	5													
	Shelly West	1983	7	2		2	2									2	
	John Schneider	1981	2	1						4	14	1	5	1			
	Lee Greenwood	1983	9	2		2		1		2	53	2	4	1			
1982	Karen Brooks	1983	1	1													
	Lane Brody	1983	1	1													
1983	Sheena Easton	1983	1	1						10	1	11	1				
	Exile	1984	3	3						4	1	1	19	2			
1984	The Judds	1984	2	2		1											
	Julio Iglesias	1984	1	1		1					5						
	Dave Loggins	1984	1	1						2	5	2	1				

Index

Page numbers of text are in roman type. Page numbers on which photographs appear are in *italic* type. (bio) refers to biographical sketch.

The author wishes to thank Kerry P. O'Neil, CPA, and David Ross for permission to use an article in O'Neil's monthly column "Dollars & Sense" appearing in *Music Row,* published by Ross, as the basis for the section "How Much Does a Successful Record Earn?"

PHOTO CREDITS

The publisher wishes to thank the following individuals and organizations for supplying photographs for this book. Numbers refer to pages on which the photographs are reproduced.

Country Music Foundation Library and Media Center, Nashville: 85 right, 110 left, 146 above right and below, 150 left, 152; Kathy Gangwisch: 115, 118 right, 172 left; Grand Ole Opry Archives: 84, 87, 89, 90 left, 108, 146 above left; Susan Hackney & Associates: 103 above; Bill Hudson & Associates, Nashville: 57; John Lomax III (photos by the author): 31 center, 47 above left, 78 below left, 82 above, 95 above (both), 133, 179; (photos collection the author): 149 left, 150 right; Barbara Mandrell Country (Bill Hudson & Associates, Nashville): 30 top left; MCA: 175; Monument Records: 154; *Music City News,* Nashville: 50 below left, 53 above left, 62 left (Henry Schofield), 88 (Tim Harden), 90 right, 92 below, 93 above, 95 below, 98, 102 below left, 103 below, 105 right, 109, 112, 113 left and center, 116, 153 (both), 158 (both), 160, 166 left, 171 (Les Leverett), 172 center below, 184, 187, 189; Willie Nelson and Family General Store, Madison, Tenn.: 60; Opryland Public Relations, Opryland U.S.A.: 24 above and center left, 25 top and bottom right, 26; Photo Fair, Nashville: 10 (all), 11 (both), 12 below right, 14 (all), 15 (all), 20 (all except top left), 21 above right, 22–23, 24 below left, 30 top right, second row from top, left and right, 70 above, 79 below left, 129, 136 above, 139, 142, 143 below left, 201, 207; RCA Records: 63 right, 122, 123 left (Larry Dixon), 193; Gordon Stoker: 149 right; Tennessee Photographic Services, Nashville: 27 below right, 74 below, 78 below right; Top Billing International: 102 above; Twitty City (Bill Hudson & Associates, Nashville): 28–29; Warner Bros. Records: 123 right; Warner-Viva Records: 125 right; WSM Archives: 75, 76 above, 85 left, 110 right.

SONG CREDITS